HOME IS WHERE THE EGGS ARE

Farmhouse Food *for the* People You Love

MOLLY YEH

WILLIAM MORROW

An Imprint of HarperCollins*Publishers*

TO NICK AND BERNIE. AND TO IRA,
WHO WASN'T BORN UNTIL AFTER THIS BOOK WAS WRITTEN
(BUT LUCKILY ARRIVED BEFORE IT WENT TO PRESS!).
I LOVE YOU ALL SO MUCH!!

"What a joyous cookbook. Molly Yeh's energy, charming storytelling, and tremendous range of recipes make this well worth the wait."

—DEB PERELMAN

"The home in Molly Yeh's brilliant *Home Is Where the Eggs Are* is a place where Seedy Halva Fairy Toasts play nice with Tahini Monster Cookies, last night's pizza party becomes today's chopped salad, and kimchi tops an inside-out cheeseburger called Jucy Lucy! In short, eggs get broken and Yeh whips up a joyfully delicious Chinese-Jewish-Midwestern omelet that shows us how cooking can be funny and fancy, silly and serious, and that the kitchen is always where the heart is."

—CAL PETERNELL

"Molly Yeh's work has always felt like it couldn't come from anyone else—it's specifically her, full of heart and personality. This new book extends that feeling into her home and family, and is so warm and lovely."

—JULIA TURSHEN

"*Home Is Where the Eggs Are* sparkles with Molly Yeh's signature sunny-side up joy, warmth, and humor. Every recipe and story remind us that there is magic to be found in everyday mealtimes, and that cooking for our family should be simple, nurturing, and utterly fun."

—HETTY LUI McKINNON

"Molly Yeh brings herself to every recipe, giving each dish a unique spice ingredient and twist! She's a human surprise and delight, and her food is brilliant!"

—DREW BARRYMORE

HOME IS WHERE THE EGGS ARE

ALSO BY MOLLY YEH
Molly on the Range
Short Stack: Yogurt

CONTENTS

RECIPES

INTRODUCTION

When they told me that everything changes when you have kids, I thought they meant that you stop doing things like watching the entire *Wet Hot American Summer* series alone in your underwear while eating potato chips every Memorial Day weekend. And that long, uninterrupted buttercream-rose-piping marathons would become nap-time frosting-blob-plopping sprints. I was prepared for the diapers (mostly) and my impending dip in Delta SkyMiles, and I even strategically scratched my dubstep itch at my best friend Rob's bachelor party in Amsterdam right before getting pregnant. But what I didn't anticipate was a pretty jarring shift in my taste buds, a newfound deeper meaning to mealtime, and a fresh perspective on food in general.

I don't mean to be too dramatic. Bananas are still gross. Fried cheese is still the queen. I'm still me. But, hi (!), it's been six years since *Molly on the Range,* and we have some major ketchup-ing to do. A lot has happened since then: I filmed ten seasons and counting of my Food Network show, *Girl Meets Farm,* we added on to our house (and moved three times because of it), acquired some more cats, endured a global pandemic, participated in the demise of the side part, and, best of all, grew our little family with Bernie (short for Bernadette) in March 2019. And I started liking olives. All of this, minus the cats, and mainly the arrival of Bernie, has shaped the way I cook now and grown it into something with even more purpose and everyday enjoyment than before.

Feeding a family is different from the kind of cooking that I did pre-Bernie, which often consisted of things like losing track of time while developing doughnut recipes for my blog before realizing that it was ten p.m. and I should probably sauté some dinner kale for Nick and me to eat on the couch in front of *Game of Thrones.* While food, to me, used to be primarily about creativity and sustenance and the occasional big Chrismukkah party, it's now also about building family traditions and memories, celebrating the everyday, and raising Bernie to have an excited relationship with food. No matter how busy life gets, sitting down to dinner as a family is one of my highest priorities, right up there with dental care, and it pauses only for Nick's sugar beet harvest. I want Bernie to grow up with a dinner table practice filled with food to look forward to, good conversation, and a space to be herself. This works out because curating three square meals a day, which actually ends up being closer to twelve when you consider Bernie's textbook-toddler tastes, is one of my very favorite parenting jobs. Which is convenient because Nick, who once tried making chicken stock in a butter warmer, was made to be the fun one.

This book is a collection of recipes that we love to eat on a regular basis, and I'm so excited to share them with you. It's food that I find satisfaction in serving to my family on any old day; no celebrations or special guests or even pants are required to get the most out of these recipes. They fit comfortably into my life as someone who gets enormous amounts of enjoyment from cooking but also just as much enjoyment in sitting outside with Bernie and sticking our hands in piles of mud (so long as there are no bugs and we are properly sunscreened). Am I saying that this is a quick-'n'-easy, everyday recipe book? No, we can't all be peanut butter on matzo. I mean, many of these recipes are indeed easy to whip up start to finish on a busy morning or between the end of a workday and Bernie's early bath time. But not all of them. Because the truth is, I don't cook for Nick and Bernie every day. Sure, I cook every day for my job, but after twelve hours of frosting a Barbie cake in front of a camera, stressing out about having the proper rainbow sprinkle distribution on her skirt, like anyone else, I require conveniences like a stash of veggie steamed buns from the deep freeze that I can throw in the microwave and get into Bernie's belly before she unleashes Hangry Bernie on me.

In my mind, cooking for my family is a bigger picture than just twenty-one individual meals smooshed together to make a week. It's about good leftover hotdish, simmering stock during nap time to fill the house with cozy smells, babka that Bernie and I baked over the weekend, homemade bread as often as energy allows, and a cake that stays moist for days so we never have to rush to finish it all before it dries out. And, yeah, of course, opening up a bagged salad, spreading PB and J on matzo when it's not even Passover, and calling it dinner happens more frequently than I brush my hair, but you won't find those recipes here.

The recipes in this book include meals that use ingredients we always have on hand, in addition to dishes I love so much that they're worth sitting down to plan and make a grocery list for. Meal planning and grocery-list making are two of my favorite Sunday activities; they don't take much time, and they go a long way in increasing the ease of hectic weeks. I always leave some holes in the weekly menu to allow for leftovers, defrosting chili from that double batch I made last month, occasional takeout, and those days that require six more rounds of cake testing than I had anticipated, and now it's dinnertime and *Nick, would you please just Google how to make spaghetti?* This is what a regular week might look like for us:

SUNDAY: Nick's pancakes with blueberries, kale giardiniera melts, chicken and stars soup

MONDAY: Blueberry smoothies, whatever recipe I'm testing that day, leftover soup

TUESDAY: Blueberry smoothies, tomatoey beans, brown rice salmon bowls (make extra rice!)

WEDNESDAY: Cookie dough oat bars and yogurt, leftover tomatoey beans with stuffed pita from the freezer, kale chip congee or cheesy kimchi fried rice with last night's rice

THURSDAY: Strawberry halva smoothies, grilled cheese and apples, a fridge-foraged salad or broccolini soup or *Nick, please make something I don't care*

FRIDAY: Strawberry halva smoothies, rainbow couscous, salami arugula pizza

SATURDAY: Toasted rugbrød with avocado, reheated leftover pizza chopped up on a salad, tahini monster cookies with Bernie, butternut soup with no-knead bread or knoephla or hotdish or something else that's kinda hearty

My priorities in the way that I cook are efficiency, function, and, of course, good taste. For the recipes in this book that don't qualify as quick, they earn their keep in other ways, whether it be by requiring minimal hands-on time (see Crusty Chocolate Chip Bread, page 28), providing nifty tricks (Hand-Pulled Noodles with Potsticker Filling Sauce, page 143), or producing results that keep on giving (bagels and hotdishes to keep in your freezer, or the Cardamom Babka/Babka Cereal one-two punch, pages 24 and 27). Most of the mains pile in vegetables so that meals can be one-dish situations; they fit in with my loose definition of a balanced lifestyle, and all of the ingredients are easily acquired in my little town or online. I have done my absolute best to lay out the steps in the most logical fuss-free way and to call for as few dishes as possible, because washing dishes is the worst, and I promise to provide as many make-ahead, freezing, and substitution tips as I can. And when it comes to the desserts and baked goods, just trust me when I say these recipes are for you

and your family only (or whoever makes up your closest inner circle: room-
mates you like, the guy you met at a club in Miami and moved in with because
your lease was up, etc.). They're treats that you can have around for a while in
a cookie jar or fridge, meaning you need not stress out about gobbling them up
before they go stale or sharing them. Sharing's for nerds. JK. Sharing's fine, it's
the small talk that kills me.

Every dish in this book serves a purpose too, whether it's to tell a story
or to share a technique or tip that I simply can't live without. I don't want to
give you recipes that are widely available on the internet already unless there's
something new and special in my version that I really need to tell you about. I
remain as passionate as ever about my biggest sources of inspiration, drawing
flavors from my Chinese and Jewish heritage, Nick's Scandinavian heritage,
our upper Midwestern home, and travels near and far. There's a reason each
recipe in this book is here, beyond just tasting good.

When you read this book, I want you to feel the joy and warmth of creating food for people you love. I don't want you to feel stressed out or like your
cooking skills, tastes, or access to ingredients are inadequate. You can make
these! You got this! These are recipes that my family and I love so much, and
in sharing them, it's my hope that you'll also enjoy making them, eating them,
and spending time with your loved ones along the way.

INGREDIENTS THAT I LOVE AND USE OFTEN

If I can get all my ingredients where I live, then I'm willing to bet that you can get them too. A majority of my staples can be found at my local grocery store and Super Target, and the rest are both easily found online and worth the wait of the shipping time. I'll be honest with you about when and how you can make substitutions, and when you shouldn't make them. To get enjoyment out of these recipes, you don't need any ingredients that are too fancy, but if you want to get fancy, then go for it!

BREAD: This book has a handful of specialty breads that I love, as well as some recipes that are to be served with great basic crusty bread as an accessory. For this crusty bread, I turn to three options over and over: Alexandra Stafford's peasant bread, Jim Lahey's no-knead bread, and take-and-bake baguettes. The former two are Googleable and super easy to make for a sourdough-inept person like myself. If you have a local bakery with good bread, I'm so jealous—go there often. If not, find a recipe (or take-and-bake brand!) that is tasty and will fit in easily with your lifestyle.

BUTTER: I generally use inexpensive generic unsalted butter for the baked goods that I make for my family or have to test over and over. But good European-style butter (usually Kerrygold or Plugrá), which has a higher fat content and contributes more richness and flavor, is worth the extra money where it counts: for special-occasion baked goods, in frostings and pie crusts and anywhere there aren't many other ingredients to hide behind, to finish dishes, and on toast.

CHOCOLATE: My chocolate preferences are like hair ties, simply all over the place. I cannot deny the joy and nostalgia that a bar of Hershey's milk chocolate brings me, and I have a stash of generic brand chocolate chips that I use all the time, in muffins, granola bars, and breads. But meanwhile, I feel weird wasting calories on a chocolate chip cookie that doesn't have chopped Valrhona or Guittard or other fancy chocolate in very specific percentages. Get in touch with your personal chocolate (and cocoa powder) preferences, learn what you like about different qualities, and choose your chocolate accordingly. I'll let you know when I feel strongly about a recipe using good-quality chocolate or cocoa, and I'll also be specific about shapes. Shapes do make a difference; the makeup of a cookie that has uniformly sized pockets of chocolate is a totally different experience than a cookie made with chopped chocolate that has a mixture of big pools and tiny shards to break up the dough. Tiny chips signify snack time and are less chocolate (and therefore healthier? lol). And when it comes to candy-coated chocolates, I go out of my way to find the pretty naturally dyed colors, like Unreal brand, or the ones found at Trader Joe's or the Whole Foods bulk section. Although there is no official distinction between semisweet and bittersweet chocolate, both are less sweet than milk chocolate, and bittersweet is generally less sweet than semisweet. You can sub semi for bitter and vice versa, and the world won't break.

COCONUT OIL: I love coconut oil so much! Unrefined coconut oil (which has coconut flavor) and refined (which is flavorless) can generally be used interchangeably, but the depth that unrefined lends is just so cozy and delightful that I tend to reach for it more often. In baked goods, unrefined coconut oil adds a subtle, warm glow of flavor that's not overpowering. Honestly, it might be my favorite baking fat (but don't tell butter). One strength of coconut oil is that it's solid at room temperature so, along with the fat and moisture you expect from baking fats, it gives some additional structural support that you wouldn't necessarily get from a liquid oil.

EGGS: Our chickens, all named Macaroni, are still well and laying! Their eggs, and in general any egg that comes from a chicken with a name and lots of space to forage, have bright yellow yolks and so much flavor. If you don't have chickens or friends with chickens, seeking out a special egg source, whether a farmers' market, local farm, or specialty store, is worth the hunt if even for just an occasional treat. Since the Macaronis' egg supply is dwindling significantly in their old age, we reserve those eggs to use where it really matters, where the eggs are the stars of the show, as in matzo brei and scrambles. For most baked goods, where the actual egg flavor can't really be detected, I turn to grocery store eggs. I almost always use large, but for things like an egg wash where the size of the egg really doesn't matter, I've omitted that specification.

EVERYTHING BAGEL TOPPING: Whoever shook up the bag of everything bagels, scooped up the stuff at the bottom, and started sprinkling it on other foods deserves a MacArthur genius grant. This very simple mix is the best savory sprinkle there is. Make your own everything bagel topping by combining equal parts dried minced onion, dried minced garlic, poppy seeds, and sesame seeds. Add kosher salt to taste and some caraway seeds, if desired. You can also use store-bought, but be aware that some store-bought brands are so heavy on the salt that it masks the other flavors. So taste yours and use your best judgment when seasoning, adding more salt to dishes if needed or omitting it if your mix is very salty.

FLOURS: I use a variety of flours in this book, and my mom will be the first to complain about this. But let me state my case: in a land where bespoke kale and obscure radishes just aren't stocked in the grocery stores, having a variety of flours in your arsenal offers a shelf-stable way of adding excitement, nuance, and even the occasional shortcut to your cooking and baking. And in some cases, health benefits! Using all-purpose flour is like drawing with the basic box of twelve crayons. Imagine what it's like to get the box of ninety-six! I keep all-purpose flour, whole wheat flour, white whole wheat flour, bread flour, almond flour, and other nut flours close by and use them often. (See page xix for more on nut flours.) High-gluten flour (for bagels), 00 flour (for extra-good pizza crust), rye flour (for rugbrød), cake flour (for steamed buns), and potato flour (for potato challah and weeknight lefse) are some of my less commonly used flours, but they're great at their jobs and last for a while, so I keep them in the further reaches of my cabinets and don't ever stress out about using them up before they go bad because of their long shelf lives. I recognize that I'm spoiled with storage space out here on the farm, so if you want to avoid having a surplus of a certain less commonly used flour, I recommend buying from the bulk section in the quantity needed. (Give them a sniff before scooping, to make sure they're fresh.) I'll tell you when substitutions are acceptable, but in general, think of wheat flours like outerwear. Cake flour is a light sweater, all-purpose is a fleece jacket, and so on up to the floor-length down parka that is high-gluten flour. Could you do your grocery run on a snowy winter day in a fleece if you can't find your parka? Sure, you'll survive. But will you *thrive?* No. I'm not here to show you how to make "pretty good bagels with all-purpose in place of high-gluten." I'm here to show you how to make *great bagels.* Because for me, picking up special groceries at the store or ordering them online isn't a burden, but spending a lot of time kneading and proofing dough and ending up with subpar bagels is. The brands I love are Bob's Red Mill (for specialty flours), King Arthur (especially for all-purpose flour, which has a slightly higher protein content than other all-purpose flours), Dakota Maid (from wheat that Nick grows!), and (when I feel like buying myself a birthday present in the form of a fifty-pound bag of 00 pizza flour) Central Milling.

FRESH HERBS: In the summer, we grow loads of basil, cilantro, dill, chives, parsley, mint, thyme, and rosemary in our garden and use them liberally. But in the winter, my only option is often those tiny clamshells that cost, like, fifty cents per leaf, and then I stress out about using them all before they wilt. The best way to keep herbs fresh is to wrap them in a damp paper towel and put them in a bag or container in the fridge. You'll be shocked how long they last.

MODERN CONVENIENCES: Pre-Bernie, I was a little snobby about using modern conveniences like pre-shredded cheese and take-and-bake baguettes, but along with the many other things that changed in my life once she was born, so too did my cheese attitude. So, yes, I use pre-shredded cheese all the time because shredding cheese is one of the hardest kitchen tasks to do with a child in your arms. (I *know* the texture isn't as good, but it's better than no cheese!) Freshly grated cheese, homemade stock, and homegrown everything are some of life's great pleasures, and you should use them when you can, but if you can't, you can still make a great meal! Everyone is welcome here, no matter your cheese situation. Store-bought chicken stock, Marzetti ranch dressing, premade pie dough, pizza dough from the pizza parlor, and even that shaky powdery Parmesan cheese, are, in the words of Queen Ina, *fine!*

NEUTRAL OIL: Neutral oil, or flavorless oil, can refer to a wide variety of oils, like canola, vegetable, grapeseed, and sunflower, to name a few. When a recipe calls for a neutral oil, choose one with a high smoke point (meaning it won't burn at high temperatures) if you'll be cooking with it. If you won't be cooking with it, then the world is your neutral oil oyster. Oils come with different health benefits, price points, and subtle flavor nuances, so take this into consideration when you shop. My neutral oil of choice is canola because it's inexpensive, has a high smoke point, and includes some nutritional benefits. "Vegetable oil" refers to a variety of different oils with varying smoke points and can sometimes contain multiple oils in the same bottle, so pay attention to the specific oils listed in the ingredients.

NUTS: I love using nuts in cooking and baking because they're tasty and a really easy way to add some protein. Roasting them just prior to using them maximizes their flavor, so I pretend to only buy raw nuts. But if you look in my freezer, you'll find bags of roasted nuts from the store, because freshly roasted nuts don't always taste as good as convenience feels. Often I can only find roasted *and* salted nuts. These are generally okay by me, since I like the added salt but, if you like, you can reduce the salt in a recipe accordingly. To roast your nuts, spread them out on a rimmed sheet pan and stick them in a 350°F oven until they're fragrant and toasty; begin checking lighter nuts at 6 minutes and heartier nuts at 10 minutes.

NUT BUTTERS: I'm pretty sure that we, as a family, keep the nut industry in business with our nut butter habit. Since we go through nut butters so quickly, we keep them at room temperature (which keeps them spreadable), but if you're a slow nut butter eater, you can extend their shelf life in the refrigerator. For anything cooking and baking related, I recommend using natural unsweetened butters to ensure that you're only adding nuts, no extra oil or sugar or other stuff. For some reason, unsalted nut butters can be really tricky to find, though, so if salted is all you can get, simply adjust the salt in the recipe accordingly or embrace the extra salt. My go-to everyday brands are Smucker's (natural) and Target Good & Gather. And for an extra treat, we love Ground Up and Eliot's.

NUT FLOURS: Nut flours are simply finely ground nuts. They add flavor, moisture, and a dense, hearty quality to baked goods. I typically buy Bob's Red Mill brand, but you can also make your own by blending nuts (raw or roasted) in a food processor until they are the consistency of a coarse flour, almost like cornmeal. If you overblend them, you will have nut butter. Store nut flours in the freezer to extend their freshness.

OLIVE OIL: I use olive oil, specifically extra virgin olive oil, whenever possible because it tastes good and makes me think I'll live to be 150 years old. My preferred brand is California Olive Ranch because it's a reliable workhorse that tastes great and is of high quality—which means that it has a higher smoke point, so you can cook at higher temperatures and even deep-fry with it without having to worry about burning it. Olive oil labels can sometimes be confusing and even misleading, making it easy to accidentally buy oil blends that include non-olive oils or low-quality oils that have low smoke points and notes of gasoline. You also want to ensure you're not accidentally buying light olive oil, which is a neutral oil but not a very cost-effective one. Stick to purchasing darker colored or opaque bottles (which protect the oil from light) and read the label carefully. Store olive oil in a cool, dark place away from heat, and don't hoard it! It's not like wine! It doesn't get better over time.

SALT: There are two kosher salt teams, Morton and Diamond Crystal. As someone who was Team Morton for years and years, I am now firmly on Team Diamond Crystal, because the granules are lighter and less salty. This has a few major advantages: it dissolves more quickly in soups and sauces, so you get a more accurate tasting before adding more salt, and it just generally makes it harder to accidentally oversalt your food. It's forgiving. I resisted joining Team DC because it's not available at my local grocery and I need to order it online. Luckily, salt lasts forever, so I'll be covered for years by the dozen boxes in my pantry. If you're on Team Morton, I feel like we could still be good friends. Just reduce the salt amounts in these recipes by about a third, okay? For finishing dishes, I recommend Maldon brand flaky salt. It adds an extra pop of sparkle, crunch, and flavor to savory and sweet dishes alike. It's pricey, but you just need a little.

SEEDS: Seeds are the reason I'm able to sleep at night knowing that Bernie is getting enough protein and iron, since she can be quite picky. Hemp seeds are soft and have a subtle, nutty flavor, so they can crash pretty much any muffin batter, granola bar, or smoothie party without killing the vibe. Flaxseeds, specifically ground flaxseeds, are a favorite food of Bernie's toy dinosaurs, so they're often requested in her morning yogurt. Millet and sesame seeds are crunchy and fun, so we just toss them into things with abandon. If I were a food, I'd love to be a seed, because they offend no one, provide great nutrients, are cute, and have long shelf lives.

SPICES: To get the most out of your spices, buy them in small quantities and replace them as frequently as you're able to (ideally every six to eight months). If you keep them for too long, you will feel like I did when I competed in the 1996 Chicago kids' triathlon before learning what a bicycle gear was: doing a lot of work for a last-place finish. Older spices don't have as much flavor, and you'll need to add more, which can make your food weirdly grainy. My favorite spice companies include New York Shuk (for Middle Eastern and North African flavors such as harissa, hawaij, baharat, shawarma, preserved lemon, and more), Diaspora (for a growing selection of spices that started with a beautiful turmeric), Burlap and Barrel (for a cardamom grinder [!] among other wonders), Penzey's, Kalustyan's, and La Boîte.

SPRINKLES: I won't let @marge287253600 and @sarge897320 from the internet yuck my yum. I *love sprinkles*! They add color and joy to sweets, and how can you not smile while eating them?! My collection lives in a dark but cozy cabinet to prevent their colors from fading. Choosing a favorite would be like choosing a favorite cheese; there are different sprinkles for different occasions. A few of my favorite brands include India Tree (specifically their naturally dyed Nature's Colors line), Beautiful Briny Sea (they produce mixes for Williams Sonoma, Fishs Eddy, and more, and they are so delicious I could eat them with a spoon), Supernatural (naturally colored and in such fun shapes!), and Sweetapolita (which makes a *sprinkle advent calendar*). And of course, super-normal grocery store sprinkles will always hold a place in my heart.

TAHINI: Tahini is a sesame paste that, when good, is luxurious and addictive, like Tayshia's season of *The Bachelorette*. But when it's bad, it's straight-up the Matt James season. There is a really wide spectrum of tahini quality, and unfortunately, bad, bitter tahini that plants itself stubbornly in its jar is all too common in the United States. Good tahini is smooth, nutty, and pourable, with just a small amount of solids piling up on the bottom of the jar. Look for tahini that's made from 100 percent Humera sesame seeds. Brands I love include Seed + Mill, Soom, Al Arz, Har Bracha, Whole Foods 365, and Wild Harvest. They might require some hunting or an internet order, but they really are worth it. Store tahini at room temperature if you plan to use it within a few months; otherwise, you can extend its life in the refrigerator.

TOMATOES: In the summer we grow a variety of tomatoes whose breeds I just refer to as "big, little, and Roma" because I'm a terrible gardener, and one perk of being married to a farmer is that I don't need to be a good gardener. We go through the majority of our summer tomatoes almost immediately, and any leftovers get preserved for soup, matbucha, and sauce. When we run out of those, I turn to Pomì or San Marzano canned tomatoes. When it comes to marinara and pizza sauce, Rao's is the only way I go. It made a sauce lover out of me.

VEGETABLES: Reliable year-round access to very good vegetables is not the strength of a region that is covered in snow most of the year (e.g., where I live). The vegetables I typically use are the most basic of the basic, the Hanes T-shirts of lettuces, cucumbers that come wrapped in plastic, and radishes that are all exactly the same size and color and shape. I've also learned to appreciate sauerkraut, kimchi, frozen vegetables, and other preserved produce. Which is all to say that you don't need access to any fancy farmers' markets for these recipes. Even the most basic of ingredients can turn into something delicious enough to eat in large quantities. (However, should you be curious about fancy lettuces and supermodel alliums, farms like the Chef's Garden and Girl & Dug offer home deliveries that are magical special treats.)

YEAST: A few years ago, I converted to only using instant yeast (versus active dry), and just like that, I never proofed yeast again, cutting down on the time and dishes standing between my mouth and a hot loaf of bread. I don't know why I wasted years of my life proofing active yeast; instant yeast needs a better marketing team. If you only have active dry yeast, you can still use it in any of these recipes, in the same quantity, but you'll need to proof it: warm up whatever milk or water is called for in the recipe to 105° to 110°F, swirl in the yeast with a pinch of sugar, and let it sit until foamy. Continue with the recipe, adding the yeast mixture when you're directed to add the liquid.

YOGURT: Greek yogurt has it all: tanginess, creaminess, versatility, probiotics, and the ability to sub in for almost any other dairy product. There are very few foods that wouldn't benefit from a plop of yogurt. I love yogurt so much that I wrote a book on it (that is now, sadly, out of print) and never get sick of it despite eating it multiple times a day every single day. Its uses are both savory and sweet, in cooking and baking, and it always manages to last way beyond its expiration date. I typically keep whole milk and 2 percent yogurt on hand and often use them interchangeably. Nonfat is fine too but predictably less rich. Non-Greek yogurts such as standard, French, and Australian are delicious but are usually best on their own, not within recipes. When you're buying Greek yogurt, check whether or not pectin or other added thickeners are listed in the ingredients. Steer clear of thickeners if you're going to be baking with the yogurt, as they can alter the texture of the final product. Look for an ingredient list that only contains milk, cultures, and maybe cream. For non-baking recipes, the presence of pectin or other thickeners is perfectly fine.

TOOLS THAT MAKE MY LIFE EASIER, AND I WANT THEM TO MAKE YOUR LIFE EASIER TOO

The tools that I typically gravitate toward on an everyday basis are sturdy, utilitarian, restaurant-grade goods that I get from restaurant supply stores. They're not beauty contest winners, but it's a small price to pay for tools that are generally inexpensive and really great at their jobs. Of course, gorgeous workhorses also exist, typically in the form of colorful cast iron, copper, and ceramic. When you find something pretty and also highly usable, love it and take care of it.

ACCORDION PASTRY CUTTER: The accordion cutter is something I fell in love with while working at the town bakery, and it allows bars, brownies, baked eggs, crackers, pie dough, and even pasta dough to be cut into uniform rectangles, squares, diamonds, and strips. Not only are perfectly parallel lines satisfying to cut and look at (and eat!), but you can also elevate even the most basic of treats by making their shapes clean and consistent. Note: When using this tool on thicker baked goods such as brownies and bars (versus thin doughs), use it for scoring, not for actually cutting. Leave the cutting to the knife. Search "accordion pastry cutter" online to find one. I recommend Ateco brand.

CAST IRON: Cast-iron skillets, braisers, and Dutch ovens are incredibly sturdy, versatile, long lasting, and just great at their jobs. They can take a lot of heat, are great at holding heat (making them my choice for frying), and can transition from stove to oven to serving table with grace. When properly cared for and seasoned, they are nonstick. I love Staub, Le Creuset, Lodge, and Great Jones. And, shameless plug, the Girl Meets Farm line at Macy's, which includes a pink cast-iron braiser.

DELI CONTAINERS: A few years ago I cleaned out our overflowing container cabinet and gave away pretty much every container that wasn't a deli container and our container stress has *drastically* decreased as a result. I buy them in three sizes (32 ounce, 16 ounce, and 8 ounce), and they all use

the same lid. They're inexpensive enough to give away to friends and not expect their return.

DIGITAL INSTANT-READ THERMOMETER: In another life I am a tattoo-covered restaurant chef who cooks hundreds of salmon fillets a night to total flaky perfection and can tell the millisecond one is done by my telepathic relationship with the fish. But in this life, in which I have no tattoos and cook fish once a week, I don't have that sixth sense and want to leave nothing up to chance, so I just temp the life out of everything because there is simply no reason not to. It's the easiest, most reliable way of telling when meats, breads, and even cookies are done. A few degrees can mean the difference between a sad, dry chicken and a moist, juicy bird. ThermoWorks makes reliable digital thermometers that provide quick readings for a range of budgets.

FISH SPATULA: Something about its odd shape makes it *way* more ergonomic to use than the traditional rectangular shaped spat. (I could actually do away with those entirely.) I use metal ones when possible and special nonstick-friendly ones when necessary.

FOOD PROCESSOR: Food processors are the go-to appliance for making dips, dressings, crackers, scones, pie dough, and crunchy toppings. (High-quality food processors can also handle homemade nut butters.) Without one, you can often find a workaround, but if you're looking to populate your kitchen with small appliances that are worthy of precious counter space, consider the food processor. Honestly, this is the place to splurge (or add to a birthday list) on a high-powered one because in most of my experience, working with low-powered food processors can be more frustrating than working with no food processor at all. My Cuisinart 14-cup food processor is a workhorse, and I recommend it 10/10.

HIGH-POWERED BLENDER: For an embarrassing profession of love for my Vitamix, you can go straight to the smoothie section on page 2. The smooth, non-gritty texture that a high-powered blender can produce is the foundation for a higher caliber of soups and smoothies (and a whole host of other foods, including grains that become flour!), and I genuinely feel like my life is better and healthier for it. A few different brands make high-powered blenders, but I can't preach enough about the Vitamix and its next-level power and reliability, and how easy it is to clean. It's a pricy investment but one very much worth considering if you're looking to get serious with your purée game.

KITCHEN RULER: Thickness, diameter, width, and other measurements are often just as important as oven temperature and ingredient amounts. The difference between a ¼-inch-thick cookie and ½-inch-thick cookie is a world of texture, and the difference between a 1-inch steak and a 1½-inch steak can be a long time on the grill. So keep a dishwasher-safe kitchen ruler with the rest of your utensils and use it often.

LIGHTWEIGHT METAL MIXING BOWLS: While big beautiful ceramic mixing bowls are great for serving and nighttime popcorn, a set of nesting metal mixing bowls is a workhorse staple. These bowls are lightweight, inexpensive, sturdy, easy to clean, and easier to use.

METAL BAKING PANS WITH PERFECT 90-DEGREE CORNERS: I find so much joy in baked goods that have perfect 90-degree corners. So unless it's for a casserole, baked pasta, or something else that's served right out of the pan, the only baking pans I use are heavy-duty metal boys with geometrically satisfying shapes. They are sturdy, and conduct heat quickly, allowing for even baking. My most used pans are the 8-inch square and 4 x 9-inch pullman loaf. Following those are the 9-inch square, 9 x 13-inch rectangle, 8-inch round, 6-inch round, and cupcake. That's all I need in life (and all you'll need for this book). My go-to brands are USA Pan, Great Jones, and Nordic Ware. I cannot stress my love for the pullman loaf pan enough, but for the tapered loaf pan enthusiast, go for the standard 4½ x 8½ x 2¾-inch (or 1-pound) metal pan and, occasionally, a 5 x 9-inch. If you only have glass or ceramic dishes when a recipe calls specifically for metal, all is not lost. You can absolutely still use them, just be prepared to add a few more minutes to the baking time and know that there could be a risk of slight overbaking around the edges before the center is done.

NONSTICK SKILLETS: Nonstick skillets are easy to use and clean, and I have no complaints about them other than that they need to be replaced every few years. Great Jones and Food52 GreenPan have some beautiful ones, but the one I feel the least bad about having to replace regularly is the less expensive restaurant-grade Tramontina.

OVEN THERMOMETER: I wrote this book while construction on our house necessitated that I work out of four different kitchens. I got to know seven different ovens, from various decades and with drastically different personalities. Some claimed they were preheated when they still had seventy degrees to go, others liked to just dip by fifty degrees whenever the heck they felt like it. It drove me crazy! It goes without saying that a (very cheap) oven thermometer saved me, and it will save you too.

SCALE: A digital scale is a life-changing tool to have in the kitchen. To read more about weighing your ingredients, turn to page xxviii. Scales come in a wide range of price points and quality levels that translate to speed, accuracy, and durability. It's important to find one that you can trust to give you an accurate quick reading (both in ounces and grams) and withstand heavy bowls of ingredients and all the spills that will happen on it. The one I use and love is Taylor brand, and it cost about forty-five dollars.

SHARP KNIVES: The sharper the knife, the less likely you are to slip while chopping a vegetable and the less likely you are to accidentally cut yourself. It's counterintuitive, but a sharper knife is a safer knife. It also makes cutting much more enjoyable, because you don't have to work as hard to cut the way you want to. I absolutely love my Misen 8-inch chef's knife and use it for practically everything (their santoku is also great). It's inexpensive and stays sharp for a while. Miyabi and Shun are also great lines of knives. The other knife I use most often is a 9.5-inch serrated knife; both Misen and Miyabi are great. That's basically it, two knives.

SILICONE SPOONULA: Spoonulas have a flatter edge on top and a rounded bowl like a spoon. The flat edge makes them extra effective at stirring and scraping the sides of batter bowls, and they're great for both cooking and baking. Any job that calls for a silicone or rubber spatula is actually best done by a spoonula. In this book I've specified silicone anywhere it should be heat-safe (otherwise any type of rubber will do). My spoonula brand of choice is GIR.

SMALL OFFSET SPATULA: If a genie put a spell on me and made me replace one of my hands with a kitchen utensil, I'd choose a small offset spatula. It has so many everyday uses beyond just frosting cakes (though you'll find it in the cake frosting section in craft stores and kitchen stores). It's more effective than a butter knife at spreading things on toast, and it's really effective at getting cupcakes and muffins out of their tins. If you're ever having trouble with anything in the kitchen, the answer is usually to reach for a small offset spatula.

SMALL TAPERED ROLLING PIN: Most of the time when I use a rolling pin, I use a smaller 10-inch one that has a slight taper, which gives me more control than a standard large one. Find one online by searching "small French rolling pin."

STANDARD SHEET PANS: Standard half (13 x 18-inch) and quarter (9½ x 13-inch) and the super-cute eighth (6½ x 9½-inch) rimmed sheet pans are the only pans I use because they stack nicely and are sturdy enough to hold up to lots of use. They're also inexpensive and make great backgrounds for

Instagram. In general I reach for lighter colored pans, but when roasting veggies, it's nice to use a darker-colored pan, which conducts more heat and will help them get extra crisp. Brands I love include Nordic Ware, USA Pan, Pampered Chef, and Great Jones. Unless otherwise specified, any mention of a sheet pan in these recipes refers to a standard half (13 x 18-inch) sheet pan, but other pans of a similar size would certainly work too. If the pan should have a rim (to prevent things like granola or nuts from rolling about), I've specified this, and if a rim is not specifically called for, then feel free to use a rimmed or rimless pan.

STAND MIXER: As a baker, I consider the stand mixer the centerpiece of the counter, a symbol of coziness and joy in the kitchen. If I saw one on MTV's *Room Raiders*, I'd want to be that person's friend immediately. If you have a big birthday, wedding, or other gift-receiving occasion coming up, then by all means, ask for the KitchenAid color that makes you happiest. But if you don't have one, don't fret—most bread doughs can be kneaded by hand, and cake batters and frostings can be made with a hand mixer.

A FEW GENERAL NOTES

ON WEIGHING INGREDIENTS: Learning to weigh ingredients changed my life, and I want it to change yours too. It makes cooking easier, more enjoyable, and more consistent. You'll also cut down drastically on the dirty dishes, and find that halving recipes or doubling them requires much less brain power. Baking with measuring cups typically requires the heavy usage of both hands, some digging around drawers for the proper cup, and a fair amount of squatting down to assess liquid measurements at eye level, all things that become a challenge with a toddler in your arms (or when laziness strikes!), and all things that can be eliminated if you rip off the bandage and adjust your brain to using weights. This adjustment process will take a few days, but as soon as you get the hang of it, you will feel a weight off your shoulders (pun intended!). Because kitchen scales can vary in accuracy levels, I do still recommend measuring very small quantities with measuring spoons, typically anything less than a tablespoon or two.

ON SALTING: Learning how to salt is the single best thing you can do to improve your cooking, and it will determine the difference between good, bad, and great results. I believe in the importance of directing you to "salt to taste," because I've cooked with both my mother and my mother-in-law (one loves salt approximately ten times as much as the other) and also because I've felt my own palate become more sensitive to salt over time. "Salt to taste" means to add the amount of salt that you prefer, but it can be a frustrating process if you're not even sure of an appropriate ballpark amount. For example, observing a proper amount of salt for pasta water for the first time can be jarring until you realize that most of it ends up down the drain. Or adding a few pinches of salt to something can feel inefficient if you're used to only pinching it between your thumb and forefinger (include your middle and even your ring finger if you want, to grasp around ⅛ teaspoon). Salting is a personal journey that will improve and also likely change over time, so focus when it's time to salt because food won't have the excitement it was meant to have without a proper amount. There are general rules for salting (salt every layer of the dish) and times when those need to be broken (don't salt the zucchini too early or else it will sweat and steam!). These are things you will pick up over time, and I am here to guide you, but there is also no such thing as overeducating yourself on how to salt, so I encourage you to read Cal Peternell's *Twelve Recipes*, Samin Nosrat's *Salt, Fat, Acid, Heat*, and any article that pops up on your newsfeed about salt.

ON OVEN RACKS: Unless an oven rack position is specified, assume the racks should be positioned in the center or close to it in order to get even heat all around. In general, if you want something crisper on the bottom, like pie, move the rack lower so that it's closer to the heat source. If you want something crisper on the top, like a casserole, move it higher, since heat rises and the very top of the oven collects a lot of heat.

ON BAKING TIME: The traditional format of baking times in recipes involves giving a range of time, like "bake until golden on the edges, 10 to 12 minutes," but this doesn't always sit well with me. What if the cookies aren't golden on the edges at 12 minutes? Should you take them out anyway? Did you do something wrong? Ovens are finicky things, and I usually disregard that top end number and rely more heavily on the visual cue ("golden on the edges"). As such, I typically feel like there is more clarity in providing a time at which you should begin checking for doneness, along with a cue for what to look for, with the understanding that if the cue isn't yet apparent, you can close the oven and check again in a bit, and not be limited by a range of time. If the time range is on the longer side (like slow cooker short ribs, where the range is hours), it's only fair to provide that range so you can better anticipate dinnertime.

BREAKFAST

I like mornings. The sleepy eyes, the funny hair, the slow-moving, soft-spoken requests for *blub-blubs* (blueberries), Al Roker delivering the weather, and strong, hot coffee out of my Zabar's mug. Our mornings are great for the same reasons that chicken Caesar salads from fast-casual restaurants are great: they're extremely predictable, almost always the same, and just perfectly enjoyable, no fireworks expected or necessary. We have a routine and we rarely stray. Bernie climbs up into my arms or her toddler tower to hang out and eat berries while I make a smoothie or spoon out some yogurt, and Nick pours his muesli into a bowl (if it's the winter) or a to-go container (in the farming season). On Sundays Nick makes pancakes, and on Saturdays we let loose with eggs or chocolate bread or even cake, nothing too extravagant.

It took me some time to come to terms with this, but I am not the kind of parent (a.k.a. my mom) who wakes up on weekends before the rest of the family to get cinnamon rolls in the oven so they can be hot and fresh when everyone comes downstairs. I find joy in waking up to Bernie chirps, brushing my teeth for the full three minutes, finding socks that match, and then strolling into the kitchen to a room-temperature scone loaf that I baked yesterday or even the day before, and leisurely toasting a slice as I help Bernie feed flaxseeds to her toy dinosaurs. I don't love being responsible for precise measurements or tying myself to an oven timer when I first wake up, but that doesn't mean we don't eat well in the morning. On the contrary, relaxation and gentle beginnings are just as delicious as yeast-risen rolls. As such, most things in this chapter are made for low-maintenance but craveworthy starts to your day: smoothies worth singing about, big-batch pantry items for grab-and-go moments, fun toasts with turbocharged flavor, and baked goods that will wait happily overnight as you slumber.

THREE SMOOTHIES

Anyone who has ever told you that "marriage isn't for them" has never used a Vitamix. The Vitamix blender we got as a wedding gift was the greatest thing to come out of getting married, tied with love and partnership and Bernie, of course. That thing is so strong it could probably purée a tractor into velvety, creamy oblivion. As a texture-first person, I'd go so far as to wish we'd gotten married sooner so that I could have had that much more time with our blender (and maybe as a bonus, skipped over an excess ex-boyfriend or two).

With a job that sometimes requires taste-testing twenty-six cakes in a day, front-loading my produce helps me feel less like garbage once dinnertime rolls around. When done right, our morning smoothies taste sweet and not vegetably, though they do pack in vegetables and other good nutrients, and the texture should be luscious and easy to guzzle. When Bernie was just starting on solid foods, I'd use green smoothies as the liquid in her oatmeal, and she actually ate it! I felt like a super parent. Now every morning we have the same routine: make a smoothie and pour it into a tall glass for me, a to-go cup for Nick, and a toddler cup for Bern. One day she'll taste a milkshake and realize what she's missing, but until then I'll sneak as many vegetables as I can into that tiny bod.

Here are some smoothie tips:

- This goes for literally everything, but for early-morning smoothies especially, weigh your ingredients. Your life will be infinitely easier if you forgo the measuring cups and just stick your blender on a scale.
- For the best, smoothest texture, blend for a little longer than you think you need to, at least a full 60 seconds.
- Get into the habit of rinsing out your blender as soon as you pour out your smoothie; it will make for painless cleanup.
- Smoothie packs to store in the freezer are very convenient. Pack everything except for the liquid into a sealable bag and store it flat so it doesn't freeze into one big solid ball that takes forever to break up. When you're ready to blend, let it sit at room temperature for a couple of minutes to thaw slightly and bend the bag a few times to break up any large chunks. Add to a blender with your liquid of choice and blend. You may need a little more liquid than normal to help it come together.
- Buy the big bags of prewashed kale and spinach and keep them in the freezer so they last longer.
- On days when all you feel like eating is bread and spaghetti but your conscience is telling you to eat a vegetable, it's okay to bribe yourself to have a smoothie by adding a slice of cake, a bar of chocolate, or a cookie directly to the blender with the produce. A blueberry cake smoothie with hidden kale is my fave.

The following are a few of our go-tos that we've made zillions of times. They are our most fun smoothies, and the directions are all the same: blend all ingredients in a high-speed blender on high for 1 to 2 minutes, until very smooth, adding more milk if needed to help it blend. Pour into glasses, sprinkle with any designated toppings, and drink immediately, because warm smoothies are gross!

ORANGE BLOSSOM DREAM SMOOTHIE

SERVES 2

1 heaping cup (180 grams) frozen chopped pineapple

1 seedless orange, peeled and separated into segments

1 medium carrot, unpeeled, trimmed and coarsely chopped

2 tablespoons (32 grams) unsweetened peanut butter or almond butter

½ cup (120 grams) plain Greek yogurt (whole milk, 2%, or nonfat)

½ cup (120 grams) milk (dairy or dairy-free), plus a little more if needed

½ teaspoon orange blossom water

⅛ teaspoon ground turmeric

Crack of black pepper

STRAWBERRY ROSE HALVA SMOOTHIE

SERVES 2

1½ cups (210 grams) frozen strawberries (sliced or hulled whole)

¾ cup (65 grams) frozen cauliflower (rice or florets)

1½ cups (360 grams) milk (dairy or dairy-free), plus a little more if needed

2 ounces (57 grams) halva, any flavor

½ teaspoon rosewater

Squeeze of lemon juice

Pinch of ground cinnamon, plus another pinch for topping

2 tablespoons (16 grams) hemp seeds or chia seeds, optional

BLUEBERRY CASHEW COOKIE SMOOTHIE

SERVES 2

1½ cups (210 grams) frozen wild blueberries

2 ounces (57 grams/1 big handful) chopped kale or baby spinach

1½ cups (360 grams) milk (dairy or dairy-free), plus a little more if needed

3 tablespoons (48 grams) unsweetened cashew butter

⅛ teaspoon ground cinnamon

¼ teaspoon pure vanilla extract

⅛ teaspoon almond extract

2 tablespoons (16 grams) hemp seeds or chia seeds, optional

Sprinkles, optional, for topping

STOLLEN GRANOLA

During one aggressive pregnancy craving for stollen, I learned why it's not as common around here as other Christmastime sweets like gingerbread and cutout cookies: it's quite the undertaking to make, and then it still kind of needs to be slathered with butter? No offense to moist stollens. But you know how pregnancy cravings work—you need these things now! So I started making other treats, like cookies and bars, with the flavor profile of stollen— loads of warm spices, orange zest, and, my favorite, almond paste—and found that granola was made to take on this challenge. The almond paste blends in visually with the toasted oats but texturally provides the slightest chew, which, to me, puts this granola in a different league from all other granolas.

MAKES ABOUT 10 CUPS

¼ cup (50 grams) packed light brown sugar

¼ cup (84 grams) honey

½ cup (100 grams) unrefined coconut oil, melted

1 teaspoon pure vanilla extract

½ teaspoon almond extract

3½ cups (315 grams) rolled oats

1 cup (128 grams) roasted or raw pistachios (see page xviii) *salted or unsalted*

7 ounces (198 grams) almond paste, grated on the big holes of a box grater (see Note)

Zest of 1 orange

¾ teaspoon kosher salt

1½ teaspoons ground cinnamon

¼ teaspoon ground cardamom

⅛ teaspoon ground cloves

⅛ teaspoon ground allspice

¾ cup (120 grams) dried cherries

¾ cup (120 grams) golden raisins

NOTE: *Almond paste can occasionally be too soft to grate. You can firm it up in the fridge for a few hours, or simply tear it with your hands into small ½-inch-ish crumbles.*

PREHEAT the oven to 300°F. Line a rimmed sheet pan with parchment paper and set aside.

IN a large bowl, whisk together the brown sugar, honey, coconut oil, vanilla, and almond extract. Sprinkle the oats and pistachios on top, followed by the almond paste, orange zest, salt, cinnamon, cardamom, cloves, and allspice, dispersing as evenly as possible. Fold together with a rubber spatula. Spread

HOME IS WHERE THE EGGS ARE

evenly on the prepared sheet pan and bake for 30 minutes, give it a stir, and then continue to bake until golden and toasty; begin checking after another 30 minutes. It may still be a little wet when it comes out of the oven, but it will dry out as it cools.

COOL completely on the pan, sprinkle on the cherries and raisins, and fold together, breaking up any clumps that are too big to eat in one bite.

STORE in an airtight container at room temperature for up to a few weeks, or in the fridge for a little longer.

COOKIE DOUGH OAT BARS

If the walls of my refrigerator could talk, they'd probably be like, "Please just stop it with the granola bars." Out of all the constants in the fridge, the most annoying are the half-empty containers of granola bars that don't have a date on them but are *probably* still good ¯_(☺)_/¯. Lactating did that to my life—it made me an obsessive granola bar maker, and I guess a forgetful one too, hence all the half-empty containers. (Who cleans out the fridge during maternity leave?!) From the time that Bernie was about three weeks old, I'd make granola bars with her strapped to me in her carrier and toss in whatever mix-ins were within arm's reach. They were something I could make without having to worry about dropping raw flour or egg on her head, and they fueled me during those first wild months of motherhood and beyond. Since then I've gone through approximately 435,785,406 variations on mix-ins, from marzipan to halva, but my favorite breakthrough came when I just tossed all of the ingredients into a food processor to produce a texture that's more like cookie dough than a regular chewy granola bar. The creaminess of the cashews, hemp seeds, and toasty oats combines with snappy chocolate chips for the new staple bar of your dessert-as-breakfast dreams. These are way too good to be forgotten in the back of the fridge.

MAKES 8 BARS

1 cup (90 grams) rolled or quick-cooking oats

1 cup (144 grams) whole raw cashews

¼ cup (32 grams) hemp seeds

1 tablespoon (13 grams) packed light brown sugar, plus more to taste if desired

½ teaspoon kosher salt

3 tablespoons (38 grams) unrefined coconut oil, room temperature, plus more if needed

2 tablespoons (42 grams) honey, plus more if needed

1½ teaspoons pure vanilla extract

2 tablespoons (30 grams) semisweet mini chocolate chips

Flaky salt

PREHEAT the oven to 350°F. Line a loaf pan with enough parchment paper to come all the way up on the long sides and allow 1-inch wings. Set aside.

SPREAD the oats on a rimmed sheet pan and toast until fragrant and slightly darker, about 10 minutes. Add to a food processor along with the cashews, hemp seeds, brown sugar, and salt and blend until very fine, like the

consistency of fine breadcrumbs. Add the coconut oil, honey, and vanilla and blend until the mixture is combined and starts to form a dough. It'll still look crumbly in the food processor, but if you squeeze some in your hand, it should stick together (if it feels a little too dry, you can add a touch more coconut oil or honey). Taste it and if you'd like it to be a little sweeter, blend in up to 1 tablespoon (13 grams) more brown sugar.

PRESS the mixture into the prepared loaf pan, spreading it out firmly and evenly. Press the chocolate chips firmly into the top and sprinkle with a pinch of flaky salt. Let firm up in the fridge for about 30 minutes, remove from the loaf pan, and slice into 8 small bars. Store in an airtight container in the fridge for up to a couple of weeks.

TOAST

My one rule about toast, which I break all the time because I love my cute red toaster, is that bread shouldn't be toasted at all; it should actually be fried. It should sizzle away in a layer of olive oil, butter, or coconut oil, until it gets those crisp golden edges and splotches all over. Its innards should still be soft and chewy, and that thin layer just below the surface should have absorbed the butter or oil, delivering luxuriousness and flavor. Toast, when made properly, should have notes of doughnut.

SO with just a tiny bit more time and fat, toast transforms from an everyday fallback breakfast into something that will make you hop out of bed and get you excited about your day. And a bonus—bread that you thought was old and stale can be revived to its original glory with a quick pan-fry.

HERE'S what to do: Heat a pan over medium heat, add a drizzle of good olive oil, a pat of butter, or a plop of coconut oil (use unrefined if you plan to top it with something sweet like jam or speculoos spread, because *yum*). Then add a slice of thick bread (fresh, day old, or even frozen), ideally ¾ inch to 1 inch, smoosh it around so that it makes full contact with the fat, and let it hang out until it reaches your desired toastiness. Flip and repeat, adding more fat to the pan as necessary. Top as desired.

SOME OF MY FAVORITE TOASTS

Olive oil fried toast (or a bagel!), cream cheese, and a slice of Swiss, Muenster, smoked Gouda, or mozzarella. Double the cheese, double the texture, double the fun.

Olive oil fried toast with smashed avocado, kosher salt, a strongly encouraged lime or lemon squeeze, thinly sliced radishes for good looks and peppery crunch, a drizzle of good olive oil to collect in pools on the radishes, flaky salt, and loads of black pepper. Inspired by the avocado toast at Lodge Bread Company in Los Angeles.

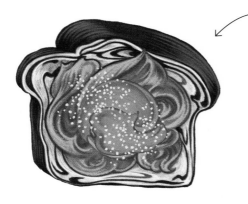

Coconut oil fried toast, sprinkled with cinnamon a little bit before it reaches desired toastiness so that the cinnamon blooms while the bread finishes. Ooh, yeah! Top it with almond butter or tahini, optional jam or honey, and a pinch of flakey salt. This is best with challah, brioche, or babka.

Mayo fried toast with a 7-minute egg topped with olive oil, flaky salt, and black pepper. Oh, mayo is a wild-card move! Spread it on before adding the bread to a dry skillet.

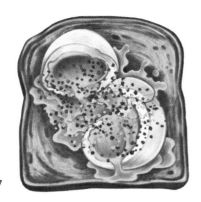

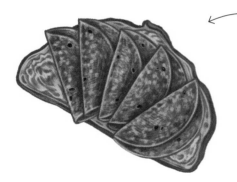

Butter fried toast with smashed avocado, black pepper, and salami. A slightly more nutritious version of my desert-island food, salami and butter on bread.

Butter fried toast with a layer of peanut butter and thin apple slices. Apple slices on toast is an awkward combination of textures, but I like it.

RHUBARB MOZZARELLA GRILLED CHEESE

Fresh mozzarella doesn't get enough credit for its ability to jump the pizza ship and get along with sweet ingredients like they're old summer camp friends. We know that ricotta can do that, because it honestly won't shut up about how great it is in doughnuts and cheesecake, but come on, mozzarella is a mild, creamy cheese too. Mozzarella can hang with both sweets and savories too. Mozzarella wants to be sandwiched with jam too.

MAKES 1 GRILLED CHEESE

2 bread slices, ideally brioche or challah or another soft, luxurious bread

1 to 2 tablespoons (20 to 40 grams) Rhubarb Rose Jam (page 15) or other rhubarb jam

About 2 tablespoons (30 grams) ricotta, optional

1½ ounces (42 grams) fresh mozzarella, torn

Flaky salt

2 big fresh basil leaves, torn

1 tablespoon (14 grams) unsalted butter

HEAT a skillet over medium heat.

SPREAD one slice of the bread with a thin, even layer of jam and the other slice of bread with either more jam or ricotta. Top one of the slices with the mozzarella and sprinkle with a pinch of flaky salt. Top with the basil and sandwich with the other slice of bread.

MELT the butter in the pan and add the sandwich, smooshing it around to get it all coated in butter. Cover and cook for a few minutes until browned, flip the sandwich, and grill it on the other side, covered, until it is browned and the cheese is melty, a few more minutes. Sprinkle with another little pinch of salt, cut in half, and have at it.

RHUBARB ROSE JAM

In the same way that caramel begs for big flakes of salt and freshly baked challah *needs* butter, in my mouth rhubarb will always ask to be paired with rose. Maybe it's because flowers and rhubarb spring up at the same time of year, or maybe I just can't resist alliteration. During rhubarb season, my bottle of rosewater jumps to the front of my pantry so I can add a little splash of it to everything rhubarb, from soda syrup to cake. It allows the rhubarb to shine while giving it that I-just-got-back-from-Paris sparkle.

MAKES 1½ CUPS

1 pound (454 grams) fresh or frozen (and thawed) rhubarb, cut into ½-inch pieces

1⅔ cups (333 grams) sugar

Juice of 1 small lemon

1 vanilla bean

1 tablespoon (15 grams) rosewater

IN a large heavy-bottomed pot, toss the rhubarb with the sugar, cover, and macerate for 1 hour, tossing occasionally. (This intensifies the flavor of the rhubarb; if you need rhubarb jam ASAP, then fine, skip this step.) Stir in the lemon juice, then split and scrape the vanilla bean and add the innards and the scraped bean to infuse the jam with vanilla flavor.

PUT on some oven mitts and an apron because things are about to get spitty. Bring the jam to a boil over high (trust me: *high*) heat and boil, stirring and scraping the bottom of the pot continuously with a heat-safe spatula so that the jam doesn't burn, until the rhubarb is broken down and the jam is thick and gloopy, 5 to 7 minutes.

REMOVE from the heat and continue stirring for another minute or two so the residual heat of the pot doesn't burn the jam. Stir in the rosewater and let cool.

DISCARD the vanilla bean and store the jam in an airtight container in the fridge for up to a few weeks.

NOTE: *There is no salt in this jam because I like to sprinkle it with flaky salt after I spread it on toast.*

SPECULOOS CASHEW BUTTER

Speculoos spread, the thick, sweet butter made of pulverized cinnamon-flavored airplane cookies, is one of the best things to sneak straight from the jar during the greatest pre-bedtime activity of standing in front of the pantry and eating tiny bites of a hundred different snacks. The problem with speculoos spread, though—and the reason I don't eat it more often—is that it doesn't serve a real nutritional purpose like a nut butter or even Nutella, which at least contains protein by way of hazelnuts. It's basically just sugar, oil, and cinnamon. And I mean no offense to those ingredients, but I would spend more time with them if they had some benefits beyond providing joy.

So this is the spread that would happen if a nut butter dressed up as speculoos for Halloween. It's nutty, warm, and not too sweet. In a move inspired by one of my favorite nut butter companies ever, Ground Up, I've loaded it with coconut, which sweetens it and makes the consistency more spreadable.

MAKES 1⅓ CUPS

1 cup (144 grams) roasted cashews (see page xviii)

1 cup (144 grams) roasted almonds (see page xviii)

1 cup (90 grams) shredded sweetened coconut

1 tablespoon (6 grams) ground cinnamon

1 tablespoon (21 grams) honey

1 teaspoon vanilla bean paste or extract

¼ teaspoon kosher salt

COMBINE all the ingredients in a high-powered food processor and blend for 10 to 15 minutes (see Note), scraping the sides occasionally, until spreadable.

STORE in an airtight container. If you expect to eat it within a month or so, store at room temperature. Otherwise you can store in the fridge to extend its freshness.

NOTE: *Not all food processors are great at making nut butter. Low-powered food processors and smaller ones aren't great for blending long enough or powerfully enough to turn nuts into butter. If you suspect that your food processor might not be powerful enough but you still want to give this a go, have some coconut oil or neutral oil on hand to add little by little in case your butter needs help achieving a spreadable consistency.*

SEEDY HALVA FAIRY TOAST

If I were a toast, I'd want to be this riff on the classic Australian and New Zealand treat, fairy bread. It's typically white bread spread with butter and covered in rainbow sprinkles, but this version is one I feel I can get away with eating on a regular basis as a grown-up human who feels guilt in the absence of a nutritious breakfast. The butter is replaced by a layer of tahini and a drizzle of honey, which makes you feel like you're eating a spreadable version of halva, the flaky Middle Eastern sesame candy. This gets covered in a mix of all the seeds from the crunchy section of your grocery store tossed with a handful of rainbow sprinkles. It has just enough whimsy to get you excited but not so much that you'd get sick of it as a daily breakfast. It has true staying power!

MAKES 1 SLICE

1 slice of multigrain toast (see page 10, ideally fried in coconut oil or butter)

Good-quality tahini (see page xxi)

Honey

Super-Fun Seed Mix (recipe follows)

Flaky salt

SPREAD the toast with a nice layer of tahini and drizzle with honey to taste. Cover the *entire* surface with Super-Fun Seed Mix and sprinkle with a pinch of flaky salt. Gobble it up, then check your teeth.

SUPER-FUN SEED MIX

COMBINE ¼ cup each millet (48 grams), hemp seeds (32 grams), sesame seeds (32 grams), flaxseeds (36 grams), and good-tasting rainbow sprinkles (40 grams). Keep in an airtight container at room temperature for a few months, or longer in the fridge or freezer. This is also great in oatmeal, muffins, granola bars, and yogurt.

SALMON AVOCADO SMØRREBRØD WITH PRESERVED LEMON CREAM

Some things I love about having married into a Nordic family:

1. My almond extract obsession is not that crazy after all.
2. Sweater culture is on a whole other level.
3. I feel a true connection with Anna and Elsa.
4. We get to go to the local branch of Sons of Norway to celebrate Syttende Mai (Norwegian Constitution Day) and eat lefse, rømmegrøt, bløtkake, and other comforting mildly flavored treats.
5. Buttered bread is so much a staple form of sustenance that it has its own one-word name, smørrebrød.

Here's my proudest smørrebrød! It's a really fun party. Like . . . yeah, it's an avocado toast and I *am* a millennial, but this is so much more than that. It's a special breakfast to celebrate the weekend, the fact that you have rugbrød in your bread box, or just being alive in an era when you can easily get avocados in the tundra.

Topping amounts may vary depending on the size of your bread, but these are the amounts I use when I have it on my fave rugbrød (page 241).

SERVES 4

Unsalted or salted butter

4 thick slices rye bread

⅓ cup (80 grams) sour cream
Greek yogurt is cool too!

1 heaping tablespoon (18 grams) finely chopped rinsed preserved lemon rind
Can sub the zest of ½ lemon + a pinch of salt.

Freshly ground black pepper

1 avocado, pitted, peeled, and thinly sliced

Flaky salt or kosher salt

3 ounces (85 grams) cold-smoked salmon, thinly sliced

2 radishes, thinly sliced

4 cornichons, thinly sliced

Crushed red pepper, optional

Handful of chopped chives or dill

Sesame seeds

Lemon wedges, for serving

HEAT a large skillet over medium heat and melt a thin layer of butter. Add the bread and toast on both sides until golden, smooshing it a little so it soaks up that butter. In a small bowl, combine the sour cream, preserved lemon, and a few turns of pepper. To assemble, dollop the preserved lemon sour cream all over the bread and then top with slices of avocado. Season the avocado with salt. Nestle in the slices of salmon, radishes, and cornichons. Top with more black pepper and crushed red pepper (if using), sprinkle with chives or dill and sesame seeds, and serve with lemon wedges.

PUMPKIN SCONE LOAF

As a wee family perpetually surrounded by baked goods (usually made in the name of "research"), we go through batches of things very slowly. A slice of challah here, a bagel there, a nibble of pancake at snacktime, a chunk of bread with soup. And so the idea of baking something that's known for being good for only a few hours out of the oven simply does not fit our lifestyle. I'm talking about scones.

The solution to this, the scone loaf, was born in time for *Molly on the Range*, and I'm proud of how many hearts it has won with its pockets of marzipan and very forgiving lifespan. So here is another version that's based on the scone queen of autumnal days, pumpkin. It has the flavor profile of a pumpkin bread, the dense crumb of a scone, and enough moisture to send Larry David into a rage. Its crunchy sugar top adds excitement and sweetness, but the interior isn't overly sweet, leaving room for a layer of jam. Or my personal favorite, cream cheese *and* jam.

MAKES 1 LOAF

2 cups (260 grams) all-purpose flour

⅓ cup (67 grams) plus 1 tablespoon (13 grams) packed light brown sugar, divided

¾ teaspoon kosher salt

2 teaspoons baking powder

½ teaspoon baking soda

2 teaspoons ground cinnamon

½ teaspoon ground ginger

¼ teaspoon freshly ground nutmeg

⅛ teaspoon ground cloves

½ cup (113 grams) cold unsalted butter, cut into ½-inch cubes

¾ cup (135 grams) semisweet chocolate chips

¾ cup (78 grams) roasted pecans or walnuts (see page xviii), coarsely chopped, optional

1 large egg

¼ cup (60 grams) buttermilk

¾ cup plus 2 tablespoons (211 grams) pumpkin purée (or half of a 15-ounce can; see Note)

1 teaspoon pure vanilla extract

NOTE: *Make two loaves and freeze one if you'd like to use up the whole can! Or use the other half of the can for Nick's pumpkin pancakes (page 41).*

PREHEAT the oven to 400°F. Grease a 4 x 9-inch pullman or standard (4½ x 8½ x 2¾-inch) metal loaf pan, line with parchment paper to come all the way up on the long sides and allow 1-inch wings, and set aside.

IN a food processor, combine the flour, ⅓ cup (67 grams) of the brown sugar, salt, baking powder, baking soda, cinnamon, ginger, nutmeg, and cloves and pulse to combine. Add the butter cubes and pulse until the butter is pea size.

DUMP into a large bowl and toss in the chocolate chips and nuts, if using. In a separate medium bowl or large measuring cup, whisk together the egg, buttermilk, pumpkin, and vanilla. Add the wet ingredients to the dry ingredients and mix with a rubber spatula or large spoon until just combined. Scrape the dough into the loaf pan and spread it out evenly. Sprinkle with the remaining tablespoon (13 grams) of brown sugar.

BAKE until the loaf is browned on top and a toothpick inserted into the center comes out clean; begin checking for doneness at 50 minutes and tent with foil if the top browns too much for your liking before the center is done. Let cool for 20 minutes in the pan, then transfer to a wire rack. Cool for at least 10 more minutes before slicing and eating.

STORE leftovers in an airtight container at room temperature. This is best eaten within 3 days but will keep for up to 5 days.

CARDAMOM BABKA

Cardamom buns, popular across Scandinavia in a variety of styles, were first marketed to me by my dad as "kind of like cinnamon rolls." We were at a snack stand on top of a mountain in Norway, and I was eight years old and intrigued by the sugary white pebbles sprinkled on top. But I soon found that cardamom was too peppery for my taste buds, so I plucked off all the pebbles and gave the underlying bun to my dad. Now that I adore cardamom, I feel as if every fresh batch of cardamom buns is an effort to make up for the bun that got away.

This babka, which is an ode to Bernie (my li'l Scandinavian Jewish loaf), is basically a bunch of cardamom buns smooshed together. Babkas are on the more labor-intensive end of the breakfast spectrum, but I appreciate the way that they fit into our lives with much less commitment than other breakfast sweets, like, say, cinnamon rolls or cardamom rolls. Individual rolls are best eaten immediately, and so I always feel the need to have company to share them with. But what's so nice about babkas is that their loaf shape can hold more moisture, last longer, and reheat in the toaster nicely. And then, when the weekend is over and the loaf has done its job, you can make Babka Cereal (page 27), so none of it goes to waste.

MAKES 1 LOAF

Dough

2½ cups (325 grams) all-purpose flour, plus more for dusting

2 tablespoons (25 grams) sugar

1½ teaspoons instant yeast

¾ teaspoon kosher salt

½ teaspoon ground cardamom

½ cup (120 grams) whole milk, warmed (105° to 110°F)

2 large eggs

6 tablespoons (85 grams) unsalted butter, room temperature

Neutral oil, for the bowl

Filling and Assembly

6 tablespoons (85 grams) unsalted butter, room temperature

¾ cup (150 grams) brown sugar (dark or light; dark for a more vibrant swirl)

1½ teaspoons ground cardamom

Pinch of kosher salt

2 tablespoons (25 grams) neutral oil

1 egg, beaten with a splash of water, for egg wash

Swedish pearl sugar, for topping (or turbinado or Belgian pearl sugar)

MAKE the dough: In the bowl of a stand mixer, whisk together the flour, sugar, yeast, salt, and cardamom. Add the milk and eggs and use a stiff rubber spatula or wooden spoon to mostly combine into a shaggy dough. Knead with the stand mixer fitted with a dough hook on medium until all of the dry ingredients are hydrated and then with the mixer still running, add the butter 1 tablespoon (14 grams) at a time until it is incorporated into the dough. When all the butter is incorporated, continue kneading for 10 to 15 minutes, until smooth and slightly sticky. The dough may appear a little too sticky at first, but keep on mixing and it should come together. Scrape the sides of the bowl occasionally if necessary to ensure everything incorporates evenly. Stretch the dough into a ball, pinching the ends under to form a taut surface, and transfer to an oiled bowl (or simply oil the stand mixer bowl and use that if it isn't too covered in dough), turning to coat the dough fully in a thin layer of oil. Cover with plastic wrap or a towel and let rise in a draft-free place until doubled in size, 1 to 2 hours.

MAKE the filling: In a medium bowl, using a stiff rubber spatula, mix together the butter, brown sugar, cardamom, salt, and oil until combined and spreadable. You can also do this in a stand mixer with a paddle. Reserve at room temperature until ready to use.

ARRANGE a rack in the lower third of the oven and preheat the oven to 350°F. Grease a 4 x 9-inch pullman loaf pan or 5 x 9-inch metal loaf pan and line it with enough parchment paper to come all the way up on the long sides and allow 1-inch wings, and set aside.

ON a lightly floured work surface, roll the dough out into a 10 x 22-inch rectangle with the wide side facing you. The dough should be slightly sticky, but if it's too sticky to work with, you can dust it with a little more flour. Spread all but about 2 tablespoons of the filling on the dough, leaving a ½-inch border on the long top edge. Starting from the bottom, roll the dough the long way into a tight log and pinch the edges to seal. Cut the log in half to make 2 shorter logs. Spread the reserved 2 tablespoons of filling along the top of one of the logs, then twist the logs together. Transfer to the loaf pan, cover loosely with plastic, and let proof for another 30 to 40 minutes, until puffy and risen by about half.

GENTLY brush the top of the babka with the egg wash and sprinkle with the pearl sugar. Place the pan on a sheet pan (to catch any drips of filling) and bake until the top is deep golden brown and the internal temperature is 190° to 195°F; begin checking for doneness at 45 minutes.

COOL for 15 minutes in the pan, then transfer to a rack to cool for at least another few minutes before slicing. Store leftovers in an airtight container at room temperature. This is best eaten within 3 days; after that, use it for French toast or Babka Cereal (page 27).

BABKA CEREAL

Every year on my birthday, Nick orders a box of my favorite things from Russ & Daughters in New York: bagels, lox, cream cheese, and babka. We take down the lox first because we couldn't live with ourselves if we ever let lox go bad, and then by the time we're done with that and all the bagels, we're left with half a babka and a craving for salads. The swirly loaf may be the beauty queen of the coffee cake world, but it's quite dense and deceptively challenging to finish in a little family. Babka French toast is one use for stale babka, but that's not what I want after a week straight of bagels. What I want is to preserve my babka long-term, allowing for a less committed experience. Enter babka cereal! The idea started off as babka chips, like bagel chips but sweet, but it quickly became clear that breaking up those chips to eat with a spoon as a Jewy Cinnamon Toast Crunch was more pleasurable. It keeps for quite some time, so my birthday celebration never has to end.

MAKES ABOUT 4 CUPS

½ loaf chocolate or cinnamon babka or the cardamom babka on page 24, a few days old

2 tablespoons (28 grams) unsalted butter, melted

1 teaspoon ground cinnamon, or to taste

2 teaspoons sugar, or to taste

¾ cup (84 grams) sliced almonds

Yogurt or milk, for serving

PREHEAT the oven to 300°F. Line a rimmed sheet pan with parchment paper and set it aside. Cut the babka into slices as thin as you can get them, about ¼ inch, and then cut the slices into little bite-size squares. (Due to babka's layered nature, these squares will not be perfect, but that's okay!) Transfer the squares and all their crumbs to a big bowl. Toss with the melted butter, then the cinnamon and sugar. Taste and add more cinnamon and sugar as desired—babkas vary drastically in sweetness and spice level, so please do taste and adjust to your liking! Toss in the almonds and spread the mixture out on the prepared sheet pan.

BAKE for 25 minutes, toss, and continue to bake until golden brown and mostly crisp; begin checking for doneness after another 25 minutes. It's okay if a couple of pieces are still slightly soft; they'll crisp up as they cool.

COOL completely on the pan. Enjoy over yogurt or with milk. Store in an airtight container at room temperature for up to a few weeks.

CRUSTY CHOCOLATE CHIP BREAD

This is what I envision chocolate babka looks like first thing in the morning before she curls her swirls and moisturizes her skin. She's crusty, disheveled, and, guess what, just as lovable! This one-bowl chocolaty bread is ideal for when you need a sweet start to your day but your toddler is sprouting molars/going through a sleep regression/has some separation anxiety and the idea of having two free hands for more than sixty seconds at a time is simply unfathomable. Or maybe you're just in the mood for a chocolaty bread with a thick crust! Either way, this loaf is a real winner, especially with good salted butter. It's true that she needs her beauty sleep (*do* read this recipe entirely before you get going), but hands-on time is about as minimal as it gets.

I think of this bread as a babka alternative for a busy yet patient person.

MAKES 1 LOAF

2 cups (260 grams) bread flour, plus more for dusting

1 cup (130 grams) white whole wheat flour or regular whole wheat flour

2 tablespoons (25 grams) sugar

2 teaspoons kosher salt

¼ teaspoon instant yeast

⅓ cup (80 grams) plain whole milk Greek yogurt

1¼ cups (300 grams) warm water (105° to 110°F)

Heaping ½ cup (100 grams) milk chocolate chips

Heaping ½ cup (100 grams) dark or bittersweet chocolate chips

IN a large bowl, whisk together the flours, sugar, salt, and yeast and create a well in the center. In a small bowl, whisk together the yogurt and water. Add the yogurt mixture to the dry ingredient well and stir with a rubber spatula to combine and form a sticky dough. Cover with plastic wrap and let rise at room temperature for 12 to 18 hours.

PLACE a large piece of parchment paper on a work surface and dust with flour.

WITH the dough still in the bowl, sprinkle the top with the milk chocolate chips, press them in with a rubber spatula, then use the spatula to fold the outside edges over the chocolate chips, in toward the center. Sprinkle this new surface of dough with the dark or bittersweet chocolate chips, give them a press, and repeat the edge-folding process, sealing the seams (using your fingers if needed) and minimizing the number of the chips poking out of the dough (no worries though if a few stubborn chips poke through). Turn this

blob out onto the floured parchment seam side down, so that you have a nice taut surface on top. Dust the surface of the dough with a little more flour, cover with plastic wrap, and let rise for 1½ hours. During the last 30 minutes of rising time, place a lidded cast-iron Dutch oven on a rack set in the lower third of the oven. (The Dutch oven should be 3 quarts or larger, and both the pot and its lid must be heatproof at 450°F.) Preheat the oven to 450°F.

CAREFULLY remove the preheated Dutch oven and take off the lid. Peel the plastic wrap off the dough and use the parchment paper to lift it up and lower it into the Dutch oven (yes—the parchment paper goes in, too). Trim any excess edges from the paper (a little overhang is fine) and cover the Dutch oven. Bake for 30 minutes, remove the lid, and continue to bake until the loaf is deeply browned on top; begin checking for doneness at 10 minutes.

USE the parchment paper to transfer the loaf to a wire rack, let it cool for about 30 minutes, cut into thick slices, and enjoy! I like this slathered with butter and sprinkled with flaky salt.

STORE leftovers in an airtight container at room temperature for up to a few days; reheat slices in a toaster oven or skillet.

HOME IS WHERE THE EGGS ARE

EVERYTHING BAGELS

After I got married and received my Minnesota driver's license, after I became a chicken mom and learned the postman's name, and after I subconsciously incorporated "ope" and "uff da" into my everyday lexicon, I realized it was time to learn how to make the thing I missed most about New York: the big chewy bagels.

Knowing this would be no small feat, I buckled up. Would I need special ingredients? Would I need New York water? Would my hands be able to shape them?? My research journey took me down countless book, internet, newspaper, and human rabbit holes; it took me to Alaska for salmon to make my own lox; and it took me right back to our farm, where I learned that the wheat that Nick grows gets ground into high-gluten flour which is then shipped to the Bronx for—you guessed it—bagels. *I moved to a bagel farm, you guys!!!*

I also learned the following:

1. Yes, you need special ingredients, but no, they are not hard to find. High-gluten flour contributes to the chewy, dense quality that separates the women from the girls. And barley malt lends that faint, can't-put-your-finger-on-it flavor. One whiff, and you'll see what I mean. Both are readily available on the internet, and both can be bought in large quantities that will keep for a while. In the event that you absolutely need bagels before the delivery truck arrives, all is not lost; substitute bread flour or all-purpose flour for the high-gluten flour and substitute honey or molasses for the barley malt. While I'd strongly prefer that you hold off on making these substitutions, since bagels take time and I want you to do this right, I'm also well aware of the crazy things that an aggressive bagel craving can cause a person to do.

2. Shaping bagels is the hardest part, but, hey, even ugly bagels are delicious (I would know). Google some bagel shaping videos!

3. No, you don't need New York water. But you do need to boil the bagels! This is the other main factor that contributes to their chewiness. When you boil the exterior, you make this special shell that prevents the dough from rising very much when it bakes. Instead, it expands inside itself to make the dense circle of bread we all know and love.

This process takes a while, but the return on investment is high. And bagels freeze remarkably well, so you can have good-as-fresh bagels any old day.

MAKES 12 BAGELS

Bagels

6 cups (780 grams) high-gluten flour, plus more for dusting if needed

2 teaspoons instant yeast

1 tablespoon (8 grams) kosher salt

2 tablespoons (25 grams) packed light brown sugar

2 cups (480 grams) warm water (105° to 110°F)

2 tablespoons (42 grams) barley malt syrup or (20 grams) powder, divided

Neutral oil, for the bowl

1 tablespoon (15 grams) baking soda

Topping

2 teaspoons poppy seeds

2 teaspoons sesame seeds

2 teaspoons dried minced garlic

2 teaspoons dried minced onion

½ teaspoon kosher salt

1 teaspoon caraway seeds, optional

1 egg white, beaten with a splash of water, for egg wash

IN a large bowl or the bowl of a stand mixer fitted with a dough hook, whisk together the flour, yeast, salt, and brown sugar. Add the water and 1 tablespoon of the barley malt and mix with a stiff rubber spatula or wooden spoon to form a stiff dough. Knead on a floured surface or in the stand mixer on medium until smooth and slightly sticky, 10 to 15 minutes, dusting with additional flour if needed to prevent sticking. Stretch the dough into a ball, pinching the ends under to form a taut surface, and transfer to an oiled bowl (or simply oil the bowl you used to mix the dough if it isn't too covered in dough), turning to coat the dough fully in a thin layer of oil. Cover with plastic wrap and refrigerate overnight.

LET the dough come to room temperature for 1 to 2 hours. Meanwhile, arrange oven racks in the upper middle and lower middle positions and preheat the oven to 450°F. Line 2 sheet pans with parchment paper, grease the parchment paper well, and set aside.

TURN the dough out onto a clean work surface, divide it into 12 equal parts, and stretch them into smooth balls, making sure to seal any dough seams well. Shape the bagels by sticking your thumb through the center of each ball and using your fingers to gently stretch out a 2-inch hole. Place the bagels on the prepared sheet pans and cover loosely with plastic wrap or a towel and let rise for 15 minutes.

BRING a large pot of water to a boil and add the baking soda and remaining tablespoon of barley malt. Lay out a clean kitchen towel near the pot of boiling water.

WORKING with 3 bagels at a time, boil them for 1 minute on each side (use a timer for this). With a slotted spoon or spatula, transfer them briefly to the kitchen towel to catch any excess moisture, and then back to the sheet pans.

TO make the topping, in a small bowl, combine the poppy seeds, sesame seeds, garlic, onion, salt, and caraway seeds, if using. Brush the bagels with the egg white and sprinkle with the topping. Bake the bagels for 10 minutes, switch the racks and rotate the pans 180 degrees, and bake until golden brown; begin checking at 6 minutes. Let cool slightly and enjoy!

I don't believe in toasting fresh bagels, because fresh bagels are perfect, but go for it with any bagel that's lost its just-baked shimmer. The best way to store bagels is to slice them as soon as they're cool and freeze them in an airtight container for up to a few months. Reheat in the toaster.

CRANBERRY WALNUT POWER BAGELS

As a Jew and former resident of New York, I am honestly so offended by this bagel. It has not one but *two* kinds of dried fruits, it will absolutely make Cynthia Nixon's bagel order seem tame if ever paired with lox, it's not even shaped like a bagel, and it's called a "power bagel," as if to imply that other bagels are somehow *not powerful*. Pfffff!

But as a Midwesterner with a nostalgic appreciation for the Aspirational Bagel Landscape of the North, I have a deep affection for these. They are inspired by the seed-packed Einstein Bros. Power Protein bagel, but . . . (How do I say this without offending the bagel shop that inspired my wanderlust for New York from a very young age? Oh, I'm just going to go for it because they need someone to tell them to step up their game, because their quality has slipped. I'm doing this out of love and for their own good.) They are better. They're plumper, denser, and more flavorful. These will certainly remind you of a cinnamon raisin bagel, however with the crunch and excitement of all the seeds and walnuts herein, well, cinnamon raisin *wishes*. I keep these in the freezer for when I want a chewy, filling breakfast that definitely doesn't include lox and for when I want to feel . . . powerful! Oh, okay, I get it now.

½ cup (60 grams) dried cranberries

½ cup (80 grams) golden raisins

1 heaping cup (120 grams) roasted walnuts (see page xviii), coarsely chopped

¼ cup (40 grams) roasted sunflower seeds

salted or unsalted

2 tablespoons (24 grams) millet

2 tablespoons (20 grams) sesame seeds

4 cups (520 grams) high-gluten flour

Bread flour or all-purpose flour is okay in a pinch. But only in a pinch.

1 cup (130 grams) whole wheat flour

1 cup (90 grams) rolled oats

½ cup (100 grams) packed light brown sugar

1 tablespoon (8 grams) kosher salt

2¼ teaspoons (1 packet) instant yeast

1 teaspoon ground cinnamon

2 cups (480 grams) warm water (105° to 110°F)

2 tablespoons (42 grams) barley malt syrup or (20 grams) powder (see Note), divided

Neutral oil, for the bowl

1 tablespoon (15 grams) baking soda

Cornmeal, optional, for dusting

NOTE: *Order barley malt online or find it at specialty/natural grocery stores. Sub honey or molasses in a pinch. But only in a pinch.*

IN a medium bowl, toss together the cranberries, raisins, walnuts, sunflower seeds, millet, and sesame seeds and set aside. In the bowl of a stand mixer fitted with a dough hook (see Note opposite), whisk together the flours, oats, brown sugar, salt, yeast, and cinnamon. Add the water and 1 tablespoon of the barley malt and mix with a stiff rubber spatula or wooden spoon to form a stiff dough. Knead on medium until smooth and slightly sticky, 10 to 15 minutes, scraping down the sides of the bowl occasionally. Resist the urge to add more flour, as the oats will absorb quite a bit of moisture. Knead in the cranberry-nut-seed mixture. (It's a *lot* of mix-ins, I know!) Stretch the dough into a ball, pinching the ends under to form a taut surface, and transfer to an oiled bowl (or simply oil the stand mixer bowl and use that if it isn't too covered in dough), turning to coat the dough fully in a thin layer of oil. Cover with plastic wrap and refrigerate overnight.

LET the dough come to room temperature for 1 to 2 hours. Meanwhile, arrange oven racks in the upper middle and lower middle positions and preheat the oven to 450°F.

TURN the dough out onto a clean work surface and roll it into a wide rectangle, about 8 by 14 inches. Use a bench scraper or knife to cut the dough in half horizontally, then divide each half into 7 rectangles to make 14 total pieces that are about 2 by 4 inches. Space them out on your work surface about an inch apart, cover loosely with plastic wrap or a towel, and let rise for 30 minutes.

MEANWHILE, bring a large pot of water to a boil and add the baking soda and remaining tablespoon of barley malt. Line 2 rimmed sheet pans with parchment paper and spray with cooking spray or dust with cornmeal. Lay out a clean kitchen towel near the pot of boiling water.

WORKING in batches of 3 or 4, boil the bagels for 1 minute on each side (use a timer for this). With a slotted spoon or spatula, transfer them briefly to the kitchen towel to catch any excess moisture, then transfer to the prepared sheet pans, spacing them 1 to 2 inches apart.

BAKE the bagels for 8 minutes, switch the racks and rotate the pans 180 degrees, and bake until golden brown; begin checking at 6 minutes. Let cool slightly, slice, and top with cream cheese, butter, peanut butter, or anything else along those lines.

THE best way to store bagels is to slice them as soon as they're cool and freeze them in an airtight container for up to a few months. Reheat in the toaster.

NOTE: *Since this is a sticky dough, I definitely recommend using a stand mixer, but if you don't have one, you can still make these. Just use a big bowl and a stiff rubber spatula or wooden spoon to mix the dough ingredients. After you mix in the water and barley malt and before you knead, cover the bowl and let it sit for 30 minutes. This will allow the flour and oats to absorb some of the moisture and make the dough easier to handle. When you're ready to incorporate the cranberry-nut-seed mixture, flatten the dough out into a big rectangle and cover it with a layer of the mixture. Press the mixture in, roll up the dough like a jelly roll, give it a few kneads, and then repeat a few more times until all the mixture is incorporated. It's a lot of mix-ins, and this process is a little sloppy, but that's okay!*

BACON WAFFLES

Walker Bros. pancake house, an institution in the Chicago suburbs, is home to an impressive stained-glass collection, homecoming morning-after brunches, and an iconic apple pancake. But what my mom and I regularly beelined for was their bacon waffles. Chopped crispy bacon dispersed throughout their unassuming yet unforgettable Belgian waffle.

This nod to those waffles is a mash-up of my go-to lachuch recipe (a bubbly pancake of Yemeni origin) and Marion Cunningham's classic waffles, both made from yeasted batters that cook up with an awe-inspiring depth that only time can create via an all-night slumber party. Which is convenient if you, too, find beating egg whites to fold into waffle batter just too much of a ruckus for a calm weekend morning.

I prefer these as standard large 7-inch round Belgian waffles. They can certainly be made with other sizes and types of waffle irons, though; just adjust the batter amount, cook time, and yield accordingly.

MAKES 6 BELGIAN WAFFLES

2 cups (260 grams) all-purpose flour

2 tablespoons (25 grams) sugar

¾ teaspoon kosher salt

2¼ teaspoons (1 packet) instant yeast

1½ cups (360 grams) water

¼ cup (56 grams) unsalted butter

1 cup (240 grams) plain whole milk Greek yogurt

2 large eggs

½ teaspoon baking soda

Cooking spray

12 bacon strips, cooked until crisp and coarsely chopped

IN a very large bowl (this batter will roughly double in size), whisk together the flour, sugar, salt, and yeast. In a microwaveable bowl or saucepan, combine the water and butter and heat in the microwave or over medium heat, swirling occasionally, just until the butter is melted. You don't want this mixture to be hot, just warm (105° to 110°F), so if it needs to cool slightly, let it sit for a few minutes. Add the warm buttery water and the yogurt to the dry ingredients and whisk until smooth. Cover with plastic wrap and let sit at room temperature overnight. This is a forgiving batter that will wait for you to sleep in, so no need to get precise about timing.

WHEN you're ready to make the waffles, put a sheet pan in the oven and preheat it to 250°F. Heat a Belgian waffle maker on high. Sniff the batter (*funky, right?*) and whisk in the eggs and baking soda. Spray the waffle iron with cooking spray and scoop in a generous ¾ cup of the batter. Scatter with a handful of bacon and cook the waffle until browned and crisp. Begin checking at 6 minutes, but waffle irons can vary in temperature, so this may take longer. Transfer to the pan in the oven to keep warm until serving, and repeat, spraying the iron with cooking spray in between each waffle. Serve these with the usual waffle-topping suspects, but know that these are perfectly delicious plain, too.

STORE leftovers in an airtight container in the fridge for up to 3 days or in the freezer for up to 3 months; reheat in a microwave or toaster.

NICK'S PANCAKES

I'm not going to sugarcoat it: Nick doesn't know how to cook. I experienced this on our first date and our second and then promptly stopped pretending to like unsalted overcooked eggs out of self-respect and appropriate boundary setting, and look where we are today! In Nick's defense, I wouldn't know the inner workings of a tractor from those of our Bernie's Little Tikes Cozy Coupe. So, the fact that a couple of years ago Nick started making our Sunday pancakes every weekend, and they've since turned into Bernie's number one favorite meal of all time (and something that I crave too), is pretty remarkable.

What I love about these pancakes is their nice dose of nutmeg and extra soft texture. They also happen to be very easy to make. After gradually, ever so gradually, introducing some of my gentle suggestions (You need not dirty all the biggest mixing bowls! A fish spatula is easier to use than a rectangular one! Use more butter! Scoop with an ice cream scoop, don't pour from the bowl!), our family has gotten to a point where if Nick goes too long without making them, Bernie will throw a tantrum and, honestly, so will I.

1½ cups (195 grams) all-purpose flour

3 tablespoons (38 grams) sugar

2 teaspoons baking powder

¾ teaspoon kosher salt

½ teaspoon ground cinnamon

⅛ teaspoon freshly ground nutmeg

2 large eggs

1½ cups (360 grams) milk (whole, 2%, or dairy-free)

½ teaspoon pure vanilla extract

¼ cup (56 grams) unsalted butter, melted and slightly cooled, plus more for the pan

Accessories We Love

Peanut butter or almond butter

Plain Greek yogurt

Maple syrup or sweetened condensed milk

Wild blueberries (fresh or frozen) or strawberries

PUT a sheet pan in the oven and turn the oven on to warm (or the lowest setting).

IN a large bowl, whisk together the flour, sugar, baking powder, salt, cinnamon, and nutmeg. In a medium bowl, whisk together the eggs, milk, and vanilla. Whisk the wet ingredients into the dry ingredients, then stir in the melted butter and mix until just combined.

HEAT a large nonstick or cast-iron pan over medium heat, melt a pat of butter, and swirl to coat. Drop in ¼-cup scoops of the batter a couple of inches apart and cook for a few minutes, until browned on the bottom and bubbles rise to the top and pop. Flip and cook for another minute or so, until browned on the other side. Transfer to the pan in the oven and continue with the rest of the batter, adding more butter in between each batch. Don't skimp on this butter.

SERVE with desired accompaniments at the table. My favorite way to eat these is with a thin layer of nut butter covering the whole pancake, a tiny drizzle of maple syrup, and a pile of frozen blueberries . . . I know the frozen blueberry thing is weird, but I like it!

STORE leftovers in an airtight container in the fridge for up to 3 days.

SOME FUN VARIATIONS

+ PUMPKIN: Mix half a 15-ounce can of pumpkin purée and 1½ teaspoons pumpkin pie spice into the batter.
+ CHIPPIES OR BACON: Sprinkle a spoonful of chocolate chips or chopped crisped bacon on each pancake after adding the batter to the pan.

EGGS

HOME IS WHERE THE MATZO BREI AND FACE MOISTURIZER ARE

In 2014, Nick and I broke our lease in downtown Grand Forks to take over the house on his family's farm after his grandma moved out. It had yellow linoleum floors, pink carpet in the bathroom, heavy curtains on all the windows, and a gigantic refrigerator in a color called "almond" anchoring the kitchen. Hanging dark cabinets made the space feel cave-like, and it wasn't long before we tore up the carpet in the bedroom to expose the plywood flooring, which aligned with our vision of some budget industrial Brooklyn aesthetic that we thought we were going for. The basement stored dozens of Nick's grandma's bowling trophies and rope knot displays from his uncle's Boy Scout troop. An orange couch from the '70s sat next to a pool table that hadn't been used in decades.

We did what we could with the kitchen, to make me feel less like a turtle in its shell during my long workdays. Per the Pinterest trends of the time, we replaced the cabinets with open shelves, counters with butcher blocks, and that big almond refrigerator with the cutest green Smeg. Except for the Smeg, it was all IKEA, all DIY, and all temporary until we could build a new house right on the farmstead.

I couldn't wait to tear this house down to build a new one. I wanted a dream house in a dream spot, farther away from the road, with more access to the yard. A big open kitchen with storage space for days. I'd draw doodles of colonials and new kitchens, and every six months we'd discover a new location on the farm where our house would sit perfectly. The kitchen would have tahini on tap and a dispenser for sprinkles. Rock walls, slides, a greenhouse in the middle!

For nearly four years, we moved from one idea to another, drawing up houses upon houses; the ideas were simply all over the place. We considered picking up and moving the original house, selling it, turning it on its head—every single possibility got its own dinnertime discussion.

Until one day, when Bernie was nine months old, I realized what Nick was patiently waiting for me to figure out: we had to stay in this house. We couldn't let it go. Suddenly it wasn't just weird pink bathroom carpet, it was carpet that kept Bernie's keppe from getting bopped as we got her ready for her first-ever baths. It wasn't just a small, dark living room, it was a cozy cocoon where we built forts and played airplane and had macaroni salad picnics. It wasn't just a house, it was a home, and we'd made our mark.

So we reworked our plans into an addition to the original farmhouse that would give us a place to work and live. The original kitchen would remain untouched and become a designated filming and work kitchen for me as we glued on a second kitchen right next to it for Bernie's after-school snacks, family dinners, and everything else we'd eat together.

I was so relieved at how right this decision felt and really excited to incorporate the old mid-century design with the new. I was also relieved that we wouldn't have to move at all; we could just scoot to the side while the construction crew built the addition. Or so I thought, lol. Apparently construction doesn't work that way. You can't just suck in your belly and move your chair in to let a construction truck squeeze behind you. We had to move three times! Three! And live in four different places: our original house, a temporary house, Nick's parents' house, and various sections of our new expanded house. Four different kitchens I cooked in while I wrote this book, you guys (so believe me when I say to get an oven thermometer).

It was an adventure with a good dose of emotion, plus some relentlessness, because COVID had just hit and we couldn't bribe our friends to help us pack or wind down at the local pizza parlor after our tough moving days. That feeling of packing away our Seder plate for long-term storage, thinking we'd be back in our house well before Passover, and then discovering that we couldn't fully unpack until the ~~middle of summer~~ following winter was something. Having to move cribs back and forth, pack up the weird miscellaneous boxes with handfuls of broken crayons and magazine articles that were never read, and having to question whether I'd need my 10-inch springform pan over the next three months and fearing that I'd find a good cheesecake recipe as soon as I sealed that box—it all happened three times over a year. Oy! But, of course, it was all so very worth it.

It also helped us reevaluate what we really need in order to feel like we are home in any given place. Spoiler alert: it isn't my clogs, and it isn't even my sprinkle collection. A house becomes a home, I learned, when I can cook in it and giggle a bunch with the people that I love. It doesn't need to be complicated, and the kitchen doesn't need to be fancy or extensive. Home, I found, is just a big batch of shallot-heavy matzo brei, Nick reading his newspaper at the table with some coffee, Bernie cuddling her bunny, and a cat or three with some allergy meds. My face moisturizer and Roku stick also help.

SALAMI MATZO BREI

Matzo brei is the answer to this complicated relationship I have with scrambled eggs where the texture is just too mushy for me to stomach unless they're first scooped up onto toast or hash browns, and I'm not always willing or able to use the extra hand necessary to make that happen. Folding softened matzo into them, however, gives you something to chew on and turns a bowl of eggs into an anytime meal worth inhaling by the gigantic, unflattering forkful. On special days, like the first day of figure skating Worlds or the week after New Year when we have a stack of cured meat left over from charcuterie boards, I make this salami version, which takes this already perfect food into eyes-rolling-to-the-back-of-the-head, should-I-get-a-tattoo-about-this territory. This is one of my top five favorite foods of all time.

HOME IS WHERE THE EGGS ARE

1 tablespoon (13 grams) neutral oil

1 large shallot, finely chopped

Kosher salt

4 plain or egg matzo sheets, broken into 1- to 2-inch pieces

4 large eggs

2 ounces (57 grams) salami, sliced or cubed

Freshly ground black pepper

Flaky salt

Small handful of chopped dill, optional, for topping

Hot sauce and ketchup, optional, for serving

HEAT a large nonstick or well-seasoned cast-iron skillet over medium-high heat and add the oil. Add the shallot and a pinch of kosher salt. Cook, stirring occasionally, for a few minutes while you prep the matzo and egg mixture. (If the pan considers smoking, turn down the heat.)

FILL a medium bowl with cool water and submerge the matzo completely for 45 seconds. (Set a timer! Matzo will go from chewy to soggy in a matter of seconds!) Drain and set aside. Crack the eggs into a medium bowl. (Use the same bowl you soaked the matzo in so you have fewer dirty dishes!) Beat them with a fork until homogeneous, then fold in the matzo.

ADD the salami to the pan and cook for a few seconds just to render a little of its fat. It shouldn't get too crispy or chewy, just pull out a little of the fat so that it lends the brei more flavor as it mingles with the rest of the ingredients.

ADD the egg mixture to the pan, spread it out with your spatula, and cook until the bottom is set. Use the spatula to gently pull the bottom cooked parts to the sides of the pan to make space for more of the mixture to cook. Repeat this gentle pulling process a few more times until everything's just about set, then turn off the heat. Continue folding, seasoning with a couple of good pinches of kosher salt as you go, allowing the residual heat from the pan to finish up cooking the eggs until they've reached your desired doneness.

TRANSFER to a serving bowl (or just serve out of the skillet), top with a few turns of black pepper, a sprinkle of flaky salt, and the dill, if using. Serve immediately with hot sauce and ketchup on the side, if desired.

DOUGHNUT MATZO BREI

I've died on so many hills while fighting for the victory of savory matzo brei that I should probably actually be dead already. The idea of sweet scrambled eggs used to be so, *so* repulsive to me. I could barely stand to look at Passover Instagram when all my friends started putting maple syrup on matzo brei! *Who are these monsters that I am friends with?* was my fifth question every year after the traditional four at the Seder.

My sweet matzo brei epiphany came one day when I was in the mood for a sweet brunch (pancakes, waffles, cinnamon rolls) but didn't want to exert the energy to make any of those things. That's when it occurred to me that I was thinking about sweet matzo brei all wrong: it's not scrambled eggs that are sweet, it's actually just a speedy hack for pancakes. Have you ever had Kaiserschmarrn? The Austrian dish that is basically scrambled pancakes? That to me is a better comparison for sweet matzo brei. Sweet matzo brei is just eggier and chewier.

So what makes this sweet matzo brei different from all the others? A finishing step of folding in some butter (frying it in oil and not butter allows the pan to get extra hot, but you still need that butter flavor) and, for the sweet element, a sprinkle of inspiration from Jami Curl's Doughnut Magic Dust, which is a cinnamon sugar that's heavy on the nutmeg to give the impression of the flavor of a sugar-coated doughnut. Try it—you'll see what I mean.

MAKES ENOUGH FOR 2 HUNGRY PEOPLE AND A BABY

2 tablespoons (25 grams) sugar

2 teaspoons ground cinnamon

½ teaspoon freshly ground nutmeg

4 plain or egg matzo sheets, broken into 1- to 2-inch pieces

4 large eggs

2 tablespoons (30 grams) heavy cream

½ teaspoon pure vanilla extract

1 tablespoon (13 grams) neutral oil

1 tablespoon (14 grams) good-quality butter (salted or unsalted)

Kosher salt

Flaky salt, optional

FIRST, make the doughnut dust: combine the sugar, cinnamon, and nutmeg in a small bowl and set aside.

FILL a medium bowl with cool water and submerge the matzo completely for 45 seconds. (Set a timer! Matzo will go from chewy to soggy in a matter of seconds!) Drain and set aside. Crack the eggs into a medium bowl (use the same bowl you soaked the matzo in so you have fewer dirty dishes!) and add the cream and vanilla. Beat with a fork until homogeneous, then fold in the matzo.

HEAT a large nonstick or well-seasoned cast-iron skillet over medium-high heat and add the oil. Add in the egg mixture and cook until the bottom is set. Use a spatula to gently pull the cooked parts to the sides of the pan to make space for more of the mixture to cook. Repeat this gentle pulling process a few more times until everything's just about set, then turn off the heat. Add the butter and a good pinch of kosher salt and continue folding, allowing the butter to melt and the residual heat from the pan to finish up cooking the eggs until they've reached your desired doneness.

FOLD in about 2 teaspoons of the doughnut dust, then transfer to a serving bowl (or just serve out of the skillet) and sprinkle with more doughnut dust to taste and a pinch of flaky salt, if desired. (You may or may not want all the rest of the doughnut dust. Leftovers can be saved and sprinkled on buttered toast, pancakes, or your next brei.)

CREAM CHEESE SCRAMBLED EGGS

Lox and cream cheese on a bagel is a classic for a reason. But, before I discovered that, my cream cheese pairing of choice was scrambled eggs. Cream cheese lends that same sort of necessary acidity to scrambled eggs that ketchup does, but with the bonus of creamy melty texture. So anyone too embarrassed to put ketchup on their eggs (you know who you are!) can now rejoice that there is another path to brightness, and those who have no ketchup shame can get a second dose of tang. The obvious topping here is a massive storm of everything bagel topping and a few bagel-adjacent scallions and dill fronds. For how little time and energy this meal takes, it punches way above its weight on flavor.

SERVES 1

A nice pat (about ½ tablespoon) unsalted or salted butter

1 large egg, beaten very well with a splash of water

1 ounce (2 tablespoons) cream cheese, cubed

Lots of everything bagel topping (see page xvi)

Flaky salt or kosher salt, if your everything bagel topping doesn't provide enough

1 scallion, green part only, thinly sliced on a very steep bias because it looks pretty

1 dill sprig, chopped or torn

Ketchup, optional, for serving

Buttered toast, for serving

HEAT a nonstick or well-seasoned cast-iron pan over medium-high heat. When it's good and hot, add the butter, swirl it around, and immediately pour in the egg. Did it make a cool sizzle sound? Good, your pan is hot enough! (If it didn't, you'll get there next time!) Quickly scatter on your cream cheese plops. By this time the bottom layer of the egg should be set. Use a spatula to pull one side of the egg in toward the other side, bunching up the bottom set part and letting the uncooked egg pool in the exposed part of the pan. Promptly push the opposite side of the egg back to the side where you started. Gently pull it around a couple more times until it's *jusssssst* set and slide it onto a plate. Sprinkle liberally with everything bagel topping and salt, if using, and finish with the scallion and dill. Serve with ketchup, if desired, and shovel up into your mouth on a slice of buttered toast.

SPINACH AND SWISS BREAKFAST SANDWICHES

When the town bakery closed and took with it their iconic slabs of hash-brown-filled eggs that were cheese-glued to a slice of bacon and sandwiched between soft, thick slices of their freshly baked bread, I mourned. They were some of the best breakfast sandwiches in the universe, which is a feat in a genre with such stiff competition. Luckily, my days of working at that bakery gave me *some* intel on how to make those eggs, but direct translation was a lost cause, since I seem to remember step one being "crack 96 eggs."

When I reworked it for our home kitchen, I snuck in some spinach, because nothing bad has ever come from a Popeye-esque start to the day, and Gruyère, because it's fancy.

The best time to serve this is on a weekend when there's a fresh potato challah pullman loaf (page 236) hanging around so that the egg slab and bread line up perfectly and create one geometrically pleasing sandwich. Smaller weekday English muffin sandwiches are a close second. So make a double batch, eat some immediately, and wrap up the rest for quick breakfasts throughout the week.

The last, most important thing I want to tell you about this sandwich, and breakfast sandwiches in general, is that they *need* the finishing step of being wrapped up in foil or parchment and sitting for a few minutes so that the toast steams and everything gets melty and gooey together. It'll make it feel more like a drive-through fast-food breakfast sandwich in the best way possible. When I die, this is what I want to be remembered for.

MAKES 4 LARGE OR 9 SMALL SANDWICHES

Eggs

1 tablespoon (13 grams) extra virgin olive oil or neutral oil

1 large shallot, thinly sliced

Kosher salt

4 ounces (113 grams/2 big handfuls) fresh baby spinach, chopped, or frozen spinach, thawed and drained

1½ cups (128 grams) frozen shredded hash browns

Freshly ground black pepper

¾ cup (3 ounces/85 grams) shredded Gruyère or Swiss cheese

6 large eggs

½ cup (120 grams) whole milk

½ teaspoon sweet paprika

A few passes of freshly grated nutmeg

Hot sauce, optional

Assembly

Flaky salt

Sliced Swiss cheese

Canadian bacon

or sausage patties, ham, regular bacon, or other breakfast meat of choice!

For large brunch-size sandwiches: sliced pullman loaf, white bread, or multigrain bread, toasted

For smaller breakfast-size sandwiches: English muffins, toasted

Ketchup, optional, for serving

PREHEAT the oven to 400°F. Grease and line a 9-inch square metal pan with enough parchment paper to allow 1-inch wings on opposite sides.

HEAT a medium skillet over medium-high heat and add the oil. Add the shallot and a pinch of kosher salt. Cook, stirring, until softened, 5 to 7 minutes. Add the spinach and another pinch of kosher salt and cook for another few minutes, until the spinach is wilted. If using frozen spinach, it's already wilted, so just stir it in (with a pinch of salt) to incorporate. Remove from the heat and set aside to cool slightly.

SPRINKLE the hash browns in the prepared pan and season with salt and pepper. Top evenly with the cheese, then the spinach mixture. In a medium bowl, whisk together the eggs, milk, paprika, nutmeg, ¾ teaspoon salt, black pepper, and a few shakes of hot sauce, if desired. Pour the mixture into the pan and bake until set; begin checking for doneness at 25 minutes.

IF serving immediately, slice into either 4 big squares or 9 smaller squares and top with a pinch of flaky salt, cheese, and Canadian bacon, and sandwich between your toasts of choice.

IF prepping for later, let cool completely in the pan, slice into squares, and refrigerate in an airtight container (or wrap individually in plastic wrap and freeze). To reheat, microwave until warmed through (about 30 seconds for refrigerated, 1 to 1½ minutes for frozen). Assemble as directed above.

WHEN the sandwiches are assembled, wrap each one individually with foil or parchment and let sit for a few minutes so that the toast steams and everything gets melty and gooey together.

BREAK out the ketchup and go to town!

LEFSE TOT BREAKFAST TACOS

At one point in time, this truly doomed restaurant space in town was occupied by an insane burrito place called Sweeto Burrito that put tots *in* their bacon/egg/cheese burrito, but not before lubricating everything with a creamy ranch-y sauce. This is never something I would order purposely unless I were hungover, but my first-timer's luck resulted in the most delicious ordering accident of all time, and one appeared in front of me like an angel from tortilla heaven. I still dream about this burrito (the space turned into a Starbucks years ago). To cure my regular craving, I make a taco inspired by that burrito, which ups the Midwestern ante by folding it into soft potato lefse. Chorizo adds the smoky meatiness that you want in the morning, and all the sauces bring it together.

Listen: it's important to get the tots really, really crispy here to add the crunchy textural excitement that a soft scrambled egg inside of a soft pancake needs. Don't have lefse in your deep freeze? Make the quick Weeknight Lefse recipe on page 244 or use flour tortillas, which will be just as delicious.

SERVES 4

14 ounces (396 grams) frozen Tater Tots

Kosher salt and freshly ground black pepper

4 ounces (113 grams) Mexican chorizo

Neutral oil or extra virgin olive oil, as needed

½ medium white onion, finely chopped

6 large eggs, beaten

1 cup (4 ounces/113 grams) shredded mozzarella, divided

8 to 10 lefse sheets (if using large lefse, fold them in halves or quarters, or use the Weeknight Lefse recipe on page 244 to make smaller 6-inch rounds), or you can sub 6-inch flour tortillas, warmed

Salsa verde

Ranch

Sriracha

Cilantro leaves

ARRANGE the Tater Tots on a rimmed sheet pan and season with salt and pepper. Bake according to the package directions, adding about 10 minutes onto the directed baking time so that they get *really* crispy.

WHILE the tots bake, make the eggs: Heat a large skillet over medium high and add the chorizo, breaking it up with a spoon and cooking until darkened, bubbly, and hot, 3 to 5 minutes. Transfer to a bowl, reserving any excess fat in the pan. If the pan is dry, add a drizzle of oil. Add the onion and a pinch of salt and cook until softened, 5 to 7 minutes. Add the eggs and scramble until mostly set. Stir in the chorizo and half of the cheese until the cheese is melted and the eggs are just set, just a few seconds more. Remove from the heat, season with black pepper (since the chorizo is salty it shouldn't need more salt, but you be the judge!), and top with the remaining cheese.

TO assemble the tacos, fill a piece of lefse with the eggs, top with some Tater Tots, drizzle with all the sauces, and sprinkle with cilantro. *Mmmmmmmmmm.*

EGGS IN A CRISPY SAFFRON RICE BASKET

When leftover rice is in the fridge and the circumstances align for a solo weekday brunch (Nick is in the fields, Bernie is at Grandma's, and I am somehow ahead in my work schedule), I treat myself to this dish that's inspired by Persian rice with saffron-stained crispy crust, tahdig. The way the egg yolk mingles with the crunchy rice creates the most splendid texture. If you don't have saffron, skipping it will still yield a pleasing moment in your day, but if you do, take a second and give yourself that extra luxury. Self-care in crispy rice form.

SERVES 1

Pinch of saffron

Kosher salt

2 teaspoons water

2 teaspoons extra virgin olive oil

¾ cup (102 grams) leftover cooked rice

I recommend jasmine or basmati

Freshly ground black pepper

1 large egg

Flaky salt

TO TOP: hot sauce, fresh tender herbs (flat-leaf parsley, cilantro, mint, or basil), sliced tomatoes, dollops of yogurt, optional

IN a mortar and pestle or a small bowl with a spoon, crush the saffron with a pinch of salt and swirl in the water. Set aside to let steep.

HEAT a nonstick skillet over medium-high heat. Add the olive oil and then the rice, breaking it up with a spatula if it's gotten lumpy in its leftover state, and stir to heat it up. Season with salt and pepper (taking into consideration whether it's been seasoned already), pat out into a 5- to 6-inch circle, and create a 2-inch well in the center to make your nest. Carefully crack in the egg, taking care not to break the yolk. Drizzle the saffron water (or 2 teaspoons plain water if not using saffron) over the rice (not the egg), cover, and cook for a few minutes, until the egg white is cooked but the yolk is still runny.

SLIP a large spatula under the whole thing and transfer to a plate or shallow bowl (it won't necessarily be one cohesive cake of rice). Season the egg with flaky salt and pepper and finish with toppings as desired.

GOAT CHEESE AND DILL BAKED EGGS

Saturdays are for going to the park and swinging, eating pizza salad
(page 130), and reading cookbooks. No Instagram allowed, and no substantial
texting either. It's what I call Shabbat Lite™, and it clears my brain to make
room for ideas and sanity while also encouraging me to be present when
pushing Bernie on the swings. Since Nick's pancakes have a semi-permanent
spot on our menu for Sunday mornings, Saturdays invite a rotating selection
of special brunches, but not too special since it's Shabbat Lite™, and if you get
stressed out making it, that defeats the purpose.

This egg dish is *kiiiiinda* like a soufflé but way more casual, making it an ideal Saturday brunch. You just whisk all the week's leftover herbs with some eggs and goat cheese, pour it into a pool of butter (which creates a crisp crust), top lavishly with flaky salt (don't forget this!), and eat immediately, because if you don't, it'll deflate. Spoon it onto a thick slice of crusty toast to feel like you're eating a strata with more textural variety.

SERVES 4

6 large eggs

3 ounces (85 grams) goat cheese, crumbled

¼ cup (1 ounce/28 grams) finely shredded white cheddar

2 tablespoons (16 grams) all-purpose flour

Scant ¼ teaspoon kosher salt

Freshly ground black pepper

½ cup (120 grams) whole milk

2 tablespoons (30 grams) heavy cream

3 tablespoons (8 grams) finely chopped dill, plus a little more for topping

1 tablespoon (3 grams) finely chopped chives, plus a little more for topping

1 tablespoon (3 grams) finely chopped flat-leaf parsley, plus a little more for topping

1 tablespoon (14 grams) unsalted butter

Flaky salt

Crusty toast, for serving

PREHEAT the oven to 425°F with a 1-quart baking dish on the center rack (I use a little 3 x 6-inch cast-iron pot, but a 3 x 6-inch cake pan or four 8- to 10-ounce ramekins would work too).

IN a medium bowl, combine the eggs, goat cheese, cheddar, flour, salt, and loads of ground black pepper and whisk vigorously until the mixture is pale and creamy. Most of the goat cheese should be blended in, but having a few crumbles left intact is a good thing. Drizzle in the milk and heavy cream while whisking, then whisk in the herbs.

CAREFULLY pull the baking dish out of the oven, add the butter, and let it sizzle and melt. Swirl the butter around so it coats the sides of the dish and let any excess pool at the bottom. Pour in the egg mixture and bake until it's puffy, set, and starting to brown on top; begin checking for doneness at 30 minutes (start checking smaller ramekins at 20 minutes). Sprinkle with additional herbs and a good pinch of flaky salt and serve immediately with good crusty toast.

FETA AND ZA'ATAR OMELET ROLL-UPS

This is inspired by the first recipe I ever saw Nadiya Hussain make on her show *Time to Eat*. It was an egg and a tortilla cooked together to create a steamy breakfast-taco-like thing that's melty and chewy in some parts and crisp and fried in others. As soon as I saw it, I dashed to the kitchen to make one and have never been so impatient for a skillet to heat in my life. The concept was so simple, so satisfying, and so clever that I proceeded to add it to our regular rotation, dreaming up different variations every week. This is my favorite one, an ode to breakfasts I fell in love with in Israel: earthy za'atar, salty feta, creamy yogurt, and piles of chopped veggies.

SERVES 1, EASILY MULTIPLIED

Extra virgin olive oil

Couple of good pinches of za'atar

1 large egg, beaten

Small handful (about 2 tablespoons) crumbled feta

One 8-inch flour tortilla

Kosher salt and freshly ground black pepper

Couple of small dollops plain Greek yogurt

Pile of chopped salad (recipe follows)

Hot sauce, optional

HEAT a medium (8- or 9-inch) nonstick skillet over medium-high heat and add a drizzle of oil. Sprinkle in the za'atar, swirl it around, and let it sizzle for a few seconds. Add the egg and swirl it around into one round thin layer. Cook until mostly set, sprinkle on the feta, and top with the tortilla, pressing it with your hand or a spatula so that it sticks to the egg. When the tortilla starts to feel warm and the egg releases easily from the pan, slide the spatula under, flip, and cook for another minute or so, until the tortilla is lightly browned. Season with salt and pepper and remove to a plate. Top with the yogurt, a strip of salad across the equator, and a few shakes of hot sauce, if desired. Roll it up, cut in half, and enjoy!

SALAD

1 Persian cucumber, diced

1 large tomato, seeded and diced

¼ medium red onion, diced

Good squeeze of lemon juice

Extra virgin olive oil

Kosher salt and freshly ground black pepper

Handful of finely chopped cilantro, flat-leaf parsley, dill, or mint, or a mix, optional

COMBINE the cucumber, tomato, and onion in a bowl, toss with lemon juice and olive oil, and season with salt and pepper to taste. Add herbs as desired. This will keep in the fridge for 2 to 3 days.

MY OTHER FAVORITE VARIATION

Sub shredded mozzarella for the feta, skip the salad and yogurt, and go straight for the ketchup.

JIANBING-ISH THINGS

While I'd like to say that these Jianbing-ish Things are inspired by a magical trip to Shanghai in which I reunited with distant family members, became friends with real-life Crazy Rich Asian Colette Bing, discovered that Colette Bing is also a distant family member (and I'm therefore suddenly the heir to a multibillion-dollar company and a fleet of private 767s), and then celebrated by buying everybody in the country these egg crepes from a street cart that has been operating continuously since the Tang Dynasty . . . We're going to have to settle on: my friend Donny introduced them to me, and I thought the concept was nifty. Because the truth is, I've been to China once and I didn't even leave the airport; I just sulked that I couldn't access Twitter.

Jianbing is a popular Chinese street breakfast that consists of a giant crepe—often made with mung bean, millet, or sorghum flour—that's cooked with an egg directly on top of it, then gets folded up with herbs, a crunchy fried thing like wonton strips or a doughnut, maybe lettuce, pickles, and hella tasty sauces. As I started making them at home, smaller and tailored to the

ingredients we keep on hand, I instantly felt more connected to my Chinese heritage and found pleasure in growing my arsenal of Chinese breakfasts beyond microwaving leftover potstickers and driving to Winnipeg for the closest dim sum. Until I finally make it to my family's homeland to eat a real one of these things, this is what I'll be making for savory pancake days. The crepe itself is very plain, acting mainly as a soft vehicle for the egg, its toppings, and a lively dunk in vinegar and soy sauce.

MAKES 6 PANCAKES

7 large eggs

¾ cup (180 grams) water

¾ cup (180 grams) milk (whole, 2%, or dairy-free)

1 tablespoon (13 grams) neutral oil, plus more for the pan

1¼ cups (165 grams) all-purpose flour

1 teaspoon sugar

Kosher salt

4 scallions, thinly sliced

4 ounces (113 grams) smoked ham (or other tasty salty meat like cooked bacon, sausage, or Canadian bacon), chopped into small pieces

Freshly ground black pepper

ADDITIONAL OPTIONAL TOPPINGS: cilantro or other tender herbs, sesame seeds, romaine or Bibb lettuce leaves, potato chips, other crunchy items, a splatter of black bean garlic sauce

Rice vinegar, for serving

Soy sauce, for serving

Sambal oelek, for serving

IN a medium bowl, whisk together 1 egg, the water, the milk, and the oil. Add the flour, sugar, and ¼ teaspoon salt and whisk until smooth.

HEAT a 10-inch nonstick skillet over medium heat. Add a drizzle of oil, swirl it around to coat, and add a generous ⅓ cup of batter, tilting the pan to help it into a thin circle. Cook the pancake until it is just about set, then crack an egg directly on top. Use the bottom of a spoon to break the yolk, very gently scramble, and spread it all over the pancake in a thin layer; it's okay if some of the egg overflows beyond the pancake. Sprinkle with some scallions, ham, a pinch of salt, and a few turns of black pepper and cook until the egg is just about set. Flip and cook for about 10 seconds, until the egg is fully set, then flip it back over so that you can add any additional toppings you want (we usually keep it simple and forgo additional toppings, but if we have romaine then, sure, I like the extra greens) and roll it up with the pancake on the outside. Transfer to a plate to serve or keep in a warm oven while you cook the remaining crepes. Serve with a dipping sauce of 1 part rice vinegar and 1 part soy sauce, plus sambal oelek to taste. Eat it with your hands if you want!

SALADS, AND THEIR SELLING POINTS

At around seven months' pregnant, we bought a brand-new deep freeze and I began the baby meal preparations that I had been looking forward to for my entire pregnancy, and then some. I was *made* to cook big batches of macaroni and cheese and Tater Tot hotdish and package them up into cute individual-size containers with colorful labels so that as sleepy new parents we could have easy access to the kind of hearty, comforting calories that everyone told us we'd crave. I stocked two deep freezes, a standard freezer, and the tiny shoebox freezer in our little Smeg fridge with meatballs, breakfast sandwiches, hotdishes with three kinds of tots, chicken and biscuits, balls of cookie dough, burritos, and even enough meals for Passover, since my due date was a week before it started. It was some next-level nesting, and I loved it. I had to keep yelling at Nick not to eat it all before Bernie arrived, but I couldn't blame him because it was all so tempting! So along with the anticipation of Bern's arrival, we were also excited about finally being able to crack into our end-of-the-world-style freezer stock.

But then the weirdest thing happened.

Completely unexpected and so very odd.

The day that Bernie was born, all I wanted was a salad. A cooling, crunchy bed of green vegetables, the opposite of what was exploding out of our freezer. I couldn't explain it. My friend Heather delivered one without me even saying anything. She just showed up at the hospital with the biggest, most satisfying salad of my life. And when we got home, Nick's mom, Roxanne, brought over stacks of Tupperware filled with piles of greens. Her salads were so gosh-darn satisfying and I ate them with so much enthusiasm that many leaves fell onto sleeping baby Bernie's head.

As someone who literally did not touch one leaf of lettuce until her late teens, this was a . . . relief? Exciting development? Identity crisis? Something that I should have spoken to my doctor about? There's probably some biological reason for this, right? Like, I needed all the nutrition I could get to breastfeed this human, or my body was desperately recovering from all the doughnuts I craved during pregnancy, or suddenly I had something more to live for? Or maybe this is just what getting older is: a necessary stop on the cycle of life that begins with applesauce and buttered noodles and ends with bulk containers of roasted cashews eaten in front of *All My Children* every single day (or was that just my grandpa?).

To be clear, my new salad obsession did not mean that I suddenly disliked bread and cheese and all things fried. I'm not here to smack-talk dairy. It just meant that my taste buds sort of shifted in their preferences, or expanded them, really. It was as if birthing a tiny human expanded my heart not only to love that tiny human more than I ever thought I could possibly love someone but also to love . . . romaine.

After a few weeks of letting other people take care of us, we were again ready to be self-sufficient humans who didn't require mother-in-law salads, so we went through bagged salad kits by the dozen. We emptied out the pre-chopped vegetables and packets of dressing and paired them with those reheated meals from the freezer, partially because we felt obligated to not let them go to waste. (Who was this person, having to eat macaroni and cheese out of guilt?) As we slowly but surely figured out how to do things beyond diaper changes, presiding over tummy time, and eating premade meals, we embraced a new normal that included making colorful, triumphant salads every day, sometimes multiple times a day.

At mealtimes we'd stick a big bowl on the counter and pile in whatever fresh vegetables we had, along with cheese, nuts, croutons, eggs, ideally some salty cured meat—whatever could fill us up. I loved the ease of these freeform fridge-foraged salads, and Nick loved the healthiness of it all, because he is one of those eat-to-survive types. This went on for a really long time, long enough for me to gradually fit into my jeans again without feeling like I was crash dieting, and eventually my old mac-and-cheese-obsessed self returned to balance out my new spinach-obsessed self. At this point I think we're just normal adults now who eat both lots of salads and lots of pasta.

Over the course of my new life as a salad fiend, I've learned that my favorite salads exercise balance. Sure, well-dressed greens are fine on their own, but they're even greater when paired with a selling point that's a little (or a lot) bad for you. Fried cheese, hot dogs, croutons inspired by Ruby Tuesday . . . you know what I mean. They're my ultimate form of balance. And they're great because I do have those days when I get to dinner feeling angry that my chocolate bread didn't rise properly. Those days, making a salad is the last thing on my mind, but if I remember that I can put tiny everything bagel cheese balls on top of it, I get super pumped.

BAGEL SALAD WITH ROASTED SALMON

In my *Honey, I Shrunk the Kids* fan-fiction holiday special, *Honey, I Shrunk the Cheeseball*, Rick Moranis crashes my annual Chrismukkah party and zaps the grapefruit-size ball of spreadable party cheese into tiny forkable salad toppers. I make bagel croutons and add roasted salmon, then we eat dinner together with tiny utensils.

SERVES 4 TO 6

Dressing

Juice of 1 lemon

1 tablespoon (15 grams) Dijon mustard

1 teaspoon honey

½ cup (100 grams) extra virgin olive oil

2 scallions, thinly sliced

Kosher salt and freshly ground black pepper

Salad

1 pound (454 grams) salmon fillet, patted dry

4 tablespoons (50 grams) extra virgin olive oil, divided

Kosher salt and freshly ground black pepper

2 large everything bagels, torn or chopped into bite-size pieces

2 tablespoons (20 grams) everything bagel topping (see Note)

4 ounces (113 grams) cream cheese, cut into ½- to ¾-inch cubes

5 ounces (142 grams) mixed baby greens

½ English cucumber, thinly sliced

½ small red onion, thinly sliced

2 scallions, thinly sliced

Handful of chopped dill

2 medium tomatoes, cut into wedges

Flaky salt

NOTE: *If you're using store-bought everything bagel topping, taste it first to make sure it's not too salty. If it is, I recommend making some yourself (see page xvi).*

TO make the dressing, in a large measuring cup, whisk together the lemon juice, Dijon, and honey. Drizzle in the olive oil while whisking continuously to emulsify. Stir in the scallions and season to taste with salt and pepper. Set aside.

PREHEAT the oven to 450°F. Coat the salmon with 2 tablespoons (25 grams) of the olive oil, season all over with salt and a bunch of turns of pepper, and

place on a parchment-lined rimmed sheet pan (skin side down if the skin is still on the salmon). On a separate rimmed sheet pan, toss the bagel pieces with the remaining 2 tablespoons (25 grams) olive oil and spread them out evenly. Stick both sheet pans in the oven and bake until the bagels are browned and crisp and the salmon is just cooked through, with an internal temperature of 120°F (for medium rare); it should flake easily with a fork. Begin checking the bagels for doneness at 5 minutes and the salmon at 10 minutes. Let cool slightly while you prepare the rest of the salad.

PLACE the everything bagel topping in a shallow bowl. Coat the cream cheese cubes all over with the bagel topping and roll them into little balls with your hands.

IN a large bowl, toss the greens, cucumber, onion, most of the scallions, most of the dill, and most of the croutons with dressing to taste. Transfer to a serving plate (or keep in the bowl). Break the salmon into pieces (discarding the skin) and add it to the top of the salad. Add the tomatoes, cheese balls, and remaining croutons. Drizzle with additional dressing and sprinkle with the remaining scallions and dill and some flaky salt.

MOZZARELLA STICK SALAD

The only food groups that I was ever really forbidden to eat growing up contained the words "cheese" and "fry," so ... cheese fries or fried cheese. The occasional fried food was fine, and cheese was encouraged in my mom's life mission to ensure I got enough calcium, but the two concepts were kept very far from each other. No matter how many times I'd ask for a post-skating-practice concession stand cheese fry or mozzarella stick, I was always met with something along the lines of how they'd clog my arteries. Now that I'm a grown-up, it's really cool that I can eat mozzarella sticks whenever I want, but of course I inherited some guilt about it, so I counteract it by eating mozzarella sticks on top of a salad.

While the idea of plopping an already perfect food on top of a salad might seem kinda kitschy, when mozzarella sticks are put on a bed of peppery crunchy arugula and briny olives with a bright creamy marinara dressing, they actually somehow become even better versions of themselves. They're a solo star *and* a team player, a regular LeBron James.

SERVES 4

Dressing

¾ cup (186 grams) marinara sauce

6 tablespoons (75 grams) extra virgin olive oil

6 tablespoons (90 grams) plain whole milk Greek yogurt

Juice of half a lemon

Crushed red pepper

Kosher salt and freshly ground black pepper

Mozzarella sticks

¼ cup (33 grams) all-purpose flour

Kosher salt

2 large eggs

½ cup (30 grams) panko breadcrumbs

¼ cup (30 grams) plain breadcrumbs

¼ cup (40 grams) grated Parmesan

½ teaspoon garlic powder

½ teaspoon onion powder

½ teaspoon Italian seasoning

Freshly ground black pepper

One 8-ounce (226-gram) block mozzarella

Neutral oil or good-quality extra virgin olive oil, for frying

Salad

5 ounces (142 grams) baby spinach

3 ounces (85 grams) baby arugula

½ small red onion, thinly sliced

1 cup (170 grams) kalamata olives, halved

One 15-ounce (425-gram) can chickpeas, drained and rinsed

1 pint (about 283 grams) grape or cherry tomatoes, halved

Handful of grated Parmesan

Handful of chopped flat-leaf parsley or torn basil leaves or both

TO make the dressing, in a large measuring cup, whisk together the marinara, olive oil, yogurt, and lemon juice and season to taste with crushed red pepper, salt, and pepper. Set aside.

SET up a standard breading station with 3 wide shallow bowls. Combine the flour and ¼ teaspoon salt in one bowl. Beat the eggs with 2 splashes of water in the second bowl. Mix the panko, plain breadcrumbs, Parmesan, garlic powder, onion powder, Italian seasoning, ½ teaspoon salt, and loads of black pepper in the third bowl.

CUT the block of mozzarella lengthwise down the center and then slice each long piece into 8 nuggets to make 16 pieces. Take each mozzarella piece through the breading procedure: coat it in the flour, then the egg, then the panko mixture, then coat in the egg mixture and panko mixture again for a double breading. This breading step can be done up to a day in advance; keep the pieces covered in the fridge until ready to use.

HEAT a large skillet, preferably cast iron, over medium-high heat. Add enough oil to generously coat the bottom of the skillet. When a breadcrumb dropped into the oil sizzles, add the mozzarella sticks, an inch apart, and fry until golden brown on all sides, a few minutes on each side. Fry in batches if necessary to avoid crowding the pan, adding more oil if the pan seems dry. You could also deep-fry the suckers! (But shallow-frying is way more convenient and does a swell job.)

WHILE the cheese fries, assemble the salad: On a large platter, spread out the spinach and arugula. Scatter on the red onion, olives, chickpeas, and tomatoes and drizzle on half of the dressing. When the mozzarella is done frying, transfer briefly to a paper towel to absorb any excess oil, then add to the salad. Top with the Parmesan and parsley and/or basil and serve with the remaining dressing.

MY DREAM GOAT CHEESE SALAD

A dream I regularly have starts with a warm crusty baguette and softened salted butter, with radishes on the side. Then we eat this chèvre chaud salad while we drink rosé and have perfect in-season cantaloupe for dessert. Time doesn't bind us, and it's floral dress weather. We're in France! It's the springtime! Life is great. In this dream I speak fluent French and can pull off that excellent *Breathless* haircut and there is prosciutto on this chèvre chaud (even though I think that might get me yelled at in France? (But it's *my* dream!)).

SERVES 4

Dressing

1 small shallot, finely chopped

3 tablespoons (45 grams) white wine vinegar

1 tablespoon (15 grams) Dijon mustard

2 teaspoons fresh thyme leaves

½ cup (100 grams) extra virgin olive oil

Kosher salt and freshly ground black pepper

Goat cheese

3 tablespoons (24 grams) all-purpose flour

8 ounces (226 grams) goat cheese, cut into twelve ½-inch coins
Use a wet knife or floss for clean cuts!

1 large egg

½ cup (30 grams) panko breadcrumbs

¼ teaspoon kosher salt

Freshly ground black pepper

Neutral oil or good-quality extra virgin olive oil, for frying

Salad

8 ounces (226 grams) mixed greens

1 small shallot, thinly sliced

6 ounces (170 grams) sliced prosciutto

12 ounces (340 grams) Campari tomatoes, sliced into wedges

Flaky salt

Accessories

Warm crusty baguette

Halved radishes

Very good butter

Flaky salt

Rosé

"Alexa, please play French café music . . ."

TO make the dressing, in a large measuring cup, whisk together the shallot, vinegar, mustard, and thyme. Drizzle in the olive oil while whisking continuously to emulsify. Season to taste with salt and pepper. Set aside.

SPREAD the flour out on a plate and coat the goat cheese all over with it.

BEAT the egg with a splash of water in a wide shallow bowl and transfer all the goat cheese to the egg to completely coat. Wipe off the flour plate, discarding any excess flour, and put the breadcrumbs on the plate, seasoning with the salt and a few turns of black pepper. Transfer the goat cheese to the breadcrumbs and coat all over. This breading step can be done up to a day in advance; keep the cheese covered in the fridge until ready to use.

HEAT a large skillet, preferably cast iron, over medium-high heat. Add enough oil to generously coat the bottom of the skillet. When a breadcrumb dropped into the oil sizzles, add the goat cheese coins, an inch apart, and fry until golden brown, a few minutes on each side. Fry in batches if necessary to avoid crowding the pan, adding more oil between batches if the pan seems dry.

WHILE the goat cheese fries, assemble the salad: in a large bowl, gently toss the greens and shallots with about half of the dressing (or to taste), then transfer to a serving plate or 4 individual shallow bowls (or keep it in the big bowl). Top with the prosciutto and tomatoes.

WHEN the goat cheese is done frying, transfer it briefly to a paper towel to absorb any excess oil, then add to the salad. Drizzle on more dressing and sprinkle with a pinch of flaky salt. Serve with a warm baguette and a plate of radishes and softened butter sprinkled with flaky salt.

SHEET PAN SALMON NIÇOISE SALAD

The charm of a Niçoise salad is that it can be arranged like a mini buffet in the middle of the table, where each component is grouped together on top of the lettuce and everybody can dish up exactly what they want: Bernie loads up on fish; I have mostly potatoes and a little of everything else (who is the real child here?); and Nick takes down all the rest. Every bite has the opportunity to be a completely different experience; some can be crunchy and briny, others can have sweetness from the tomatoes. Of course, the salty potatoes-only bites are what I truly look forward to. This sheet pan version streamlines some prep and adds roasted, crispy texture.

1 pound (454 grams) rainbow fingerling potatoes, quartered

6 tablespoons (75 grams) extra virgin olive oil, divided

Kosher salt and freshly ground black pepper

8 ounces (226 grams) haricots verts, trimmed

4 large eggs

½ cup (120 grams) white wine vinegar

¼ cup (60 grams) Dijon mustard

2 teaspoons fresh thyme leaves

½ small red onion, finely chopped

1 head butter lettuce, leaves separated

One 4- to 6-ounce (113- to 170-gram) hot-smoked salmon fillet, broken into large chunks

1 pint (about 283 grams) grape or cherry tomatoes, halved

1 cup (170 grams) Niçoise or kalamata olives

PREHEAT the oven to 425°F.

TOSS the potatoes with 1 tablespoon (13 grams) of the olive oil, ½ teaspoon salt, and a few grinds of pepper on a rimmed sheet pan and arrange them cut side down. Roast for 15 minutes.

MEANWHILE, toss the haricots verts with 1 tablespoon (13 grams) of the olive oil, ¼ teaspoon salt, and a few grinds of pepper and place on a second rimmed sheet pan. Nestle the eggs in their shells in nests of haricots verts so they don't roll all over.

GIVE the potatoes a toss and put them back in the oven, along with the second sheet pan. Continue to roast until the potatoes are golden brown and crispy in spots and easily pierced with a fork and the haricot verts are tender and crisp in spots, about 15 minutes more.

WHEN the eggs come out of the oven, immediately submerge them in a bowl of ice water and let sit for a couple of minutes. Peel and quarter them.

TO make the dressing, in a large measuring cup, whisk together the vinegar, mustard, thyme leaves, and red onion. Drizzle in the remaining 4 tablespoons (50 grams) olive oil while whisking continuously to emulsify.

MAKE a bed of lettuce leaves on a serving platter. Arrange the potatoes, haricots verts, salmon, eggs, tomatoes, and olives on top of the lettuce and drizzle with some of the dressing. Sprinkle with salt and a few grinds of black pepper. Serve the remaining dressing on the side. Enjoy!

PRETZEL CHICKEN NUGGET SALAD
WITH HONEY MUSTARD DRESSING

One of the great similarities between New York City and the Midwest is a solid diner culture that champions atmosphere, familiar faces, and servers who will bring you and your crying baby a half-filled mug of hot water to heat a bottle without having to ask for it. Diner menus here have things like knoephla, hotdish, and mettwurst to reflect the flavors of the region, and they are absolute gems. When I find myself at a diner past breakfast time, my order of choice is a cup of knoephla soup and a crispy chicken salad, or chopped up chicken nuggets on a bed of iceberg lettuce and wedges of tomatoes covered in sweet-like-candy honey-mustard dressing. The fried chicken provides the textbook greasy diner experience while the lettuce and tomatoes check my grown-up box for, uh, health.

I crave this combo more often than we go to diners, though, so here's a version I make at home. The chicken nuggets are baked, so I don't have to be too delusional about trying to be healthy on a weeknight, but they're coated in pretzels to take up the slack in the flavor and crunch department. It takes a lot for me to crave a crouton-less salad, but if you think of these chicken nuggets as . . . meat croutons . . . you, too, can crave this.

Chicken

½ cup (104 grams) mayonnaise

3 tablespoons (45 grams) Dijon mustard

1 teaspoon garlic powder

1 teaspoon onion powder

Freshly ground black pepper

4 heaping cups (200 grams) mini pretzels

1 pound (454 grams) boneless, skinless chicken breasts, cut into ½- to ¾-inch strips

Olive oil cooking spray or other cooking spray

Dressing

½ cup (120 grams) plain Greek yogurt (whole milk or 2%)

¼ cup (52 grams) mayonnaise

2 tablespoons (30 grams) Dijon mustard

2 tablespoons (42 grams) honey

2 tablespoons (30 grams) apple cider vinegar

1 tablespoon (13 grams) extra virgin olive oil

Kosher salt and freshly ground black pepper

Salad

8 ounces (226 grams) mixed greens

½ small red onion, thinly sliced

2 medium tomatoes, sliced into wedges

TO make the chicken, preheat the oven to 425°F. Line a rimmed sheet pan with parchment paper and set aside.

IN a medium bowl, combine the mayo, mustard, garlic powder, onion powder, and black pepper. In a food processor or zip-top bag with a rolling pin, crush the pretzels into about 2 cups of fine crumbs (a few slightly small chunks are okay) and place them in a wide shallow bowl. Coat the chicken strips all over with the mayo mixture, then coat them all over with pretzels. Transfer to the prepared sheet pan and space them out evenly. (Discard any extra crushed pretzels.)

COAT the chicken thoroughly with cooking spray and bake until the coating is crisp and the chicken is cooked through and no longer pink, with an internal temperature of 165°F; begin checking for doneness at 12 minutes. Let cool for a few minutes, then chop into bite-size pieces or snip with kitchen scissors.

TO make the dressing, in a large measuring cup, whisk together the yogurt, mayonnaise, mustard, honey, vinegar, and olive oil and season to taste with salt and pepper.

TO assemble, arrange the mixed greens on a serving plate and top with the onion, tomatoes, and chicken. Dress as desired and enjoy!

RAINBOW COUSCOUS SALAD WITH CHICKPEAS AND FETA

There was a couscous veggie salad that I used to get at the now-closed Balducci's behind Juilliard that would bring me energy and respite in the middle of days spent practicing the same 209* notes on the xylophone over and over in order to minimize my chance of missing any of those notes when it counted: at orchestra auditions. I couldn't tell you how many notes I ended up missing at the only orchestra audition I ever took, but I can tell you that the Balducci's salad was charmingly lemony, tossed with a perfect amount of fresh green herbs, and super jolly due to the fact that Israeli couscous looks like a ball pit for Barbies. It wasn't too fancy or anything, but there were many days when, if I wasn't eating that salad in a practice room, I was thinking about it in a practice room. Which was probably one of the earlier signs of my shift in brainpower allocation from music to food. But that is neither here nor there.

I've been making a salad inspired by that Balducci's salad for years. There was even going to be one in *Molly on the Range*, but it got cut, and I'm glad about that, because this new version serves even more function in my life. It has chickpeas and feta, which weren't in the original, but they fit in seamlessly with the confetti'd ball-pit-like nature and make this a full dinner, a one-bowl picnic.

SERVES 4

5 tablespoons (63 grams) extra virgin olive oil, divided

One 15-ounce (425-gram) can chickpeas, drained, rinsed, and dried very well

Kosher salt and freshly ground black pepper

Zest and juice of half a lemon

2 garlic cloves, finely chopped

8 ounces (226 grams) Israeli couscous, cooked according to the package directions
Orzo also works!

2 Persian cucumbers, diced

1 pint (about 283 grams) grape or cherry tomatoes, quartered

1 orange bell pepper, diced

4 radishes, thinly sliced

½ medium red onion, diced

½ bunch (about 20 grams) flat-leaf parsley, finely chopped

6 ounces (170 grams) feta, crumbled

*Porgy and Bess, for the one person who was wondering.

HEAT a large skillet over medium-high heat and add 1 tablespoon (13 grams) of the olive oil. Add the chickpeas and cook, tossing occasionally, until browned, 10 to 15 minutes. They might start to pop, and that's okay! Season with salt and pepper and remove from the heat to cool slightly.

IN a large bowl, combine the remaining 4 tablespoons (50 grams) olive oil, the lemon zest and juice, garlic, a good pinch of salt, and a few turns of pepper and whisk vigorously to combine and emulsify. Add the couscous, cucumbers, tomatoes, bell pepper, radishes, onion, most of the parsley, and most of the feta and fold together. Taste and adjust the seasoning as desired. Transfer to a serving bowl (or don't!) and top with the chickpeas, remaining feta, and remaining parsley.

THIS salad is great at any temperature and can be made a day or two in advance. Store it in the refrigerator but let it sit out for a bit before serving, just to take the chill off.

ROTISSERIE CHICKEN FATTOUSH WITH SUMAC VINAIGRETTE

As someone who works from home, the idea of working outside of the home is appealing for two reasons: (1) you can pack cute desk lunches in bento boxes and (2) you can pick up a rotisserie chicken on the way home. The romance of walking into a warmly lit home on a dark, stormy evening, carrying a juicy grocery store chicken feels vaguely Norman Rockwell (with a dash of Sandra Lee).

Rotisserie chickens contain the power to turn the quickest meals into flavor explosions. I wish there was a rotisserie chicken perfume. When the garden herbs are plentiful and there's leftover pita from the weekend, I get all carnivorous and tear up a chicken over this take on a fattoush, the Levantine salad with the defining feature of pita croutons. It's a crisp, colorful salad held down by creamy avocados and brought together with a bright vinaigrette that gets its shine from vinegary sumac.

If you don't have sumac, you can leave it out and add a little lemon zest to taste. And if you don't have homemade pita on hand (or the laffa on page 252), then maybe you have access to a great Israeli restaurant or bakery that sells those super-thick fluffy pitas? They really are the bee's knees. If not, grocery-store-bought pita is okay!

Dressing

1 garlic clove, finely chopped

2 tablespoons (30 grams) white wine vinegar

Juice of 1 lemon

¾ teaspoon ground sumac

½ cup (100 grams) extra virgin olive oil

Kosher salt and freshly ground black pepper

Salad

2 large pitas, torn into bite-size pieces

2 tablespoons (25 grams) extra virgin olive oil

Kosher salt and freshly ground black pepper

1 head butter lettuce, leaves separated, or 6 to 8 ounces (170 to 226 grams) chopped romaine

2 Persian cucumbers, thinly sliced

4 radishes, thinly sliced

2 scallions, cut into 1-inch pieces

2 avocados, pitted, peeled, and sliced

½ cup pickled red onions or ¼ medium red onion, thinly sliced

Meat from half a rotisserie chicken, coarsely chopped

1 handful each of coarsely chopped dill, flat-leaf parsley, and mint leaves

Flaky salt, optional

PREHEAT the oven to 450°F.

TO make the dressing, in a large measuring cup, whisk together the garlic, white wine vinegar, lemon juice, and sumac. Drizzle in the olive oil while whisking continuously to emulsify. Season to taste with salt and pepper. Set aside.

TOSS the pita with the olive oil, a pinch of salt, and a few turns of pepper and spread out on a rimmed sheet pan. Toast in the oven until browned; begin checking for doneness at 5 minutes. Let cool slightly.

IN a large bowl, gently toss together the lettuce, cucumbers, radishes, scallions, avocados, onions, pita croutons, chicken, and herbs, and dress to taste. Sprinkle with a little flaky salt, if desired, and enjoy.

HOT DOG CHOP WITH AVOCADO RANCH

One of the crueler facts about this world is that my dream of living past 120 years old with an active and vibrant retired life, complete with daily mahjong games and sunset walks with Nick, is just not compatible with my other dream of eating hot dogs, and only hot dogs, every day for three meals a day. My love for the wiener knows no shame: with mayonnaise, with nacho cheese, wrapped in Pillsbury Crescents, at Twins games where I secretly root for the White Sox, in those sweet buns from the bakeries in Chinatown . . . I've never met a hot dog I didn't like. Because of my lofty retired life dreams, I typically reserve hot dogs for special occasions like holiday parties or bat mitzvahs where I can sneak over to the kids' buffet unnoticed, but if the hankering strikes or a pack in the fridge is about to expire and I find myself programming them for a regular old Wednesday, they're going to be on top of a salad. But let me tell you: there is nothing consolatory about this salad. It has this tangy creamy avocado ranch that is worth dirtying up the food processor for and croutons inspired by the best salad bar croutons there are, from the one-and-not-only Ruby Tuesday. They're oily, salty, crisp on the outside, and soft in the middle. When everything is arranged in a color-block pattern, you'll forget that hot dogs were meant to be nestled into bread. This is extra special in the summer when corn is at peak sweetness, but I'm also not at all opposed to making this in the winter when the corn comes from the freezer.

SERVES 4 TO 6 (OR 2 IF YOU'RE EATING WITH NICK)

Dressing

½ large avocado, pitted and peeled

¼ cup (60 grams) buttermilk

¼ cup (52 grams) mayonnaise

Juice of 1 lemon

¼ cup (15 grams) coarsely chopped chives or scallions, plus more for topping the salad

¼ cup (10 grams) coarsely chopped dill, plus more for topping the salad

¼ cup (10 grams) coarsely chopped flat-leaf parsley, plus more for topping the salad

1 teaspoon sugar

Kosher salt and freshly ground black pepper

Salad

2 tablespoons (25 grams) neutral oil, plus more for oiling the grill

2 ears corn or about 1 cup (136 grams) frozen corn kernels

4 hot dogs

Kosher salt and freshly ground black pepper

5 ounces (142 grams) pumpernickel bread, cut into ¾-inch cubes (about 2½ cups cubes)

¼ teaspoon garlic powder

12 ounces (340 grams) romaine, coarsely chopped

2 hard-boiled eggs, peeled and chopped

½ pint (about 142 grams) grape or cherry tomatoes, quartered

½ small red onion, finely chopped

TO make the dressing, add the avocado, buttermilk, mayonnaise, lemon juice, chives or scallions, dill, parsley, sugar, a good pinch of salt, and a few turns of pepper to a blender or food processor and purée until smooth. Set aside.

HEAT an oiled grill, grill pan, or large skillet over medium-high heat and grill the ears of corn and hot dogs on all sides for a few minutes, until char marks appear. (If using frozen corn, you can place a skillet right on the grill.) Remove to a cutting board and, when cool enough handle, cut the kernels off the cob and season with salt and pepper. Cut the hot dogs into bite-size pieces.

TO make the croutons, heat a large skillet over medium heat and add the 2 tablespoons (25 grams) oil. Add the pumpernickel cubes and cook, tossing occasionally, until crisp and toasty on the outside but still chewy on the inside, 4 to 6 minutes. Remove from the heat and season with a good pinch of salt and the garlic powder.

TO assemble the salad, add the romaine to a large bowl and arrange all the toppings in a pretty color-block design on top. Sprinkle with additional herbs. Get a good look, take a pic if you want, and then toss everything together with dressing to taste.

TAHINI CHICKEN SALAD

Maybe it was because they were always creeping in the shadows of the cream cheese case at the bagel store, maybe it was because they seemed to be hiding secrets behind their uncomfortably opaque dressing, maybe it was because my friend Rob always farted the smelliest farts when he would eat them, but for a very long time, since birth, I held a fierce aversion to mayonnaise-based salads. What could ever be the point of eating cold food from the diet section of the menu if it looked that gross and wasn't even remotely healthy? I hate inefficiency, and mayonnaise-based salads, I thought, were anything but efficient.

Some time after I moved to Grand Forks, however, I realized I would starve in certain situations if I kept this annoying attitude up. So I gradually came around to them—first to egg salad, upon realizing that it's basically just eggs in two different forms mushed together; then to macaroni salad, since it's hard to screw up pasta; and eventually to the wider world of creamy salads. This chicken salad was the first I ever foamed at the mouth for, because the tahini, which takes the place of some of the usual amount of mayo, gives me comfort, while loads of lemon and dill saturate it with life. But the true conversation topic comes from the crispies on top: chopped up crispy chicken skin, a.k.a. Jewish bacon, a.k.a. chicken gold. It's a texture and flavor party, and everyone is invited, even you, my former mayo-hating self!

MAKES 4 CUPS

1 tablespoon (13 grams) neutral oil

2 pounds (908 grams) bone-in, skin-on chicken thighs, patted dry

Kosher salt and freshly ground black pepper

¼ cup (56 grams) good-quality tahini (see page xxi)

¼ cup (52 grams) mayonnaise

2 tablespoons (30 grams) water

¼ teaspoon freshly grated nutmeg

Zest and juice of 1 lemon

Crushed red pepper

2 large celery stalks, finely chopped

4 scallions, thinly sliced

3 tablespoons (8 grams) chopped dill

PREHEAT the oven to 425°F.

ADD the oil to a 10- to 12-inch oven-safe (ideally cast-iron) skillet and swirl to coat. Season the chicken thighs liberally all over with salt and pepper, place them skin side down in the skillet, smoosh them around to coat in oil, and

turn over and smoosh around again so that they're skin side up and coated in oil. Stick in the oven until cooked through with an internal temperature of 165°F at the thickest part; begin checking for doneness at 20 minutes. Transfer the thighs to a cutting board and drain off all but a thin layer of fat from the skillet.

HEAT the skillet over medium-high heat. Remove the chicken skins from the thighs, taking care to ensure that the skins stay intact, and place them in the skillet. Cook undisturbed until golden brown and very crispy (reduce the heat if the pan starts smoking), 8 to 10 minutes. Meanwhile, remove the bones from the chicken thighs and finely chop the chicken. Once the skin is crispy, remove it to a paper towel to drain any excess fat, then transfer to a cutting board and finely chop.

IN a large bowl, mix together the tahini, mayonnaise, water, nutmeg, lemon zest and juice, and a couple of pinches of crushed red pepper until smooth. Add the chicken, celery, scallions, most of the dill, and most of the chicken skin and fold to coat evenly. Taste and season with salt and pepper, if desired, (the chicken is pretty salty and peppery already, so you may not need to add more). Top with the remaining chicken skin and dill and serve!

STORE leftovers in an airtight container in the fridge for up to 3 days.

CRUNCHY ASIAN SLAW

Did everybody's mom in the '90s make that salad where you use a packet of "Oriental" ramen seasoning to make the dressing and then toast the unboiled noodles to add on top? It's only just recently occurred to me how hilarious that concept is, but also how tasty and functional. Everyone needs a crunchy Asian salad in their life for when they have to use up the other half of the cabbage from making potstickers or the hand-pulled noodles on page 143, or they just need a crunchy, refreshing counterpoint to a pile of steamed buns. This very versatile slaw is great on its own as a side or topped with something substantial as a main dish.

SERVING SUGGESTIONS: Top with chopped roasted salted peanuts, toasted sesame seeds, sriracha peas, wasabi peas, or, *yes*, toasted dried ramen noodles. Make it into a full meal with grilled chicken, salmon, or potstickers (!) on top, or have steamed buns on the side, or pile it on a hot dog with Kewpie mayo and teriyaki sauce!!

SERVES 4 TO 6

Dressing

¼ cup (60 grams) unseasoned rice vinegar

½ cup (100 grams) neutral oil

2 tablespoons (42 grams) honey

2 tablespoons (30 grams) soy sauce

1 tablespoon (15 grams) Chinese hot mustard

1 tablespoon (13 grams) toasted sesame oil

1 tablespoon (15 grams) sambal oelek or sriracha

Salad

½ medium head red or Napa cabbage, very thinly sliced or shredded

1 large carrot, trimmed and coarsely shredded

½ medium red onion, very thinly sliced

½ bunch (about 20 grams) cilantro, coarsely chopped

4 scallions, thinly sliced

IN a large bowl, whisk together the vinegar, oil, honey, soy sauce, mustard, sesame oil, and sambal oelek or sriracha. Add the cabbage, carrot, onion, cilantro, and scallions and toss to combine. (If you have the time and patience, let it sit for 15 minutes or so to let the cabbage soften slightly. If you don't, no big deal.) Top as desired and enjoy!

SOUPS

When I hear the word "house," I think of an exterior: a white two-story colonial with black or green shutters, a red door with a big brass knocker, and ideally a layer of snow dusted over everything. It could be on a postcard or in a snow globe; I have no idea who lives there. A retired university English professor or Sandy Cohen–type lawyer. But when I envision "home," I'm suddenly in the kitchen, wearing an oversize sweater and hearing giggles from Bernie in the next room as she builds block towers or dances with Nick. There might be figure skating or a Harry Potter movie on the TV in the background, or my family's faces on the phone as we FaceTime through dinner prep. One thing is for sure: there is soup on the stove. It's simmering away, exuding warmth in every sense and elevating the day to peak coziness. You can light every candle in a house, pile on the blankets, and cover hard floors with thick sheepskin rugs you got from the As-Is IKEA section, but it's the pot of simmering soup that truly makes a house a home. (Oops, should the title of this book actually be *Home Is Where the Soup Simmers?*)

Soup is a necessary character in our story of winter and fall. Every August, toward the end of the month, the heat in this region switches off and in comes the chill. This chill stays until April or May, and until then, we survive on warm things.

My absolute favorite meals in the whole entire world are soup, specifically when Bernie helps me taste-test it. I ladle a little bit out into one of her bowls and sit down on the kitchen floor with her before we take tiny bites. We discuss . . .

"Is it too salty?"

"No."

"Does it need anything?"

"No."

"Does it—"

"*Sup!*"

That's my cue to get more. She loves soup and I love watching her eat soup, because she does cute dances while she eats, and when she wants more she says, "*Sup!*" with a great emphasis on the "p" sound. She's rarely hungry by dinnertime since she fills up on taste tests, but that's fine by me.

Just like salads, soups also have to have a selling point. Because if you break down the ingredients, most soups are kind of just like liquidy salads. They need things to make you crave them—a carby cheesy creamy hook. Those hooks can come in the form of star-shaped noodles, a pile of salty breadcrumbs, good cheese, or a required accessory of crusty toast.

The number one rule of soup is that it requires time for it to be good. But what some of these recipes lack in speed, they make up for in ease. My chicken soup veggies are cut on the chunkier side, which reduces prep time drastically; the only chopping required in my Parmesan beans is decapitating a head of garlic; and my sheet pan squash soup is essentially shoving some stuff into the oven and then going to sing *Frozen* songs with Bernie.

CHICKEN AND STARS SOUP

The most gratifying requirement of being a Jewish mother is having a chicken soup practice. This soup doesn't have to be an original recipe or contain secrets that make it the best. It honestly doesn't even have to be that great—you just need to make it, because no matter what, your kids and your kids' kids will both need it and love it.

When it came time for me to develop my personal practice, I harked back to a time in middle school when I would bring a red plaid thermos of Campbell's chicken and stars soup for lunch every single day. Pouring little cups of that steaming hot soup dotted with those soft, comforting noodles in the middle of my school day made me feel like I was cozy at home. Since it wasn't the "normal" PB and J, it was a one-way ticket to nerddom, but I loved those soupy stars so much more than the idea of sitting at the popular table. (And so my personal brand was born?) These days I make very big, very thick cutout star noodles, as if those tiny noodles of my past have grown up with me.

Sunday afternoons are when I make my soup. It's my workout rest day, so instead of riding the exercise bike when Bernie takes her nap, I build a stock and get it simmering while I stamp out as many noodle stars as I can before she wakes up. If Bernie's earliest memory is waking up to a house that smells like chicken soup, I will feel like I have succeeded as a parent.

I load my soup with big slices of vegetables, because vegetables saturated in soup are Bernie's favorite, and bigger slices are quicker to chop, easier for her to eat with her hands, and less likely to disintegrate into mush if the soup simmers for an extra long time. Like any good Jewish chicken soup, this is heavy on the dill—but the nutmeg and lemon are the sleeper hits, infusing even more depth into an already flawless food. Contrary to some "rules," I cook my noodles directly in the soup instead of in a separate pot of boiling water, because, well, I honestly like it for all the reasons they tell you not to do it. (The noodles get mushy! The broth gets cloudy!) I *love* mushy noodles. I love the way the cloudy starch from the noodles thickens the soup so much that I sometimes also dump in any excess dusting flour instead of throwing it out. It makes you feel like you're at a deli where the soup has been simmering all day long, or even since yesterday.

Soup

One 3½-pound (1.6-kilogram) whole chicken

2 medium yellow onions, 1 quartered and 1 chopped

2 medium parsnips, trimmed, 1 cut into large chunks and 1 cut into ¼-inch slices

3 large carrots, trimmed, 1 cut into large chunks and 2 cut into ¼-inch slices

3 large celery stalks, 1 cut into large chunks and 2 cut into ¼-inch slices

2 garlic cloves, peeled and smashed

2 thyme sprigs

6 flat-leaf parsley sprigs, 3 whole and 3 chopped

12 dill sprigs, 6 whole and 6 chopped, plus more for serving

2 bay leaves

1 teaspoon whole black peppercorns, plus ground black pepper

Kosher salt

Zest and juice of half a lemon

A few passes of freshly grated nutmeg

Egg noodle stars

2 cups (260 grams) all-purpose flour, plus more for dusting

1½ teaspoons kosher salt

¼ teaspoon freshly grated nutmeg

2 large eggs

¼ cup (60 grams) water

FOR the soup base, in a large pot, combine the chicken, quartered onion, parsnip chunks, carrot chunks, celery chunks, garlic, thyme, the 3 whole parsley sprigs, the 6 whole dill sprigs, the bay leaves, and the peppercorns. Add cold water to cover and come up just below the top of the pot, about 5 quarts. Bring to a boil and then reduce the heat to simmer at a low bubble, uncovered, until the chicken is very tender, about 1½ hours (or longer if you have the time—up to 6 hours, topping off with more water if the stock dips below the chicken and veggies), skimming off any scum (there won't be much) and, if desired, some fat.

WHILE the stock simmers, make the stars: In a medium bowl, whisk together the flour, salt, and nutmeg, add the eggs and water and mix to form a dough. Knead for 5 to 7 minutes, until smooth. Cover with plastic wrap or a damp towel and let rest for 20 minutes. On a floured surface, roll out the dough to ⅛ inch thick, dusting with more flour as needed to prevent sticking, and cut out stars with a bite-size star-shaped cookie cutter (or other small cookie cutter!). Dust the stars with flour so they don't stick together and set them aside on a sheet pan. Reroll the scraps and repeat to use up the rest of the dough. (If you don't have the patience for all these cutouts, you can also just use a knife to cut long skinny noodles.) Set aside until ready to use.

CAREFULLY strain the stock, discarding all of the solids except for the chicken. You should have 3½ to 4½ quarts of stock. Set the chicken aside to cool briefly while you put together the rest of the soup. Return the strained stock to the pot and bring it to a simmer. Add the chopped onion, sliced parsnip, sliced carrots, sliced celery, chopped parsley, chopped dill, noodles, and 1 tablespoon salt and simmer, covered, until the vegetables and noodles are tender, 30 to 40 minutes.

MEANWHILE, pull the chicken off the bones and chop it into bite-size pieces. Season the chicken with salt and, when the vegetables and noodles are tender, add it to the soup along with the lemon zest and juice, nutmeg, and ground black pepper. Taste and add more salt if needed. This is important: the amount of salt in a chicken soup can mean the difference between unappetizing chicken tea and the elixir of bubbe love that it should be. So don't skip this step, and don't rush it either. Taste your soup. If it doesn't make you smile reflexively, add more salt, about a ½ teaspoon of it, and give it a few good stirs so it can dissolve. Taste and repeat as needed until it tastes good.

GARNISH with fresh dill and serve.

LEFTOVERS

AS A MUSHY NOODLE FAN, I store the soup all together and look forward to the next day when the soup will taste even better and the noodles will be even softer. I recognize that not everyone loves a mushy noodle, though, so if you're in this category and you expect to have leftovers, cook the noodles separately in salted boiling water to your desired doneness and store the drained leftover noodles separately as well. Leftovers will keep in the fridge for up to 3 days or in the freezer for up to 3 months.

TOMATOEY PARMESAN BEANS

A few years ago, Ali Slagle published a stunningly simple recipe in the *New York Times* for canned beans cooked in milk that opened my eyes to how special canned beans can become when you make the right choices: use a whole dang head of garlic, don't skimp on the butter, and don't underestimate the power of a bay leaf. Since first making Ali's recipe, we've gravitated toward a couple variations that have become staples for when we need something hearty that's not pasta, that's healthy-ish and protein-y but that doesn't require a trip to the store for fresh vegetables and meat, and—most of all—is easy, because we're all hungry and Bernie will only allow me to put her down for the amount of time it takes to chop the top off of a head of garlic. That last point is crucial in my enjoyment of this recipe; it is truly a dump-and-go recipe that requires minimal prep. The Parmesan rind adds another dimension as well as a fun treat when it gets all soft and gooey. (If you don't have a stray rind lying around, chop it off your current block, since you'll be grating a lot of that block onto these beans as well!) We try to let this simmer forever so that the flavors bloom into the best versions of themselves, but if we're too hungry to wait that long, a shorter simmering time is A-OK. Just compensate with a little more salt or Parmesan. These beans are primarily vehicles for Parmesan and an excuse to eat thick toast with garlic on it, so don't take these serving directions as suggestions; they are part of the package.

SERVES 2 TO 4

2 tablespoons (28 grams) unsalted butter

1 garlic head

One 15-ounce (425-gram) can cannellini beans, drained and rinsed

One 15-ounce (425-gram) can chickpeas, drained and rinsed

One 28-ounce (794-gram) can chopped or whole peeled tomatoes

1½ cups (360 grams) low-sodium chicken or veggie stock

1 Parmesan rind, plus a good amount of freshly grated Parmesan for serving

1 bay leaf

Kosher salt and freshly ground black pepper

2 big handfuls of chopped or torn kale, chard, baby spinach, or other sturdy greens, optional but encouraged

Crusty toast, for serving

Extra virgin olive oil

Flaky salt

IN a large pot, melt the butter over medium heat. Chop the top off the head of garlic so that all the cloves are exposed and discard any of the peels that are about to fall off (but in general you want the head to stay together). Add the garlic to the pan cut side down and cook for a few minutes, until browned around the edges. Stir in the beans, tomatoes, stock, Parmesan rind, bay leaf, a couple of good pinches of salt, and a bunch of black pepper. (If using whole peeled tomatoes, break them up a little with your spoon.) Bring to a boil, reduce to a simmer, cover, and cook until the garlic cloves are smooshy, about 30 minutes, or longer if you have the patience, stirring occasionally. Stir in the greens a few minutes before you plan on serving and let wilt. Taste and add more salt and pepper as needed.

RETRIEVE the garlic head, scoop out the softened cloves with a knife (or carefully smoosh with your fingers since it will be hot), and spread them on your crusty toast. Ladle the beans into bowls (avoiding the bay leaf), finish with a drizzle of olive oil, black pepper, a little flaky salt, and a storm of Parmesan and serve with the garlicky toast. Bring the Parmesan to the table to add more as you eat—this is crucial.

VARIATION
CREAMY PARMESAN BEANS

FOLLOW the directions for the Tomatoey Parmesan Beans but omit the tomatoes, increase the stock quantity to 1¾ cups (420 grams), and add a handful of chopped cooked ham if you happen to have some. Finish with 2 tablespoons (30 grams) heavy cream.

SERVE with lemon wedges and crushed red pepper.

BROCCOLINI SOUP WITH BREADCRUMBS AND POACHED EGGS

I have this great app idea that I need you to promise me you won't steal. It's called Soup of the Day, and it tells you what the soup of the day is at all the restaurants in your area. Then you can just think in your brain, "Hm, I feel like knoephla today," and you don't have to call every restaurant to find it. You can just go on my app and have it tell you that Darcy's Diner has it and if you click a button, your phone will call Darcy's to order it. It's the ideal app for a soup-forward lifestyle.

Anyway, this broccolini soup grew out of an aversion I have to broccoli-cheese soup. I'm always disappointed when I hear that it's the soup of the day, because it makes my belly hurt. So much goop, so much cheese . . . Are we sure this isn't just macaroni and cheese that forgot its noodles? It's too much for me, but it doesn't need to be that way. We can have a more agreeable broccoli soup! Here's how: first, use broccolini! It's milder and sweeter (and less . . . farty?) than regular broccoli. Second, you don't need that much cheese: a strong cheese will add a lot of flavor without having to add too much of it, so it won't feel weighed down. And third, skip the cream altogether and rely on a runny egg yolk to contribute richness. The breadcrumbs add some good crunchy texture and are an easy carby element if you're out of bread.

We like this soup in the spring, when our bodies start to crave more, brighter vegetables but the snow is still raging outside, overstaying its welcome.

SERVES 4

2 tablespoons (25 grams) extra virgin olive oil

1 medium yellow onion, chopped

Kosher salt

½ teaspoon crushed red pepper

12 ounces (340 grams) broccolini, cut into ½- to ¾-inch pieces

1½ pounds (680 grams) russet potatoes, chopped into ½- to ¾-inch pieces

6 cups (1.4 kilograms) low-sodium chicken or vegetable stock

Freshly ground black pepper

4 ounces (113 grams) shredded Parmesan, pecorino, sharp white cheddar, or Gruyère

Juice of half a lemon

Accessories

2 tablespoons (28 grams) unsalted butter

1 cup (60 grams) panko breadcrumbs or crumbled day-old crusty bread

Kosher salt and freshly ground black pepper

4 eggs

Extra virgin olive oil

Flaky salt

Sriracha

HEAT a large pot over medium-high heat and add the olive oil. Add the onion and a pinch of salt and cook, stirring occasionally, until softened, 5 to 7 minutes. Add the crushed red pepper and cook for another minute. Add the broccolini, potatoes, stock, 1 teaspoon salt, and a bunch of ground black pepper, cover, and bring to a boil. Reduce to a simmer and cook, stirring occasionally, for 20 to 30 minutes, until a fork pokes easily into a potato

CAREFULLY ladle about three-quarters of the mixture into a blender and purée until very smooth. You may need to do this in batches as you don't want to fill your blender more than halfway when you're puréeing hot stuff. Return the mixture to the pot, over low heat, and add the cheese, stirring until melted. Stir in the lemon juice, taste, and adjust the seasonings as desired.

TO make the accessories, heat a medium saucepan or deep skillet over medium heat and melt the butter. Add the breadcrumbs, a pinch of salt, and a few turns of pepper and cook for a few minutes, stirring often, until the breadcrumbs are golden. Remove to a bowl. Wipe out the saucepan and fill it with about an inch of water. A few minutes before you're ready to serve, bring the water to a low simmer. Carefully crack in the eggs, taking care not to break the yolks. Simmer until the whites are opaque but the yolks are still soft and jiggly, 2 to 4 minutes. Remove with a slotted spoon to a plate lined with a paper towel (or, if you're a speed demon, you've already ladled the soup into bowls while the eggs poached and can put them directly into the soup). Ladle the soup into shallow bowls and accessorize each with a poached egg, a drizzle of olive oil, a pile of breadcrumbs, a pinch of flaky salt, some good turns of black pepper, and a splatter of sriracha. Enjoy!

SHEET PAN ROASTED SQUASH SOUP

Puréed veggie soups are basically just hot smoothies, so we frequent them for the same reasons that we love shoving fruits and vegetables into our bods via our morning smoothies. When there's squash from the garden and apples from the trees, Bernie paints them with olive oil and they roast while we go off to twirl and dance. Whole cloves of garlic nested with lots of olive oil in the squash bowls get kind of confited while the apples and veggies pick up lots of roasty flavor. It takes some time, which is mostly hands off, but if you'd like to speed it up, you could peel and chop the squash into chunks so that it softens quicker.

Everything gets puréed into a soup that's a simple kind of comfort; it's not about the fireworks here. But this is important: it's served with a big plate of hot crusty bread in the center of the table along with prosciutto and mayo or Boursin or good butter—anything fatty and decadent to reward the fact that none of you left this page after seeing this soup referred to as a "hot smoothie." *Ew, David.* Ideally, this bread is a loaf of Alexandra Stafford's peasant bread (Google it! It's so great!), but on busier days it's a take-and-bake baguette, baby!

One 2½- to 3-pound (1.1- to 1.4-kilogram) butternut squash, halved lengthwise and seeds removed

1 Honeycrisp apple, cored and cut into big wedges (skin on)

1 Granny Smith apple, cored and cut into big wedges (skin on)

1 large onion, peeled and quartered

3 tablespoons (38 grams) extra virgin olive oil

3 garlic cloves, peeled

Kosher salt and freshly ground black pepper

4 cups (960 grams) low-sodium chicken or vegetable stock, plus more if needed

2 teaspoons green hot sauce, plus more to taste

Dollops of plain Greek yogurt for serving

Accessories

Hot crusty bread with prosciutto and mayo or Boursin or butter or anything else along those lines

PREHEAT the oven to 400°F. Line a rimmed sheet pan with parchment paper.

PLACE the squash halves on the sheet pan, cut side up. Arrange the apples and onion around them. Divide the olive oil between the divots in the squash and add the garlic cloves. Dip a pastry brush into the olive oil and use it to brush the squash, apples, and onion with a thin layer of oil, leaving the excess in the divots. Sprinkle with 1 teaspoon salt and loads of black pepper and roast until the apples and onion are soft and have some charred edges; begin checking at 30 minutes.

TRANSFER the apples, onion, garlic, and excess oil to a blender. Continue to roast the squash until a spoon easily pokes into the flesh; begin checking at 45 minutes, but depending on the size and shape of your squash, it could take closer to 60 minutes. To the blender, add enough stock to get the mixture blending, then blend until very smooth. Pour into a large pot and simmer while the squash finishes roasting.

SCOOP the flesh from the squash into the blender and add enough stock to get the mixture blending, supplementing with some puréed apple and onion mixture if necessary. Blend until very smooth and add to the pot along with any remaining stock. Stir and bring to a simmer. Thin out with more stock (or water), if desired. Add the hot sauce. Simmer, covered, for as long as your hunger and schedule will allow, stirring occasionally, but if you're very hungry, you can eat it immediately. Taste and adjust the seasoning as desired.

SERVE with dollops of Greek yogurt and more black pepper. Enjoy with your bread-y accessories of choice!

BAHARAT CHILI WITH CORNBREAD ON TOP

Every few months in the winter, I get a craving for chili that simply will not quit. Unlike watching *Pitch Perfect 2* or eating hot dogs, it's not something that I'm always 100 percent in the mood for. But when I am and a beautiful chili promptly presents itself, it's like the heavens have opened up and rained down flying baby bunnies. Bonus points go to the chili with cornbread on it; when cornbread is crunchy on top and soaked with chili on the bottom, that is big living. This chili has my heart because it gets a visit from baharat ("spices" in Arabic), a spice blend that's common in Middle Eastern cooking and has a combination of savory flavors like cumin and coriander and warm tones like cinnamon and nutmeg. This recipe is heavier on the beans than it is on the turkey and has a few golden raisins stirred in toward the end that are like tiny sweet bursty surprises. Earth's Gushers.

Don't skimp on the yogurt when dishing up. It's a necessary hit of creamy acidity that also cuts down on the time the chili takes to cool off enough so that you don't burn your mouth.

SERVES 4 TO 6

Chili

4 thick-cut bacon strips

1 medium yellow onion, chopped

2 medium carrots, trimmed and chopped

1 jalapeño, seeded and finely chopped

Kosher salt

2 garlic cloves, finely chopped

1 tablespoon (6 grams) baharat

1 tablespoon (8 grams) chili powder

Freshly ground black pepper

1 pound (454 grams) ground turkey, 93% lean

Two 15-ounce (425-gram) cans chickpeas, drained and rinsed

One 15-ounce (425-gram) can cannellini beans, drained and rinsed

One 28-ounce (794-gram) can fire-roasted diced tomatoes

3 cups (720 grams) low-sodium chicken stock

½ cup (80 grams) golden raisins

Cornbread

1 cup (160 grams) cornmeal

1 cup (130 grams) all-purpose flour

1 tablespoon (13 grams) sugar

1 teaspoon kosher salt

1 teaspoon baking powder

½ teaspoon baking soda

1 large egg

½ cup (100 grams) extra virgin olive oil

1 cup (240 grams) plain Greek yogurt (whole milk or 2%)

Accessories

Dollops of plain Greek yogurt

Chopped flat-leaf parsley, optional

IN a large Dutch oven or other oven-safe pot, crisp up the bacon over medium heat. Transfer to a paper towel to drain any excess grease, let cool slightly, coarsely chop, and set aside. Keep the bacon grease in the pot and increase the heat to medium high. Add the onion, carrots, jalapeño, and a pinch of salt and cook, stirring occasionally, until softened, about 10 minutes. Add the garlic, baharat, chili powder, and a few turns of black pepper and cook, stirring, until fragrant, about a minute. Add the turkey, season with ¾ teaspoon salt, and cook, breaking up the meat with a spoon, until browned. Add the bacon, chickpeas, cannellini beans, tomatoes, and stock. Bring to a boil, reduce to a low simmer, and cook, uncovered, for 40 minutes, stirring occasionally.

MEANWHILE, make the cornbread. Preheat the oven to 400°F.

IN a medium bowl, whisk together the cornmeal, flour, sugar, salt, baking powder, and baking soda. In a separate medium bowl or large measuring cup, whisk together the egg, olive oil, and yogurt. Right before the chili is done simmering, add the wet ingredients to the dry ingredients and mix until just combined. Set aside briefly while you stir the golden raisins into the chili and taste and adjust the seasoning as desired. Use an ice cream scoop or large spoon to dollop the cornbread mixture all over the top. Bake until the cornbread is lightly golden; begin checking for doneness at 25 minutes.

SERVE with the yogurt and a sprinkle of parsley, if using, and enjoy!

KALE CHIP CONGEE

If congee were a clothing item, it would be that pilly oversize sweater that you got fifteen years ago that just gets cozier in its old age. No matter how many times you go to your closet to choose a sweater on a chilly day, hoping that you will emerge swaddled in delicate cashmere like a chic woman of comfort, your cozy sensibility always gets the best of you, and you inevitably determine that the simple, humble, very old ketchup-stained sweater is your actual happy place.

Congee is not fancy or flashy. It doesn't even really require more than two ingredients; it is just a straight shot to comfort. In essence, congee is rice cooked for forever in loads of stock or water.

Toppings are always a choose-your-own adventure, which translates, for us, to taking the jar of kimchi and whatever sauces are in the fridge and plopping them on the table. A giant pile of kale chips functions like crackers in that some get soft and chewy and some stay crisp. When we're going wild, we chop up unsweetened doughnuts (well, deep-fried biscuits from a can, haha) as a nod to the traditional addition of youtiao, Chinese crullers. We almost always use brown rice in the name of health, which takes longer to cook than white rice, but that just means more time to make "pom-pom soup" with Bernie on the floor of the kitchen.

SERVES 3 TO 4

Congee

1½ cups (270 grams) short-grain brown rice, rinsed

10 cups (2.4 kilograms) low-sodium chicken stock

2 whole scallion stalks, trimmed

Two 1-inch pieces of ginger (no need to peel them)

Toppings

8 ounces (226 grams) coarsely chopped kale

2 tablespoons (25 grams) extra virgin olive oil

¾ teaspoon kosher salt

4 large eggs

Suggested Accessories

Sliced scallions

Chopped kimchi

Chopped unsweetened doughnuts

Fried garlic chips

Toasted sesame oil

Sambal oelek or other hot sauce

Soy sauce

IN a large pot, combine the rice, stock, scallions, and ginger and bring to a boil. Reduce to a simmer, cover, and cook for about 90 minutes, stirring occasionally so the rice doesn't stick to the bottom of the pot. Cook until the rice has broken down and the mixture is thick and porridge-like. You can adjust the consistency to your liking by cooking it longer, uncovered, to make it thicker or by adding more stock or water to make it thinner.

TO make the kale chips, preheat the oven to 350°F. If you've just washed your kale, make sure that it is very dry (alternatively, do what I do and buy the prechopped, prewashed kale). Toss the kale with the olive oil and spread across 2 rimmed sheet pans. Season with the salt. Bake until crispy; begin checking for doneness at 12 minutes. Let cool on the pan.

TO make the eggs, bring a pot of water to a simmer and gently lower in the eggs. Simmer for exactly 7 minutes, then stop the cooking by submerging the eggs in an ice bath or running them under cold water. Peel and slice in half for the perfect runny egg. (For a hard-boiled egg, simmer for 10 minutes instead.)

LADLE the congee into bowls, discarding the ginger and whole scallions, and top with the eggs, a big handful of kale chips, and other accessories as desired. Put the sauces on the table and pass them around. I like a small drizzle of sesame oil and a splattering of sambal oelek. If I think it needs more salt, I drizzle in a little soy sauce.

STORE leftovers in an airtight container in the fridge for up to 3 days. They'll thicken up, but you can thin them out with more stock or water.

PIZZA FRIDAY

Our Pizza Friday tradition is alive and well and, thanks to Bernie, populated with lots of clown-like vegetable smiley faces. For our entire life together (and, for me, since childhood), Nick and I have eaten pizza every Friday night. We've only strayed from it for monumental reasons, like my being in labor. Bernie's arrival shook things up a little (even post-labor) because planning a pizza stone preheating and dough rising dance that's supposed to coincide with a sacred toddler bedtime ritual requires some Justin Peck–level choreography. But no *Goodnight Moon* recitation can keep us from hot melty cheese.

The routine we commonly perform is a two-part event. Part one is where Bernie and I pinch off little balls of dough and make mini pizzas with olive eyes, tomato noses, and spinach hair, which we sit down to enjoy, as Bernie's full supper and Nick's and my amuse-bouches. Part two is after bedtime, when Nick and I eat our actual non-smiley-face pizza and get a little drunk by splitting one can of local beer. The term "date night" makes me kind of cringe, but that's basically what it is. The rule is that we have to watch an actual movie or something dramatic that's outside of our realm of quotidian *Curb Your Enthusiasm* or *House Hunters* episodes. But sometimes by the time we've watched all the trailers, discussed all our options, researched them on Rotten Tomatoes, and settled on the thing, our pizza is eaten, the beer is warm, and it's past our bedtime. We are really so boring. But our pizza isn't.

A NOTE ON DOUGH: *Unless otherwise noted (as in Caesar Salad French Bread Pizza, page 119, and House Veggie Pizza, page 126), the pizza dough called for refers to a classic mixture of flour, water, salt, and yeast that ideally has had time overnight to ferment and develop flavor. Use your favorite recipe (I alternate between Jim Lahey's no-knead dough, Joe Beddia's Pizza Camp dough, and Alexandra Stafford's less-time-intensive no-knead dough, all easily Googleable); or your favorite store-bought dough; or ask your local pizza parlor if you can purchase some of theirs. If you want to up your homemade dough game, order a bag of type 00 flour, which is very finely ground flour made from durum wheat that results in a crust slightly less chewy than one made with all-purpose. Whatever dough you use, make sure that it's at room temperature before you start. If your dough has been in the refrigerator, let it sit for at least 1 good hour, up to 3 or 4 hours, covered, at room temperature before using.*

BROCCOLINI, SAUSAGE, AND LEMON DEEP-DISH PIZZA

Out of all the pizzas that have made their way into my belly, I identify most closely with this one. As a Chicago native, I have a love for deep-dish pizza in my DNA; a go-to recipe is required for when we've gone through the last of the Goldbelly'd Lou Malnatis in the freezer. This broccolini sausage pie isn't a re-creation of a classic Chicago pizza, because I'm typically wont to leave that up to the pros; this version is puffier, doesn't require sauce (we'll get to that . . .), and has crispy cheese around the edges. Everything here works so nicely together because the heartiness of the ingredients matches the heftiness of the dough, so they all bake at the same rate and you don't have to fret about precooking the broccolini or sausage. The fatty sausage enriches everything around it (wouldn't you like to be more like sausage?), and the lemon brightens up each thick bite. I can literally never decide if this pizza should have sauce or not, so I'm including it as a dunking/drizzling option that you can add at the end.

MAKES ONE 10-INCH DEEP-DISH PIZZA, EASILY DESTROYABLE BY TWO HUNGRY ADULTS WHO ATE SALADS ALL WEEK (WE USUALLY DOUBLE THIS)

2 tablespoons (25 grams) extra virgin olive oil, plus more for drizzling

1 pound (454 grams) pizza dough, room temperature

2 garlic cloves, thinly sliced

8 ounces (226 grams) fresh mozzarella, roughly torn

⅓ cup (80 grams) whole milk ricotta
ricotta con latte if you can find it!

Zest of 1 lemon

4 ounces (113 grams) broccolini, cut into ½-inch pieces

Kosher salt

4 ounces (113 grams) raw Italian pork sausage, casings removed

Freshly grated Parmesan

Crushed red pepper

Marinara sauce, warmed, for dunking or drizzling, optional

PREHEAT the oven to 450°F.

SWIRL the olive oil around the bottom and sides of a 12-inch cast-iron skillet or 10-inch round cake pan and add the dough. Pat out the dough so that it covers the bottom and comes up about an inch on the sides (it will kinda shrink in the oven). Scatter the garlic, mozzarella, dollops of the ricotta, and the lemon zest over the dough, all the way to the edge.

IN a small bowl, toss the broccolini with a drizzle of olive oil to coat and scatter over the pizza. Season with a good pinch of salt. Top the pizza with small pinches of the sausage and bake until the cheese is splotchy; begin checking for doneness at 20 minutes. Shower with Parmesan and a couple of pinches of crushed red pepper. Run a knife or offset spatula around the edge and use a spatula to transfer the pizza to a cutting board. Slice and enjoy with marinara for dunking or drizzling, if desired.

CAESAR SALAD FRENCH BREAD PIZZA

French bread pizza was totally "mom food" growing up. There was always a stash of it in our freezer that only my mom would go near, and she usually had it while I was eating my after-school Hot Pocket. Sometimes I'd steal bites, always being sure to steer clear of the ends because they were hard and overcooked, though for the most part I stuck to my Hot Pockets. They were better. But as soon as Bernie was born and I became a mom, the switch in my brain that controls feelings toward French bread pizza (which is apparently next to the anxiety dial and the switch that turns a "bathroom" into a "potty") was flipped, simple as that. French bread pizza takes remarkably well to my kink for salad on pizza. I know—it's polarizing, salad on pizza, but when you see it in this form—folded over like a sandwich—it may help you realize that salad belongs on a pizza just like lettuce belongs on a sandwich. It adds a cooling crunch! It's also easier to eat salad on a pizza in sandwich form because the salad is contained better.

This is the ultimate quick pizza, not just because you forgo any homemade dough for a loaf of bread from the grocery store bakery, but also because other conveniences like pre-shredded mozz, shaky powdery Parmesan, and a bagged salad kit are consistent with the overall vibe. So honestly, just lean in.

MAKES 4 SANDWICHES

1 French bread loaf from the grocery store bakery

2 tablespoons (25 grams) extra virgin olive oil

4 garlic cloves, finely chopped

½ cup (124 grams) pizza sauce

2 cups (8 ounces/226 grams) shredded mozzarella

Pinch of dried oregano

A few handfuls of chopped grilled chicken, optional

9 ounces (255 grams) romaine, chopped

Totally cool if they're from a bagged salad kit.

Caesar dressing, store-bought or homemade, if you're feeling fancy (recipe follows)

Crushed red pepper

Freshly ground black pepper

Grated Parmesan

PREHEAT the oven to 425°F.

SLICE the French bread in half lengthwise (try to keep from cutting through all the way on one long end so you can open it up in one big piece) and place cut side up on a sheet pan. Brush the innards with the olive oil and sprinkle evenly all over with the garlic. Spread on the pizza sauce and cover with the mozzarella. Sprinkle with the oregano and top with chicken, if using, and bake until the cheese is melted and the edges are toasty; begin checking for doneness at 10 minutes.

MEANWHILE, in a large bowl, toss the romaine with dressing to taste.

CUT the pizza into 4 big pieces crosswise (they will create 4 big sandwiches), then top with the salad and sprinkle with crushed red pepper, black pepper, and Parmesan. Fold over, smash a little, and enjoy!

CAESAR DRESSING

MAKES ABOUT 1 CUP

¼ cup (30 grams) grated Parmesan

½ cup (120 grams) plain Greek yogurt (whole milk or 2%)

2 tablespoons (25 grams) extra virgin olive oil

1 tablespoon (15 grams) Dijon mustard

2 shakes Worcestershire sauce

Zest and juice of half a lemon

1 garlic clove, finely chopped or grated with a fine zester

Lots of freshly ground black pepper

¼ teaspoon kosher salt

IN a medium bowl, combine all the ingredients and whisk until smooth. Taste and adjust the seasoning as desired. Store in the fridge until ready to use (this can be made a day or two in advance). Store leftovers (if there are any) in an airtight container in the fridge for up to 3 days.

SALAMI AND ARUGULA PIZZA

In case my salad-on-pizza messaging from the last recipe was unclear, here is a more refined argument. Peppery arugula amplifies peppery salami, cuts its richness, and provides a tangle of joy on top of a chewy thin-crust pie. I won't shut up until you experience this. For the most graceful salad pizza experience: cut the pizza before adding the salad, only top what you intend to eat immediately (so that the greens stay crisp and leftovers can be assembled with proper attention to topping temperatures), and fold your pizza slices when eating so they go down like little sandwiches.

MAKES TWO 10-INCH PIZZAS, TO SERVE 2 TO 3

1 pound (454 grams) pizza dough, room temperature

All-purpose or type 00 flour, for dusting

½ cup (124 grams) pizza sauce

8 ounces (226 grams) fresh mozzarella, roughly torn

½ small yellow onion, thinly sliced

12 thin slices (3 to 4 ounces/85 to 113 grams) deli salami

3 ounces (85 grams) baby arugula

Juice of half a lemon

1 tablespoon (13 grams) extra virgin olive oil

Flaky salt or kosher salt

Freshly ground black pepper

Crushed red pepper

Freshly grated Parmesan

ARRANGE a rack in the center of your oven with a pizza stone if you have one (or a rimless baking sheet if you don't) and preheat it to 500°F, ideally for at least an hour.

DIVIDE the dough in half and stretch it into 2 balls, tucking the ends under and pinching them together so there's a smooth, taut surface. Set each on a lightly floured 10-inch square piece of parchment paper, cover with plastic wrap or towels, and let sit for 30 minutes.

FLATTEN the balls of pizza dough into 9- to 10-inch rounds, dusting with flour as necessary to prevent sticking. Spread each dough round with ¼ cup (62 grams) of sauce, going almost all the way to the edge, and top with the mozzarella, onion, and salami. Working with one at a time, slide the pizza (and the parchment) onto the stone and bake until the crust is golden and the salami is crisp around the edges; begin checking for doneness at 7 minutes.

IN a large bowl, toss the arugula with the lemon juice and olive oil and season with salt, loads of black pepper, and crushed red pepper.

WHEN the pizzas are done, slice them into quarters and top each with a big pile of arugula. Cover with lots of Parmesan.

HAM AND POTATO PIZZA

Living in meat-and-potatoes country, I've accepted that the concept of going out to dinner with the intention of ordering a big, beautiful salad is about as reliable a plan as ice fishing in June. The strength of our local menus lies in bison burgers and ribs, not little gems and bespoke olives. Now, while I'd totally back a campaign for Chez Panisse to offer drone delivery within a 2,000-mile radius, I also don't want to kid anyone: I *lovvvvve* meat and potatoes. And this pizza is an ode to that. Potatoes on pizza is the ultimate carb-on-carb act; the way the potatoes melt down into the cheese and become one with the thick, oily crust is pure bliss. Ham brings smoky, salty bits of excitement, and spinach checks the box for vitamins and color. Don't hold back with the ranch drizzle here. This is a sauceless pizza, so the texture police will thank you for this. Also, welcome to the Midwest!

MAKES 1 THICK-CRUST HALF-SHEET-PAN PIZZA, TO SERVE 3 TO 4

3 tablespoons (38 grams) extra virgin olive oil, divided, plus more for brushing

2 pounds (908 grams) pizza dough, room temperature

2 large garlic cloves, thinly sliced

1 medium shallot, thinly sliced

12 ounces (340 grams) fresh mozzarella, roughly torn

6 ounces (170 grams) thick-cut ham, chopped

2 handfuls of baby spinach

12 ounces (340 grams) Yukon gold potatoes, cut into ⅛-inch-thick slices

Kosher salt and freshly ground black pepper

Ranch

Crushed red pepper

Freshly grated Parmesan

Handful of chopped flat-leaf parsley

PREHEAT the oven to 450°F.

COAT a rimmed half sheet pan with 2 tablespoons (25 grams) of the olive oil, add the dough, and press the dough all the way to the edges. If the dough starts to fight you as you press it, leave it to sit for 10 to 15 minutes so that the gluten can relax, then go at it again. Brush the top with a thin, even layer of olive oil and scatter on the garlic, shallot, mozzarella, ham, and spinach. (Scatter the cheese all the way to the edge so you get some crispy bits!)

IN a large bowl, toss the potatoes with the remaining tablespoon (13 grams) of olive oil and arrange in an even layer on the pizza, doing your best to avoid overlapping them. Sprinkle with a good pinch of salt and a bunch of turns of pepper. Bake until the crust is golden and the cheese is splotchy brown; begin checking for doneness at 30 minutes. If you'd like a little more color on the potatoes, stick the pizza under the broiler for a few minutes. Top with a drizzle of ranch, crushed red pepper, loads of Parm, and the parsley. Cut into big squares and enjoy!

HOUSE VEGGIE PIZZA

Sometimes we arrive at Pizza Friday after a week of being lazy about our morning smoothies, eating test runs of new macaroni and cheese recipes for dinner, choosing to sit on the couch at night and watch *The Bachelorette* instead of doing an ab workout while watching *The Bachelorette*, and also picking at the birthday cake that's been sitting out on the counter since Nick's birthday the previous week, and exchange glances with each other that say, "We gotta have pizza now?" Life is so tough. The thing about Pizza Friday is that, well, you can't just skip it and have a salad; that would be like Mercury going into retroretroretrograde. So the compromise we resort to (which does not taste like a compromise at all) is building our pizza on a whole wheat crust and covering it with a blanket of greens. The greens get a little crispy in the oven, so you almost feel like you're eating kale chips on a pizza, and the crust is thin and satisfyingly chewy. In an ode to my Chicago roots, this crust calls for butter (twice) and Barnaby's-style pleating (IYKYK!!), and in an ode to my home now, I can't resist adding ranch at the end.

Dough

¼ cup (56 grams) unsalted butter, melted

¾ cup (180 grams) warm water

1 teaspoon kosher salt

1 teaspoon sugar

1 cup (130 grams) all-purpose flour, plus more for dusting

1 cup (130 grams) whole wheat flour (or more all-purpose)

Toppings

1 tablespoon (14 grams) unsalted butter, melted

⅓ cup (83 grams) pizza sauce

8 ounces (226 grams) shredded whole milk mozzarella or roughly torn fresh mozzarella or a combination of both

2 large garlic cloves, thinly sliced

½ small red or yellow onion, chopped

½ green bell pepper, chopped

2 ounces (57 grams/1 big handful) chopped kale

2 ounces (57 grams/1 big handful) baby spinach

Extra virgin olive oil

Kosher salt and freshly ground black pepper

Ranch

Freshly grated Parmesan

Crushed red pepper

ARRANGE a rack in the lower third of the oven and preheat it to 475°F.

TO make the dough, in a large bowl, whisk together the butter, water, salt, and sugar. With a rubber spatula, stir in the flours until combined. Turn the dough out onto a lightly floured surface and knead for 5 minutes, adding additional all-purpose flour if it gets too sticky. Form into a ball, cover with plastic wrap or a damp towel, and let sit for 30 minutes.

LINE a sheet pan with parchment paper. On a floured surface, using a rolling pin, roll the dough out into a big rectangle, about 13 x 18 inches, adding more flour as needed to prevent the dough from sticking to the surface or your rolling pin. Transfer the dough to the pan and crimp the edges to make a crust.

TO top the pizza, brush the edges with the butter and then spread on the sauce, followed by the mozzarella, garlic, onion, and bell pepper. Cover everything with the kale and spinach and drizzle the greens with olive oil. Sprinkle with a good pinch of salt and a few turns of black pepper.

BAKE until the cheese is splotchy with brown marks and the crust is golden; begin checking for doneness at 15 minutes. Drizzle with ranch, then top with lots of grated Parmesan and crushed red pepper. Cut into squares and enjoy!

PAN-FRIED GARDEN PIZZA

What this summertime pizza lacks in cheese and salty meat, it makes up for in the fact that it's built on what is basically a big flat doughnut. It's a fun, rustic way to use up garden veggies, showcasing the sweetness of peak-season corn, zucchini, tomatoes, and eggplant if that's your thing. You really can't go wrong with the toppings here if they've been sourced from your backyard or a friend's. All these goodies are held in place via a zingy garlic bean dip on a squishy fried crust that doesn't require you to turn the oven on.

MAKES TWO 10-INCH PIZZAS, TO SERVE 2 TO 3

1 pound (454 grams) pizza dough, room temperature

All-purpose or type 00 flour, for dusting

4 tablespoons (50 grams) extra virgin olive oil, divided, plus more as needed

1 small zucchini, diced

Kernels from 1 ear sweet corn (about 1 cup/136 grams)

½ small red onion, thinly sliced

1 jalapeño, thinly sliced, or ½ bell pepper, diced

Other garden goodies that would be fun to add or substitute for any of the above: diced eggplant, summer squash, chopped green beans.

Kosher salt and freshly ground black pepper

1 batch (1 heaping cup) Zingy Navy Bean Dip (page 247)

Don't feel like making this? I won't tell anyone if you use store-bought garlic hummus instead.

12 grape or cherry tomatoes, quartered

Handful of fresh basil, torn

A few squeezes of fresh lemon juice

Flaky salt

Crushed red pepper

DIVIDE the dough in half and stretch it into 2 balls, tucking the ends under and pinching them together to create a smooth, taut surface. Set on a lightly floured surface, cover loosely with plastic wrap or a towel, and let sit for 30 minutes.

HEAT a 12-inch (ideally cast-iron) skillet over medium-high heat and add 1 tablespoon (13 grams) of the olive oil. Add the zucchini, corn, onion, and pepper, spread them out evenly, and let cook until browned, 10 to 15 minutes, tossing only very occasionally so that they can develop some nice color. Season with salt and pepper, transfer to a plate, and wipe out the skillet.

WHILE the veggies cook, flatten the balls of pizza dough into 10-inch rounds, dusting with flour as necessary to prevent sticking.

RETURN the skillet to medium heat and add the remaining 3 tablespoons (38 grams) of olive oil. When the oil is hot, carefully transfer 1 dough round to the skillet. Fry the dough for about 5 minutes, until golden on the bottom. If the dough puffs up, you can gently press it down with a spatula. Using two spatulas, carefully flip the dough and cook for 3 to 5 more minutes, until golden on the other side. Transfer to a plate and repeat with the remaining dough, adding more oil to the skillet if needed. If the dough comes out of the skillet looking excessively oily, there is no shame in blotting it with a paper towel.

TOP each pizza with a thick layer of Zingy Navy Bean Dip and a pile of the grilled veggies, tomatoes, and basil. Sprinkle everything with squeezes of lemon, flaky salt, and crushed red pepper. Slice and enjoy!

LEFTOVER PIZZA SALAD

The quintessential day-after-Pizza-Friday lunch is *leftover pizza salad!* It's for when you want leftover pizza for Saturday lunch but feel like you should maybe have a vegetable after eating all that pizza last night. It's the best of both worlds: hot gooey cheesy pizza and cold crunchy refreshing greens. It's also a great clean-out-the-fridge move so you can use up the rest of last night's pizza toppings.

A LOOSE GUIDE FOR BUILDING YOUR OWN LEFTOVER PIZZA SALAD

START with your pizza: ideally one medium slice per person, more or less, depending on what you have and your hunger level. Preheat the oven to 350°F. Chop the pizza into bite-size squares, scatter on a parchment-lined rimmed sheet pan, cheese side up, and bake until hot and crisp on the edges (they'll still be chewy in the middle!); begin checking for doneness at 5 minutes, but if it's a thicker slice, it'll take longer.

BUILD your salad: In a large bowl, toss in your greens, 1 to 2 big handfuls per person. I prefer chopped romaine or a mix of chopped romaine with whatever leftover tender greens I have, such as spinach or arugula. Add the remainder of last night's onion, pepper, a handful of kalamata olives, and/or grape or cherry tomatoes, chopped in your desired size and shape. Add a drained can of chickpeas if you'd like to bulk things up! Or leftover pepperoni! Give it a hit of fresh basil! Cucumbers are good too, maybe even mushrooms if you're a mushroom person.

FOR the dressing, try a red wine vinaigrette: In a large measuring cup, whisk up 1 part red wine vinegar to 2 parts olive oil and add a dollop of Dijon, a pinch of sugar, a pinch of dried oregano, and salt and pepper to taste. Ranch is also great.

TOSS everything together and cover with grated Parmesan and black pepper. Yay!

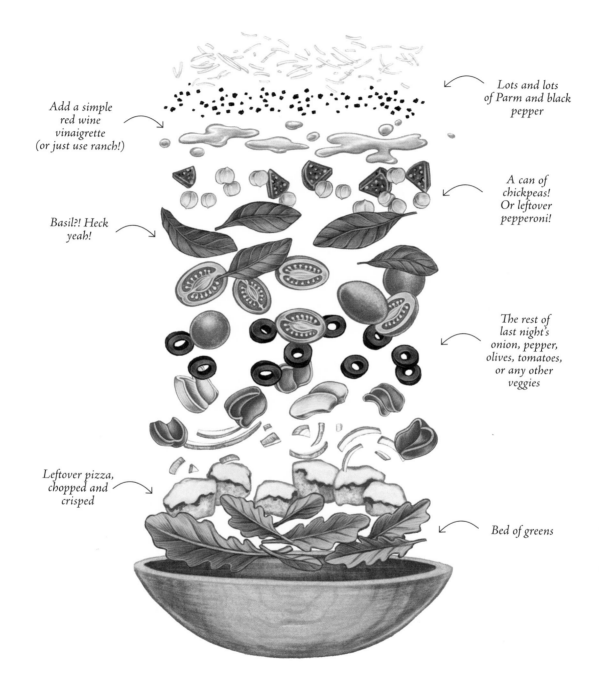

Lots and lots
of Parm and black
pepper

Add a simple
red wine
vinaigrette
(or just use ranch!)

A can of
chickpeas!
Or leftover
pepperoni!

Basil?! Heck
yeah!

The rest of
last night's
onion, pepper,
olives, tomatoes,
or any other
veggies

Leftover pizza,
chopped and
crisped

Bed of greens

PASTA + GRAINS

Dinnertime in our house sounds the same almost every night: *Wheel of Fortune* hums in the background at a volume just loud enough for me to hear when Pat Sajak announces the final puzzle so I can crane my neck from the table and take a peek to see if I can solve it before the contestant does (it happened twice); Nick and I catch up on our days as we trade off reading a book to Bernie; and Bernie chants the name of whatever she is eating, which in her perfect world is always either noonulls (noodles), pas*taaa*, or *fice* (plain white rice). Honestly, Bern, same. When we have a pile of carbs on the menu for dinner, I look forward to it all day long: the ease of it, the look on Bernie's face when she digs in, the super-nostalgic bite of plain buttered rice that I eat in secret while standing over the pot before mixing it with whatever vegetable we're having. And then there's the shovel, the big sloppy bites, what my dad would call "fulfilling our BFR" or Bulk Food Requirement, which is the name he's given to the Yeh family condition of valuing quantity of food ever so slightly more than quality. Noodles simply taste best when inhaled without grace. There is always room for seconds and—later in the nighttime when we're about to go to bed and the leftovers are in the fridge, still kinda lukewarm—thirds.

Here are some pasta and grain dishes that are worth putting on the stretchy pants for. I generally include some major vegetable and protein action to provide balance and make them one-pot meals, but there are certainly some exceptions (Bernie cannot be fooled by veggies in the mac and cheese), which call for a simple sautéed vegetable on the side or my shameful habit of putting an open bag of spinach on the table with a jar of Marzetti ranch next to it and calling it a side salad.

PRESERVED LEMON PAPPARDELLE WITH FRIED PINE NUTS, ZUCCHINI, MINT, AND FETA

When Henry James said that famous quote about how the most beautiful words in the English language are "summer afternoon," I think he actually meant "preserved lemon pappardelle with fried pine nuts, zucchini, mint, and feta." Those ingredients together are poetry to my ears (and mouth). Between the funky preserved lemon, buttery pine nuts, salty feta, sweet zucchini, and fresh mint, this pasta leaves no flavor stone unturned.

SERVES 4

2 medium zucchini, sliced into ¼-inch coins

6 tablespoons (75 grams) extra virgin olive oil, divided

Kosher salt

12 ounces (340 grams) pappardelle

¼ cup (35 grams) pine nuts

4 garlic cloves, finely chopped

½ teaspoon crushed red pepper, plus more to taste

2 tablespoons (32 grams) finely chopped rinsed preserved lemon rind

or sub the zest and juice of 1 lemon

1 cup (4 ounces/113 grams) crumbled feta

Freshly ground black pepper

1 lightly packed cup (24 grams) mint leaves, coarsely chopped

Flaky salt

Lemon wedges, for serving

ARRANGE a rack at the bottom of the oven and preheat the oven to 425°F. Bring a large pot of water to a boil.

TOSS the zucchini with 2 tablespoons (25 grams) of the olive oil and spread out in an even layer on a rimmed sheet pan. Roast until golden brown on the bottom; begin checking at 12 minutes.

ADD a small handful (about a heaping tablespoon) of salt to the boiling water. Add the pappardelle and cook to ever-so-slightly shy of your desired doneness per the package instructions. Drain, reserving ½ cup (120 grams) of the pasta water.

RETURN the pot to medium-high heat and heat the remaining 4 tablespoons (50 grams) olive oil. Add the pine nuts and cook, stirring, for a couple of minutes, until golden. Use a slotted spoon to remove to a paper-towel-lined plate. To the pot, add the garlic, crushed red pepper, and preserved lemon and cook, stirring, for 1 minute, until fragrant. Add the reserved pasta water, then the pasta. Add most of the feta and loads of black pepper and toss toss toss toss toss, until the pasta is coated, glossy, and a little creamy from the feta. Toss in most of the mint leaves. Taste and adjust the seasoning as desired. Transfer to a serving bowl (or don't and serve right out of the pot!), pile the zucchini on top, and season with a nice pinch of flaky salt. Sprinkle on the pine nuts, remaining feta and mint, additional crushed red pepper and black pepper as desired, and garnish with lemon wedges for squeezing on at the table.

FUNERAL HOTDISH

If Chinese Hotdish is my stripper name and Busy Day Hotdish is a fantasy version of myself who juggles it *all* perfectly while looking very hot, then Funeral Hotdish is my indie band in which I live out teenage dreams of playing pop music on the marimba. It'd sound like Arcade Fire meets Aqua meets pre-12-tone Schoenberg with just a touch of the Oneders. All of those influences would plop into your lap in a seamless album, like the one-pot-wonder that it is. One-Pot-Oneder. That's our first hit. A Tom Everett Scott appreciation song.

Speculation around here dictates that this ultra-comforting meal gets its name because it's often served at funerals (I haven't been to enough funerals to personally confirm, pu pu pu) and maybe because it's red like blood? Gross. My other guess is that it just had a brilliant marketing team, because anytime you serve it, it is an instant conversation topic. It's the center of attention because of its quirky title. And, like, what did it even do to deserve it? Nothing! Look at this recipe! It is *so* outrageously easy and disproportionately delicious. Usually it's made with ground beef, but I like taking a shortcut to more flavor by using sausage. The result is super-soft noodles that always take me back to eating Hamburger Helper as a kid, not too much sauce, just enough peas to provide the illusion that your toddler is eating vegetables, and a blanket of cheese. There is nothing not to love here.

SERVES 3 TO 4

1 pound (454 grams) Italian pork sausage, casings removed

One 28-ounce (794-gram) can chopped tomatoes

2 cups (208 grams) elbow macaroni noodles

1½ cups (360 grams) vegetable or chicken stock

¾ cup (96 grams) peas, fresh or frozen

Kosher salt and freshly ground black pepper

1 cup (4 ounces/113 grams) shredded cheese
I like a mix of mozzarella and Parmesan.

Handful of chopped flat-leaf parsley or torn basil, optional, for topping

HEAT a large pot over medium-high heat. Add the sausage and cook, breaking it up with a wooden spoon, until browned and cooked through, about 7 minutes. Add the chopped tomatoes, noodles, and stock and bring to a boil. Reduce to a simmer, cover, and cook, stirring occasionally, until the noodles are tender; begin checking for doneness at 25 minutes. Stir in the peas (if they're frozen, they'll thaw pretty much immediately when stirred in). Season with salt and pepper to taste. Top with cheese (you can stick it under the broiler to get extra melty if you'd like, but the cheese will get pretty melty from the heat of the noodles regardless) and herbs, if desired.

EMERGENCY PASTA

When you're so hungry that not even the arrival of your most recent Sephora shipment can stop you from walking to the kitchen, there are two concepts that just won't cut it: salad and following a strict recipe. Hanger calls for pasta, and this pasta calls for anything you have on hand.

Cook half a box of small pasta in heavily salted water, drain, and reserve a cup of the cooking water.

Toss in a few good handfuls of chopped greens, shaved brussels sprouts, broccoli florets, or other green veggies that are hiding in your fridge (and a good pinch of salt!) and cook for a few minutes, until tender. Grate in a couple of garlic cloves and cook for another minute.

Heat a large skillet over medium-high heat, add a drizzle of oil, and brown a pound of sausage or crisp a can of chickpeas or throw in a big handful of chopped roasted chicken.

*Reduce the heat to medium low, add
the pasta, and toss with a couple of big
handfuls of grated Parmesan, the zest and
juice of half a lemon, black pepper
and crushed red pepper to taste, and
pasta water as needed until glossy
(you may not need all of it).*

*Finish with a few pats of butter or
dollops of mascarpone, ricotta, cream
cheese, or sour cream!*

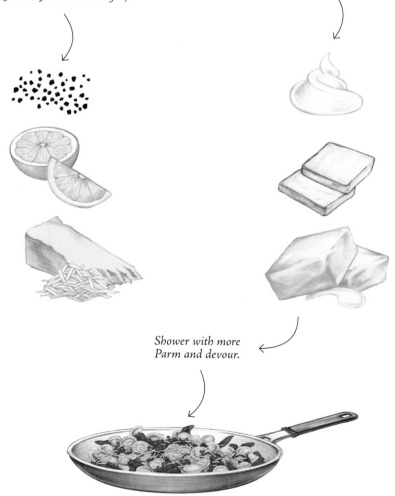

*Shower with more
Parm and devour.*

STOVETOP YOGURT MAC AND CHEESE

This is not a mac and cheese for guests or even really Instagram. It's for you to enjoy out of the pot when you're ravenously hungry and cannot be bothered to make a béchamel but you're still in possession of just enough motivation to prevent you from opening up a box with the powdery cheese. No offense to the box with the powdery cheese, but this version is honestly almost as easy.

It's a loose descendant of Diane Kochilas's genius yogurt pasta that uses Greek yogurt as the base for an Alfredo-like sauce. The result strikes a very respectable level of creaminess without being too heavy, helping it sit comfortably in the rotation of weeknight meals.

This is best eaten immediately, with Raffi playing in the background and sliced apples on the side.

SERVES 4 TO 6

Kosher salt

1 pound (454 grams) small shell pasta
Chickpea pasta also works!

1½ cups (360 grams) Greek yogurt (whole milk, 2%, or nonfat)

12 ounces (340 grams) grated melty cheese
My fave is mozzarella—but cheddar, Jack, Gouda, Swiss, or a mix are all great!

A few passes of freshly grated nutmeg

Pinch (or 2 or 3) of onion powder

Freshly ground black pepper

OPTIONAL CONDIMENTS: sriracha, ketchup, ranch . . . the usual suspects!

BRING a large pot of water to a boil and add a small handful (about a heaping tablespoon) of salt. Cook the pasta just short of your desired doneness according to the package directions (it will complete cooking once it's in with the sauce). Reserve 1 cup (240 grams) of the pasta water, then drain the pasta. Put the pot back on the stove over very low heat and add the reserved pasta water, the yogurt, and the cheese. Stir with a silicone spatula or wooden spoon until just combined (it'll be kinda lumpy since the cheese won't be melty yet), then add the pasta. Fold and fold and fold for a few minutes until the cheese is melty and the sauce has thickened and sticks to the pasta. Don't fret if it looks a little curdled and funky at first, just keep on folding. Season with nutmeg, onion powder, black pepper, and more salt as desired. Serve immediately with your desired condiments and enjoy!

HAND-PULLED NOODLES WITH POTSTICKER FILLING SAUCE

These noodles are the result of two strong forces in my life: (1) my habit of drooling on my phone every time I see Xi'an Famous Foods' super-thick hand-pulled noodles on my Instagram feed and (2) my failed mission to make homemade potstickers for Bernie on a regular basis on account of they always take about six times longer to make than I want them to and I feel like I'm being a bad mom by folding potstickers instead of singing Elmo with her (I tried doing both at once but got winded after Snuffy's verse). These forces combined when my older sister, Stoopie, texted me a picture of a huge bowl of hand-pulled noodles that she had just made, saying "These taste like Doughy Part!! You have to make them!!" "Doughy Part" was our name for thick, chewy potsticker wrappers when we were kids, and it was one of my very favorite foods. Just the wrappers.

I immediately got to work following the directions that Stoopie texted, adding baking soda to my dough for bounciness and crisping them up in a pan before putting them in a big pot with all my go-to potsticker filling ingredients, and, OMG, fell in *luvvv*. It felt like I was eating a giant bowl of cut-up potstickers, and it took way less time than actually making potstickers.

This sauce has all the hallmarks of a great potsticker filling: loads of ginger, scallions, and vinegar. But a perk to this sauce form is that you can sneak in way more cabbage than you would if you were making potstickers. In a potsticker filling, it'd be too wet, but here, the moisture from the cabbage is used to the sauce's advantage. *Cha-ching!* And bonus, camouflaging thinly sliced cabbage in noodles is the best toddler parent magic trick there is.

While hand-pulling noodles is much less time-consuming than pleating dozens of dumplings, I do need to be clear that it takes significantly more time than just using premade noodles. If hand-pulling noodles doesn't fit into your lifestyle today, I've included a shortcut for you!! All it takes is boiling store-bought pappardelle with some baking soda in the water to mimic the hand-pulled noodle bounce and faint flavor. They'll be a little less chewy and charming than the hand-pulled route but still *dannnng* good.

Noodles

3 cups (390 grams) all-purpose flour

½ teaspoon baking soda

1 cup (240 grams) water

Kosher salt

Neutral oil

Sauce

Neutral oil, if needed

1 pound (454 grams) ground chicken or pork

Kosher salt

4 scallions, thinly sliced

1 tablespoon (9 grams) finely chopped fresh ginger (from about a 1-inch piece)

½ medium napa cabbage, thinly sliced

Use the other half to make the Crunchy Asian Slaw on page 92!

1 teaspoon sugar

2 tablespoons (30 grams) soy sauce, plus more to taste

2 teaspoons toasted sesame oil

1 tablespoon (15 grams) sambal oelek, plus more for serving

2 tablespoons (30 grams) unseasoned rice vinegar

TO make the noodles, in a medium bowl, whisk together the flour and baking soda. In a measuring cup, whisk the water with ¾ teaspoon salt until dissolved. Stir the water into the flour with a spoon or spatula until you have a shaggy dough. Turn it out onto a work surface and knead until you have a smooth, stiff dough, about 5 minutes. Cover with plastic wrap, and let it rest for 20 minutes. Knead it for 5 more minutes and then divide it into 3 equal parts. Use a rolling pin to roll them out into long skinny ovals, about 12 x 3 inches. Brush the ovals on both sides with a thin layer of oil. Set them on a sheet pan, cover with plastic wrap, and let sit for 30 minutes, or up to 60.

NOW get your sauce ready! Heat a large pot over medium heat. If you're using chicken, add a tablespoon (13 grams) of oil, then the chicken. If you're using pork, no need to add oil; just add the meat to the pot. Season the meat with a couple of pinches of salt and cook, breaking it up with a wooden spoon. When the meat is cooked, assess your fat situation: if you're using chicken and the pot seems dry, add a drizzle of oil to the pot. If you're using fatty pork and there seems to be an excessive amount of fat, drain it off, leaving a tiny bit to help cook the veggies. Add the scallions (reserving some of the green parts for topping) and ginger and cook for a minute, until fragrant. Add the cabbage and a pinch of salt and cook, tossing occasionally, until wilted, 7 to

10 minutes. Stir in the sugar, soy sauce, sesame oil, and sambal oelek and turn down to simmer while you cook the noodles.

BRING a large pot of water to a boil and season with a small handful (about a heaping tablespoon) of salt. Work with one oval of dough at a time and keep the others covered. Cut the oval crosswise into six 2-inch-thick strips, then gently pull the ends of each strip to create one long noodle. Slapping the noodles on the counter a couple of times as you pull helps them stretch. Pull each one as long as you can, and if they break, it's okay; we are not professionals. (Or maybe you are! I don't know!) If the noodles are fighting being stretched, that is your sign to cover them back up and let them rest for 15 to 30 more minutes before trying again. Place the pulled noodles on a sheet pan or spread them out on your counter and don't let them touch each other. Repeat with the rest of the dough to make a total of 18 long noodles.

WHEN you're done pulling (pat yourself on the back!!), boil the noodles in 3 batches for 2 minutes each. Transfer directly to the sauce *or* see below for directions to crisp them up in a pan before transferring to the sauce. Using tongs, toss the noodles with the sauce, adding 1 to 2 ladles of pasta water as needed until glossy. Toss in the vinegar. Taste and adjust the salt level as desired. Top with more sambal oelek and scallions and demolish.

FEELING XTRA?

TO mimic the crisp texture of pan-fried potstickers, heat a large nonstick pan over medium-high heat and add a drizzle of oil. When a batch of noodles is done boiling, transfer to the pan and cook undisturbed until they're lightly browned and crisp, 5 to 7 minutes, then transfer to the sauce. You can crisp up all the noodles this way or just a batch or two to add textural excitement to the finished dish.

NOODLE SHORTCUT

You will need:

Kosher salt

1 tablespoon (15 grams) baking soda

12 ounces (340 grams) pappardelle

And all you do is:

BRING a large pot of water to a boil and season with a small handful (about a heaping tablespoon) of salt. Add the baking soda and cook the pasta according to package directions. Continue as directed above.

PEANUT NOODLES WITH CHARRED SCALLIONS, STEAK, AND BROCCOLINI

I have a hypothesis that all people, no matter how strongly they identify with Larry David, edge slightly closer to being outdoor people once they have kids. Fresh air is to kids what that first sip of coffee in the morning is to adults, and seeing their smiles when faced with a sandbox or dirt pile is enough to encourage anyone to endure the elements and gross bright sun. Sunscreen in cute packaging helps.

When my tolerance for bugs and free-flowing breezes increased with the arrival of Bernie, we started grilling more. One of my go-to moves is making a big bowl of peanut noodles during nap time (since they're addictive at any temperature, they're the perfect make-ahead component), then at dinnertime I grill up a steak and veggies, plop them on top of the noodles, splatter them with condiments, and dig in.

Kosher salt

1 pound (454 grams) noodles or pasta of your choice

⅓ cup (85 grams) unsweetened creamy peanut butter

¼ cup (60 grams) soy sauce

2 tablespoons (25 grams) toasted sesame oil, plus more for serving

2 tablespoons (42 grams) honey

2 large garlic cloves, finely chopped

¼ teaspoon crushed red pepper

Neutral oil

Two 1-inch-thick New York Strip steaks (8 to 10 ounces/226 to 283 grams each), room temperature

Freshly ground black pepper

12 ounces (340 grams) broccolini

8 scallions, trimmed

1 lime, halved

Sambal oelek

Flaky salt

BRING a large pot of water to a boil and season with a small handful (about a heaping tablespoon) of salt. Cook the noodles to the desired doneness. Drain, reserving ¼ cup (60 grams) of the pasta water.

IN a large bowl, whisk together the peanut butter, soy sauce, sesame oil, honey, garlic, and crushed red pepper until smooth. Add the noodles and toss to combine, adding the pasta water if the sauce is too thick to coat the noodles. Set aside until ready to serve. These are great hot, cold, or at room temp, so feel free to do this step a day in advance.

PAT the steaks dry and season generously all over with salt and pepper.

HEAT a grill, grill pan, or large cast-iron skillet over medium-high heat. Toss the broccolini and scallions with a drizzle of oil and season with salt and pepper. Cook the scallions, broccolini, and lime (cut sides down) until charred, flipping the scallions and broccolini occasionally, about 4 minutes for the scallions and 8 to 10 minutes for the broccolini, until they are just tender. Set aside.

ADD the steak and cook until a nice golden crust has formed on both sides and the internal temperature is 125°F (for medium rare), 3 to 4 minutes per side. Transfer to a cutting board and let rest for 5 minutes. Slice against the grain.

THINLY slice the scallions and toss with the noodles. Top with the steak and broccolini. Squeeze the lime halves over everything. Drizzle with a little bit of sesame oil and sambal oelek to taste and sprinkle the steak with flaky salt.

CRISPY COCONUT RICE WITH SHRIMP

To make a Chinese hotdish, church cookbooks will tell you to open up cans of water chestnuts, toss in a bag of crispy lo mein noodles, and hold everything together with cream of mushroom soup. I'm no detective, but anyone who knows anything about Chinese people and their lactose intolerance (which I miraculously grew out of, leaving it all to my sister) could tell you that a Chinese person likely did not write those recipes. So, in my mission to come up with our own Chinese hotdish tradition, I tried doing simple one-to-one swaps with coconut milk. I even experimented with the lo mein noodles, but then things got weirder and I thought, well, what if the required crispy element of this hotdish was actually on the bottom—in the form of crispy rice—rather than on top? What if the creamy element came via a proper coconut rice rather than a sauce to hold it all together? What if we just sautéed some shrimp? Do scallions count as the vegetable, and does this really need to be baked? I guess I just demonstrated one of those memes that sub every ingredient in a cookie recipe to result in a baked ham, because the result was definitely not a hotdish, and it was definitely more Southeast Asian than Chinese. But it's darn tasty.

SERVES 4

2 cups (360 grams) jasmine rice, rinsed

One 13.5-ounce (382 gram) can full-fat coconut milk

1½ cups (360 grams) water

1½ teaspoons kosher salt

1½ tablespoons (19 grams) sugar

4 tablespoons (50 grams) neutral oil, divided

8 scallions, thinly sliced

1 garlic clove, finely chopped

1 pound (454 grams) medium to large shrimp, peeled, deveined, and thawed/patted dry, if frozen

Kosher salt and freshly ground black pepper

Zest and juice of half a large lime, plus lime wedges for serving

Sambal oelek

Handful of chopped cilantro

IN a large lidded nonstick or well-seasoned cast-iron skillet or pot, combine the rice, coconut milk, water, salt, and sugar. Cover, bring to a boil, reduce to a simmer, and cook for 20 minutes. Turn off the heat and let sit, covered, for 15 minutes. Fluff with a fork and transfer to a wide shallow bowl, spreading the rice out so it can cool slightly. You can do this step up to a day in advance, keeping the rice uncovered or loosely covered in the fridge.

RETURN the pot to medium heat, add 3 tablespoons (38 grams) of the neutral oil, and heat until a grain of rice dropped into the pot sizzles immediately. Toss the rice with most of the scallions (reserving some of the green parts for topping), add to the pot, spread it out evenly, and cook, undisturbed, until browned and crispy on the bottom, 5 to 10 minutes. Check the doneness by scraping up a little bit of the rice, peeking, and then putting it back if it needs more time.

WHILE the rice crisps, cook the shrimp: heat a large skillet over medium-high heat and add the remaining tablespoon (13 grams) of oil. Add the garlic, cook for 30 to 60 seconds, until fragrant, then add the shrimp. Season with salt and pepper and cook for a few minutes, turning occasionally, until the shrimp are pink, opaque, and cooked through. Remove from the heat.

WHEN the crispiness of the rice has been confirmed, scrape the bottom of the rice up with a stiff spatula, and fold the crispy bits, along with the lime zest, into the rest of the rice. Taste and add more salt, if desired, and transfer to a serving plate. Top with the shrimp, squeeze the lime juice on top, splatter with sambal oelek, and top with the remaining scallions and the cilantro. Serve with lime wedges and more sambal oelek, to taste.

CHEESY KIMCHI FRIED RICE

I can't stress enough how big of a challenge it is to find great vegetables at the store in the winter, get them home before they wilt, and still feel like eating them after being out in the cold all day vegetable schlepping. It's a risky sequence that doesn't always work out. So we find solutions! One of them is going to Arizona in January. But the rest of the time we stick to sturdy roots and squashes, frozen things, loads of alliums, pretending that ketchup is a vegetable, and *drumroll* jars of preserved cabbages! Sauerkraut is a staple in this region because many people around here have German ancestry, but sauerkraut's hot Korean cousin, kimchi, is also, in my very strong opinion, ideal for Midwestern kitchens. Not only does it last for a while in the back of my fridge, saving me at dinnertime when all the fresh vegetables have gone on vacation, but it also weaves seamlessly into the kinds of hearty, warming dishes that we crave when it snows.

Kimchi fried rice is one of my most shovel-able foods. I could shovel mountains of it into my mouth on any given night and be so happy. To add the extra layer that we need in the colder months, I like taking inspiration from Korean corn cheese and melting cheese on top.

SERVES 3 TO 4

3 tablespoons (42 grams) unsalted butter, divided

4 large eggs, beaten

Kosher salt and freshly ground black pepper

1 medium yellow onion, chopped

4 scallions, thinly sliced, white and green parts separated

One 14-ounce (396-gram) jar cabbage kimchi, drained and chopped, brine reserved

2 garlic cloves, finely chopped

4 cups (600 grams) cooked short-grain white rice

Day-old rice will absorb more flavor but 60% of the time I don't plan that far ahead and end up using freshly cooked rice, and it's still GR8!

¾ cup (102 grams) corn kernels, fresh or frozen

Chopped cooked hot dogs, optional

1 teaspoon toasted sesame oil

1½ cups (6 ounces/170 grams) shredded mild melty cheese

I like a mix of mozzarella and provolone.

Sriracha

HEAT a large oven-safe nonstick or cast-iron skillet over medium-high heat. When it's good and hot, add 2 teaspoons of the butter, swirl it around, and immediately pour in the eggs. Scramble to your liking, transfer to a cutting board, season with salt and pepper, give 'em a rough chop, and set aside.

WIPE out the skillet, return it to the stove over medium heat, and add the remaining butter. Add the onion, the white parts of the scallions, chopped kimchi, and a good pinch of salt and cook, stirring occasionally, until soft, 7 to 10 minutes. Add the garlic and cook another minute. Add the rice, corn, eggs, hot dogs (if using), and sesame oil and toss to combine. Season to taste with salt and the reserved kimchi brine. Spread everything out in an even layer and cook, undisturbed, for about 3 minutes, until the bottom starts to get crisp (it will continue to crisp in the oven). Top with an even layer of cheese and stick it under the broiler for a few minutes, until the cheese is melty and splotchy with brown marks. Top with the scallion greens, and serve with sriracha.

SKILLET CHICKEN WITH RAMP RICE AND BOK CHOY

Every spring for ramp season I turn into our largest farm cat, Sven, when the mice are out: a *hunter*. Grand Forks is not like New York, where greenmarkets have ramps aplenty for the few weeks they're in season and my ramp guy, Donny, will trade a messenger bag of them for twenty dollars on a street corner in Midtown. North Dakota is at the very western edge of the ramp zone, and there's a much lower demand here for trendy alliums with extremely limited seasons, so springs have passed where I just plumb haven't found them. One April, I asked my assistant, Hayden, to keep his eyes peeled and, if he found them, to pounce. Well, he pounced all right. He showed up at my door a few days later with enough ramps to feed a small (very hip, bearded, wire-rimmed-glasses-wearing) army. That spring we gobbled up this winner of a chicken dinner like the ramp fiends that we are.

Ramps taste like sunnier scallions with garlic-scented deodorant on, and what they bring to this chicken and rice dish is *joy*. Chicken and rice, especially chicken and *schmaltzy* rice, are joyous already because chicken thighs honestly don't need anything more than salt, pepper, and a good hot skillet to the skin to be tasty, but the wild leeks bring with them the optimism of spring and longer days ahead.

SERVES 3 (OR 2 WITH LEFTOVERS!)

2 pounds (908 grams) bone-in, skin-on chicken thighs

Kosher salt and freshly ground black pepper

1 tablespoon (13 grams) neutral oil

2 bunches of ramps (about 8 ounces/226 grams), thinly sliced, white and green parts separated

Sub scallions if you don't have ramps

¼ cup (60 grams) dry white wine

1 cup (180 grams) basmati rice, rinsed

1½ cups (360 grams) water

3 baby bok choy heads, quartered lengthwise

Handful of chopped chives

SEASON the chicken thighs generously all over with salt and pepper. Heat a large lidded oven-safe (preferably cast-iron) skillet over medium-high heat and add the oil. Add the chicken thighs skin side down and cook, undisturbed, until the skin is golden and crispy and doesn't really fight you when you try to flip it, 8 to 10 minutes. Flip and cook for 5 more minutes, then remove to a plate skin side up.

REDUCE the heat under the pan to medium, and add the white parts of the ramps and a pinch of salt. Cook, stirring occasionally, until softened, 3 to 5 minutes. Add the ramp greens and cook until wilted. Add the wine, stir, and use your spatula to scrape up the tasty bits stuck on the bottom of the pan. Stir in the rice, water, and ½ teaspoon salt and spread out evenly in the pan. Nestle the bok choy in one layer on top of the rice, season it with salt, and nestle the chicken into the bok choy. Raise the heat to high and bring to a boil. Reduce the heat to a simmer, cover, and cook until the rice is tender and the chicken is fully cooked with an internal temperature of 165°F; begin checking for doneness at 20 minutes. Uncover and stick it under the broiler for a few minutes so that the chicken skin remembers that it is supposed to be crispy. Sprinkle with chives and serve.

TWO FAVORITE GRAIN BOWLS

If I ever want to feel like a cool mom, I put on my high-waist wide-leg jeans and Glossier Boy Brow and make grain bowls. (Is all that stuff still cool?) The bowls start with a scoop of fluffy grains and get adorned with a buffet of pretty toppings: a protein as the anchor, something pickled for acidity, fresh veggies and/or herbs galore, a creamy dressing, and a super-fun crunchy element on top. Crushed crackers, everything bagel seasoning, um, *Cheetos?* It's a little party in a bowl. Sometimes it's annoying to have to prep a gazillion little things for just one stinkin' meal, but the best part about all of these components (even poached eggs!) is that you can prep big batches of them in advance so you can have the easiest second stinkin' meal tomorrow, and even a third the next day. As such, I recommend prepping as much as possible in lidded containers to make it easier to store and use leftovers. *What? You can poach eggs in advance??* Yes, just transfer them to a container of cold water when you're done cooking and keep them in the fridge for a day or two. When it's time to serve, dunk 'em in hot water (but not boiling) until warm.

Following are two of our favorite grain bowls that make us feel satisfied, nourished, and a little bit trendy, at least by the standards that existed when we left Brooklyn a decade ago. As a toddler parent, I love the function of grain bowls because they take well to swap-outs based on whatever ingredients you have on hand and whatever ingredients your kid has decided she hates this week even though she loved them last week. Which is to say: don't feel the need to stick to these recipes too rigidly; have some fun with them!

BROWN RICE BOWLS WITH SMOKED SALMON, MAYO, AND CRUSHED CRACKERS

Kewpie mayonnaise is a little sweeter and richer than regular mayonnaise, making for a nice glossy dressing. (If you're all out, you can sub in other mayo; add another pinch of sugar to the dressing.) Crushed Ritz crackers make everything better, but oyster crackers (or the Spicy Ranch Snack Mix on page 260) are also a worthy addition.

SERVES 4

Rice

2 cups (360 grams) short-grain brown rice, rinsed

3 cups (720 grams) water

1 teaspoon kosher salt

1 tablespoon (12 grams) sugar

1 tablespoon (15 grams) unseasoned rice vinegar

Dressing

½ cup (120 grams) Kewpie mayonnaise

2 tablespoons (30 grams) unseasoned rice vinegar

½ teaspoon kosher salt

1½ teaspoons sugar

2 scallions, thinly sliced

1 tablespoon (9 grams) finely chopped fresh ginger (from about a 1-inch piece)

1 garlic clove, finely chopped

Assembly

4 radishes, thinly sliced

2 tablespoons (30 grams) unseasoned rice vinegar

Pinch of sugar

Pinch of kosher salt

Neutral oil

2 or 3 baby bok choy heads, quartered lengthwise

Flaky salt

8 ounces (226 grams) thinly sliced cold-smoked salmon

4 small handfuls of mixed greens

12 Ritz crackers, coarsely crushed

FIRST, get the rice going: Combine the rice, water, salt, sugar, and rice vinegar in a medium saucepan. Bring to a boil, reduce the heat to a simmer, cover, and cook until the rice is tender and the water is completely absorbed; begin checking at 30 minutes. Remove from the heat and let sit, covered, for 10 minutes, then fluff with a fork.

MEANWHILE, prep everything else: To make the dressing, in a medium container or bowl, whisk together the Kewpie, rice vinegar, salt, and sugar until smooth, then stir in the scallions, ginger, and garlic and set aside. To pickle the radishes, in a medium container or bowl, toss together the radishes, rice vinegar, sugar, and kosher salt and set aside. To make the bok choy, heat a large skillet over medium-high heat and add a nice drizzle of oil. Add the bok choy and cook, turning occasionally, until the stems are tender and the leaves are deep golden brown, 3 to 5 minutes. Sprinkle with a good pinch of flaky salt.

TO assemble, scoop the rice into shallow bowls. Top each with some slices of salmon, a few pieces of bok choy, a small handful of mixed greens, and some pickled radishes. Drizzle with the dressing to taste. Sprinkle with some of the crackers, then bring the crackers to the table so you can sprinkle more on as you eat.

FARRO BOWLS WITH POACHED EGGS AND GREEN TAHINI

Farro is a chewy, hearty grain that always manages to fill me up faster than I anticipate. I find it most convenient to cook it like pasta (boiling in a big pot and draining the excess water) versus measuring out an exact amount of water as is common with rice.

SERVES 4 TO 6

Green tahini

¼ cup (10 grams) coarsely chopped flat-leaf parsley

¼ cup (10 grams) coarsely chopped dill

2 scallions, coarsely chopped

1 garlic clove, peeled

Juice of half a lemon

½ cup (112 grams) good-quality tahini (see page xxi)

6 tablespoons (90 grams) cold water, plus more if needed

Kosher salt and freshly ground black pepper

Assembly

Kosher salt

2 cups (360 grams) farro, rinsed

2 tablespoons (25 grams) extra virgin olive oil

1 medium shallot, thinly sliced

2 tablespoons (30 grams) white wine vinegar

Pinch of sugar

4 to 6 eggs

1 pint (about 283 grams) grape or cherry tomatoes, quartered

3 radishes, thinly sliced

Fresh tender herbs (a mix of flat-leaf parsley, dill, and scallions, or any other herbs you like)

Hot sauce, optional

Everything bagel topping (see page xvi)

Flaky salt or kosher salt, if your everything bagel topping doesn't provide enough

Lemon wedges

TO make the green tahini, combine all the ingredients in a food processor and blend until smooth. It should be thick but drizzle-able. If it's too thick, add a little more water. This can be made a day or two in advance and kept in a container in the fridge. It'll firm up in the fridge, so thin it out with a little water before serving if you go this route.

TO cook the farro, bring a large pot of water to a boil, season with a small handful (about a heaping tablespoon) of salt, and add the farro. Cook until soft but still with a tiny bite; begin checking for doneness at 20 minutes. Drain and toss with the olive oil.

WHILE the farro is cooking, in a medium bowl or container, toss together the shallot, vinegar, sugar, and a pinch of salt and let the shallot soften and get a little pickle-y for a few minutes or up to overnight.

TO poach your eggs, fill a skillet with about 1 inch of water and bring to a low simmer. Carefully crack in the eggs, taking care not to break the yolks. Simmer until the whites are opaque but the yolks are still soft and jiggly, 2 to 4 minutes. Remove with a slotted spoon to a plate lined with a paper towel. Don't overcrowd the pan and cook your eggs in batches if necessary.

TO assemble, scoop the farro into shallow bowls. Top each with a big plop of the tahini sauce; an egg; and little piles of pickled shallots, tomatoes, radishes, and herbs. Add hot sauce, if desired, and sprinkle liberally with everything bagel topping and salt (if there isn't enough in your everything bagel topping). Serve with lemon wedges for squeezing.

HOTDISHES + FAMILY STYLE

Sometimes I wonder what my former self would think if she found out that her future child would have a North Dakota birth certificate and that "uff da" would be one of her first sentences. She'd be very confused, and likely concerned for this child's access to a deli and Nordstrom. I'd tell her not to worry, that Bernie lives on matzo ball soup and wears a hunter green sale rack Juicy velour hoodie often. She says "keppe" and "schlep" and not yet "oy vey," but she knows what it means (and it's basically "uff da"). Plus she gets to grow up with all the delights of this place: reliable heavy snowfall, high-quality hockey culture, fierce appreciation for hard work and butter, a complete absence of traffic, family members everywhere, a rhubarb patch, two apple trees, cookies in salad, and a rotating selection of hotdishes.

It makes me *soooo* happy that Bernie will grow up with hotdish.

When I tell my local friends that I didn't try hotdish until I moved here, some of them seem to genuinely wonder if I starved. Even I start to question what the heck we were doing wasting our time with Hamburger Helper when it could have been a hotdish. (No offense, Hamburger Helper.) That's how ingrained it is into the fabric of suppertime here. And with good reason—it's easy to make and easy to love.

For those who don't know hotdish, let me introduce you. A hotdish is a specific type of casserole that contains a full meal in a dish: veggies, a protein, and a carb element, most famously Tater Tots. It's all held together by a sauce of some sort, classically a can of condensed creamed soup, but a tomato base is acceptable too. Its charm is in its ability to evoke nostalgia and make you fall in love despite an often mushy and brown appearance. Hotdishes are experts at feeding a large family, bringing comfort to anyone going through a big life event, and staying warm in the oven when Nick says it will just take him five minutes to put away the tractor but it actually takes him thirty.

Church cookbooks have full sections of them, and towns have festivals and competitions in their honor. As a veteran East Grand Forks Heritage Days Hotdish Competition judge, I'm proud to report that I've eaten enough hotdishes to make up for my hotdishless childhood. And at home, I've made more variations than we've had snowstorms, which is, well, a lot. So here are some of our favorites, along with some other really great hearty mains that don't quite fit the definition of a hotdish but are lovable all the same.

Most of the recipes in this chapter are typically weekend dinners for us. They're things I like to cook at a leisurely pace (with movies or figure skating competitions on in the background), to really let the veggies cook down and fill the house with warmth. Many of them, the hotdishes especially, are great candidates for freezing half to defrost on short notice in the weeks or months to come.

CLASSIC TOT HOTDISH

As a Tater Tot enthusiast with an endless desire to tinker, I will be experimenting with the hotdish equation until the cows come home. I will switch up the seasonings, sneak in vegetarian proteins, add "trendy" vegetables, and, yeah, I'll eventually try to gracefully sprinkle in everything bagel seasoning . . . but no new spin on a hotdish will ever come as close to giving Nick that new-Star-Wars-movie excitement as the classic: beef, creamed soup, flaccid veggies, tots. There's a reason it's a classic, and it's that it's as comforting as cuddles from a big furry puppy. It doesn't need anything fancy, no specialty this or that; even adding parsley at the end sometimes feels wrong (but, hey, we are living in the Instagram age, so do it if you want). All it needs is love and good tot arrangement.

My version forgoes store-bought creamed soup for a velvety smooth sauce you make yourself, ideally with dreamy homemade stock as the base (but store-bought is great too). I've added just a couple of tiny extra sparks—some beer for acidity and nutmeg for warmth—but nothing to take away from the nostalgia of it all. Consider this its no-makeup makeup look.

While we don't typically add cheese, many families around here do, either under the tots or on top. Frozen French fries can be subbed for tots (which resembles the classic Busy Day Hotdish), and ground turkey or that new meatless meat can be subbed for beef. I get my personal freak on by covering my whole bowl with ketchup, which both cools it down so I can eat it faster without burning my mouth and adds bright acidity.

1 tablespoon (13 grams) neutral oil

2 medium shallots, finely chopped

Kosher salt

2 pounds (908 grams) ground beef, 93% lean

12 ounces (340 grams) frozen chopped green beans

¼ cup (56 grams) unsalted butter

½ cup (65 grams) all-purpose flour

¼ cup (60 grams) pale ale
or sub with low-sodium chicken stock

2¼ cups (540 grams) low-sodium chicken stock

½ cup (120 grams) heavy cream

Freshly ground black pepper

1 teaspoon fresh thyme leaves

¼ teaspoon freshly grated nutmeg

2 pounds (908 grams) frozen Tater Tots

Accessories

If you're feeling wild: a few big handfuls of shredded cheddar, for topping

If you're feeling fancy: chopped flat-leaf parsley, for topping

If you're feeling like you and I should be BFFs: ketchup, for serving

ARRANGE a rack in the upper third of the oven and preheat the oven to 450°F.

HEAT a large skillet over medium-high heat and add the oil. Add the shallots and a pinch of salt and cook, stirring, until softened, 5 to 7 minutes. Add the ground beef and season it with 1 teaspoon salt. Brown the beef, breaking it up with a wooden spoon or spatula. Stir in the green beans and cook for a few minutes, until thawed. Use a slotted spoon to transfer the mixture to a 9 x 13-inch casserole dish and spread it out evenly. Set aside while you make the creamed soup.

DISCARD the juices that remain in the skillet, wipe it out, and return to medium heat. Melt the butter and whisk in the flour to make a paste. Cook, whisking, for 2 minutes. Whisk in the pale ale, then add the chicken stock very gradually, in 3 or 4 additions, whisking continuously and allowing the mixture to thicken before each addition. Whisk in the heavy cream, a bunch of turns of black pepper, the thyme, and the nutmeg. Increase the heat and continue whisking frequently until it just begins to simmer, then reduce the heat to low and simmer very gently for 5 minutes, whisking occasionally. Taste and adjust the seasoning as desired. Pour or ladle the mixture all over the ground beef and fold together to incorporate. Top with perfectly aligned rows and columns of Tater Tots (adding a layer of cheese under or over the tots, if desired) and season with salt and pepper.

BAKE until the tots are golden brown and crispy on top; begin checking for doneness at 35 minutes (or a few minutes earlier if you have cheese on top). If you want to get the tots even crispier, finish with a few minutes under the broiler. Let cool slightly, top with parsley, and/or serve with ketchup, if desired.

TO MAKE AHEAD: Complete the steps up through topping with tots (and cheese, if using), assembling in a 9 x 13-inch metal casserole dish. Let cool, wrap in plastic or foil, and refrigerate or freeze until ready to cook. It'll last 2 days in the refrigerator and 3 months in the freezer. If reheating from the fridge, proceed as directed but add on a few more minutes in the oven to ensure that it's heated through. To reheat from frozen, cover loosely with foil and bake at 350°F for an hour, then uncover, increase the heat to 450°F, and bake until the tots are golden brown and the innards are heated through; begin checking for doneness at 20 minutes. Let cool slightly, top with parsley, and/or serve with ketchup, if desired.

TURKEY WILD RICE HOTDISH

Turkey wild rice hotdish doesn't get as much love in this visual world because it doesn't have a glamorous coat made of Tater Tots, but that's okay—*more for us*. This might be one of the best-kept secrets of the Midwest because, in everyone else's defense, I don't know that you can fully love it until you close your eyes and eat it. At least that's how it was for me when I first tried Nick's mom Roxanne's version. It looked terrible (by nature, not by fault of Roxanne!) but tasted like a warm hug. It was love at first bite. And just like with Tater Tot hotdish, I will never tire of trying to fold nontraditional additions like dates and ras el hanout into this format, but there is a reason this too is a classic. The two defining features of a wild rice hotdish are the nutty wild rice that lends body and chew and the crispy cracker top, which is best when you use Ritz. Town House would be good too, or even Cheez-Its. Leftover Thanksgiving turkey is great for this (top with leftover stuffing if you have it!), but you can also swap out the turkey for chicken (a rotisserie chicken!).

SERVES 4 TO 6

¾ cup (135 grams) wild rice, rinsed

2 cups (480 grams) water

Kosher salt

¼ cup (56 grams) unsalted butter

1 large yellow onion, finely chopped

2 large carrots, trimmed and finely chopped

2 large celery stalks, finely chopped

6 tablespoons (49 grams) all-purpose flour

2½ cups (600 grams) low-sodium chicken stock

½ cup (120 grams) heavy cream

Freshly ground black pepper

2 teaspoons finely chopped rosemary

¼ teaspoon freshly grated nutmeg

4 cups (about 515 grams) shredded cooked turkey

2 sleeves Ritz crackers, coarsely crushed

2 tablespoons (25 grams) neutral oil or extra virgin olive oil

Chopped flat-leaf parsley, for topping

PREHEAT the oven to 375°F.

IN a medium saucepan, combine the wild rice, water, and ¼ teaspoon salt and bring to a boil over high heat. Reduce the heat to a simmer, cover, and cook for 30 minutes, until al dente. Drain the rice and set it aside.

TO make the creamed soup, in a large pot, melt the butter over medium-high heat. Add the onion, carrots, celery, and a pinch of salt and cook, stirring occasionally, until soft, 10 to 15 minutes. Stir in the flour and cook for another 2 minutes. Reduce the heat to medium and add the chicken stock very gradually, in 3 to 4 additions, while whisking continuously and allowing the mixture to thicken before each addition. Whisk in the heavy cream, a bunch of turns of black pepper, the rosemary, and the nutmeg. Increase the heat and continue whisking frequently until it just begins to simmer, then reduce the heat to low and simmer very gently for 5 minutes, whisking occasionally. Taste and adjust the seasoning as desired.

IN a 9 x 13-inch casserole dish, layer a third of the soup, then half of the rice and half of the turkey. Repeat, then top with the remaining third of the soup mixture. Toss the crackers with the oil and distribute them over the top.

COVER with foil and bake for 20 minutes, uncover, and continue baking until the crackers are golden; begin checking at 10 minutes. Let cool slightly, top with parsley, and enjoy!

TO MAKE AHEAD: Complete the steps up through topping with the crackers, assembling in a 9 x 13-inch metal casserole dish. Let cool, wrap in plastic or foil, and refrigerate or freeze until ready to cook. It'll last 2 days in the refrigerator and 3 months in the freezer. If reheating from the fridge, proceed as directed but add on a few more minutes in the oven to ensure that it's heated through. To reheat from frozen, cover loosely with foil and bake at 350°F for an hour, uncover, increase the heat to 375°F, and bake until the crackers are golden brown and the innards are heated through; begin checking for doneness at 20 minutes. Let cool slightly, top with parsley, and enjoy!

CHICKPEA TOT HOTDISH

Some of my favorite Labor Day weekends in recent history have been spent as the lunch lady at an adult summer camp outside of Fargo. It's exactly as awesome as it sounds: building menus of nostalgia-inspired foods to serve on cute trays, reliving my childhood summer camp memories (but with loads of booze), and busting out some hella sweet moves at the Saturday night dance.

A major part of menu planning for this weekend is working out the jigsaw puzzle of dietary restrictions that comes with the territory of feeding 150 millennials. It's actually really satisfying to piece it all together and discover new vegan cheeses along the way. One year after cranking out dozens of beefy, creamy Tater Tot hotdishes for the masses, I turned my focus to the vegan/gluten-free campers and made them a chickpea harissa hotdish that came out so good it should have been the main attraction. The chickpeas went swimming in a wine-spiked tomato sauce that was smoky and just spicy enough to shine. On top, the tots did their job of delivering salty, crispy nostalgia. Now, while I don't think I can physically eat a harissa-covered chickpea without impulsively reaching for the feta and yogurt dollops, that obviously de-veganizes it, so feel free to leave these out or sub in dairy-free alternatives.

6 tablespoons (75 grams) extra virgin olive oil

1 medium yellow onion, finely chopped

2 large carrots, trimmed and finely chopped

2 large celery stalks, finely chopped

Kosher salt

4 garlic cloves, finely chopped

2 teaspoons Aleppo pepper or smoked paprika

Freshly ground black pepper

1 tablespoon (16 grams) harissa paste or (6 grams) dried harissa

1 tablespoon (15 grams) tomato paste

½ cup (120 grams) dry white wine

Two 15-ounce (425-gram) cans chickpeas, drained and rinsed

One 28-ounce (794 gram) can chopped tomatoes

½ cup (120 grams) water

1 teaspoon sugar

2 pounds (908 grams) frozen Tater Tots

A few squeezes of lemon juice

Chopped cilantro and flat-leaf parsley, for topping

Crumbled feta, optional, for topping

Dollops of plain Greek yogurt, optional, for serving

ARRANGE a rack in the upper third of the oven and preheat the oven to 450°F.

HEAT a large (at least 3½-quart, ideally oven-safe) skillet, braiser, or Dutch oven over medium high heat and add the olive oil. When the oil's hot, add the onion, carrots, celery, and a pinch of salt and cook, stirring occasionally, until soft, 10 to 15 minutes. Add the garlic, Aleppo pepper or paprika, and a few turns of black pepper and cook, stirring, for another minute. Add the harissa, tomato paste, and white wine and cook, stirring occasionally, until the wine is reduced by half, 3 to 4 minutes. Stir in the chickpeas, tomatoes, water, sugar, and 2 good pinches of salt and increase the heat to bring the mixture to a boil. Reduce to a simmer, cover, and cook for 15 minutes, stirring occasionally. Taste and adjust the seasoning as desired.

IF your skillet isn't oven-safe, transfer its contents to a 9 x 13-inch casserole dish (or something of a similar size); if it is oven-safe, keep the mixture in the skillet. Cover with a layer of tots. Season with salt and pepper. Bake until the tots are golden; begin checking for doneness at 35 minutes.

TOP with a few squeezes of lemon juice; the herbs; and feta, if using; and serve with dollops of Greek yogurt, if desired.

TO MAKE AHEAD: Complete the steps up through topping with tots, assembling in a 9 x 13-inch metal casserole dish. Let cool, wrap in plastic or foil, and refrigerate or freeze until ready to cook. It'll last 2 days in the refrigerator and 3 months in the freezer. If reheating from the fridge, uncover and proceed as directed but add on a few more minutes in the oven to ensure that it's heated through. To reheat from frozen, cover loosely with foil and bake at 350°F for an hour, then uncover and increase the heat to 450°F and bake until the tots are golden brown and the innards are heated through; begin checking for doneness at 20 minutes. Top with a few squeezes of lemon juice, the herbs, and feta, if using, and serve with dollops of Greek yogurt, if desired.

VEGGIE SUPREME WHITE BEAN HOTDISH

Pizza hotdish seems to be one of the less common hotdishes of the world, and I think it's because pizza is perfect already and doesn't need to be hotdished. Which isn't to say pizza hotdish isn't tasty; it's basically pepperoni pizza toppings tossed with pasta and ground beef. It just doesn't exactly serve a purpose in our kitchen. But in a move inspired by Deb Perelman's famous Pizza Beans (gigante beans in tomato sauce under a thick layer of cheese), I started subbing out the pasta and meat in pizza hotdish for, you guessed it, beans, and the whole thing morphed into this pizza-adjacent casserole that I feel a whole lot better about serving my family on a non-pizza night. It's loads of veggies and beans, bound together by cheese, all cozy under a blanket of breadcrumbs dressed up like garlic bread.

SERVES 4 TO 6

3 tablespoons (38 grams) extra virgin olive oil, divided

1 medium yellow onion, chopped

1 green bell pepper, chopped

Kosher salt

4 ounces (113 grams/2 big handfuls) baby spinach, chopped

4 garlic cloves, finely chopped, divided

½ teaspoon dried oregano

Crushed red pepper

One 2.25-ounce (64-gram) can sliced black olives, drained and rinsed

Two 15-ounce (425-gram) cans cannellini beans, drained and rinsed

One 28-ounce (794-gram) can chopped or whole peeled tomatoes

¼ cup (56 grams) mascarpone, (60 grams) ricotta, or (56 grams) cream cheese

2 cups (8 ounces/226 grams) shredded mozzarella, divided

¾ cup (45 grams) panko breadcrumbs

Freshly grated Parmesan

Handful of torn basil leaves

PREHEAT the oven to 450°F. Heat a large (at least 3½-quart, ideally oven-safe) skillet, braiser, or Dutch oven over medium-high heat and add 2 tablespoons (25 grams) of the olive oil. Add the onion, bell pepper, and a pinch of salt and cook, stirring occasionally, until soft, 7 to 10 minutes. Add the spinach and a pinch of salt and cook, stirring, until wilted. Stir in half the chopped garlic, the oregano, and a pinch or two of crushed red pepper and cook, stirring, for a minute until fragrant. Add the olives, beans, tomatoes, and 1 teaspoon salt and increase the heat to bring to a boil. (If using whole peeled tomatoes, break them up a little bit with your spoon.) Reduce to a simmer and cook, uncovered, stirring occasionally, for 10 to 15 minutes to let the flavors meld. Stir in the mascarpone (or ricotta or cream cheese) and a big handful of the mozzarella until melted. Taste and adjust the seasoning.

IF your skillet isn't oven-safe, transfer its contents to a 9 x 13-inch casserole dish (or something of a similar size); if it is, keep the contents in the skillet. Top with the remaining mozzarella, sprinkling it all the way to the edge. In a small bowl, toss the panko with the remaining tablespoon (13 grams) of olive oil, the remaining garlic, and a pinch of salt. Scatter the panko all over the top of the mozzarella and bake until the cheese is melty and the breadcrumbs are lightly browned; begin checking for doneness at 15 minutes. Top with a storm of Parmesan, basil, and a sprinkle of crushed red pepper and enjoy!

TO MAKE AHEAD: Complete the steps up through topping with breadcrumbs, assembling in a 9 x 13-inch metal casserole dish. Let cool, wrap in plastic or foil, and refrigerate or freeze. It'll last 2 days in the refrigerator and 3 months in the freezer. If reheating from the fridge, uncover and proceed as directed but add on a few more minutes in the oven to ensure that it's heated through. To reheat from frozen, cover loosely with foil and bake at 350°F for an hour, uncover, increase the heat to 450°F, and bake until the breadcrumbs are lightly browned and the innards are heated through; begin checking for doneness at 15 minutes. Top as above and enjoy!

HAWAIJ CHICKEN POTPIE

From the time Bernie was born until her first tiny teeth poked through her gums, I dreamt about her introduction to solid food. Every day we'd walk outside and check to see how the apples on our trees were progressing so that we could make applesauce for her first feast. I combed my cookbooks for the best-looking recipe and spent hours online researching baby dishes and spoons. I couldn't wait to see the look on her face when she finally got to eat something that wasn't breast milk, or grape-flavored baby Tylenol on vaccine day.

When the apples were finally ready, I picked them with her strapped to me in her carrier, peeled them as she napped, and made the smoothest ever applesauce with just a hint of cinnamon. The birds were chirping, the sun was out, it was a magical day, exactly how I envisioned it . . . until she had absolutely no interest in eating. She had one bite and then one more, and without even so much as a smirk of acknowledgment, she continued about her day as if the most exciting milestone in all her five months of life thus far hadn't just occurred.

"This is supposed to be the best day of your life, Bernie! You get to eat *food* now! And food is the best thing of all besides you, so it's time to get really *really* excited!!!!" I tried telling her. But it seemed she was already plotting out her life as one of those eat-to-survive types, and as someone who comes from a long line of family on both sides who 10,000 percent live to eat, I was at a loss for words.

Her staunch neutrality on solid food lasted for months, throughout the purées and soft steamed sweet potatoes. She'd unenthusiastically eat only what she needed to in order to have the energy for her actual interests of digging in the sandbox and going in the Jolly Jumper. She never saw the meal as the main event. Which is the opposite of how I was as a kid, and still am. Every party, concert, playdate, or skating competition that I went to growing up was *actually* about the birthday cake or Lunchable on the lawn at Ravinia or macaroni and cheese with hot dogs in it or concession stand noodles in a cup. Shouldn't Bernie be genetically programmed to understand this?

But then Christmas came and we had these potpies, and suddenly the floodgates opened up. One bite, and it was as if it had just occurred to her that *food is actually the best*. She inhaled it, carrots and chicken and all. And then asked for more. And more!! And *omg where is this all going?* Nick and I asked each other. I was impressed. She picked a good first food to love. From there, she discovered a love of chicken noodle soup, chicken and dumpling soup, any other chicken stewy thing, and other über-comforting foods that gave us a glimpse into who she is. She's a cozy toad, and I love that about her!

These pies are schmaltzy and spiced with the Yemeni spice blend hawaij for soup, which is heavy on the turmeric and cumin and adds a buttery quality. It doesn't overpower in these pies; it just helps a good classic potpie become a more glamorous and well-traveled version of itself. You could make one big pie, but the puff pastry element comes together most gracefully in an individual serving. You also get more crispy bits that way.

MAKES 4 PIES, TO SERVE 4

6 bone-in, skin-on chicken thighs, patted dry

Kosher salt and freshly ground black pepper

2 tablespoons (25 grams) neutral oil

1 medium yellow onion, chopped

3 large carrots, trimmed and thinly sliced

3 large celery stalks, thinly sliced

1 teaspoon grated fresh ginger

1 tablespoon (8 grams) hawaij spice for soup (store-bought or homemade, recipe follows)

6 tablespoons (49 grams) all-purpose flour

2½ cups (600 grams) low-sodium chicken stock

½ cup (20 grams) chopped flat-leaf parsley

¼ cup (10 grams) chopped dill

¾ cup (96 grams) peas, fresh or frozen

½ cup (120 grams) heavy cream

1 sheet puff pastry, thawed overnight in the refrigerator or for about 45 minutes at room temperature

1 egg, beaten with a splash of water, for egg wash

Flaky salt

Sesame seeds

PREHEAT the oven to 425°F.

SEASON the chicken thighs generously all over with salt and pepper. Heat a large oven-safe (preferably cast-iron) skillet, braiser, or pot over medium-high heat and add the oil. Add the chicken thighs skin side down and cook, undisturbed, until the skin is golden and crispy and doesn't really fight you when you try to flip the thighs, 8 to 10 minutes. Flip and transfer the pan to the oven for 10 to 15 minutes, until the chicken is cooked through with an internal temperature of 165°F. (You can cook the second side just on the stove for an additional 15 to 18 minutes instead of using the oven, but it might get spitty!) Transfer the chicken to a plate, leaving the fat in the skillet.

HEAT the skillet over medium heat and add the onion, carrots, and celery and a pinch of salt. Cook, stirring occasionally, until softened, 7 to 10 minutes. Add the ginger and hawaij and cook for another minute, until fragrant. Whisk in the flour and cook, whisking, for 2 more minutes. Add the chicken stock very gradually, in 3 or 4 additions, whisking continuously and allowing the mixture to thicken before each addition. Stir in the parsley, dill, and peas, then reduce the heat to low and allow it to hang out (stir it occasionally) while you prepare the chicken. Pull the chicken off the bones, discard or snack on the skin, chop the meat into bite-size pieces, and add it to the pan. Stir in the heavy cream. Taste and adjust the seasoning as desired.

LADLE into four ½-quart ovenproof bowls or cocottes. On a work surface, roll out the puff pastry sheet so that it's big enough to cut into 4 squares that are about an inch larger than the bowls in diameter. Brush the edges of the bowls with egg wash and then lay the puff pastry squares on top of the bowls, gently pressing around the bowl edges. Brush the tops with egg wash, sprinkle with a pinch of flaky salt, and cover liberally with sesame seeds. Cut 2 slits in the center of each and place them on a rimmed sheet pan, which will make them easier to transfer and also catch any mixture that overflows in the oven. Bake until the pastry is golden; begin checking for doneness at 20 minutes. Let cool slightly and serve.

TO MAKE AHEAD: Assemble the potpies in individual metal dishes, allowing the chicken mixture to cool before topping with the puff pastry. Cover with foil (not too tight so it doesn't stick to the egg wash) and freeze for up to 3 months. To reheat, place the foil-covered pies on a rimmed sheet pan and bake at 400°F for 40 minutes; carefully uncover and continue to bake until the pastry is golden and the innards are heated through; begin checking for doneness at 15 minutes. Let cool slightly and serve.

HAWAIJ SEASONING FOR SOUP

COMBINE 2 teaspoons ground turmeric, 2 teaspoons ground cumin, 30 turns or ½ teaspoon ground black pepper, ½ teaspoon ground ginger, ½ teaspoon ground coriander, and ¼ teaspoon ground cardamom.

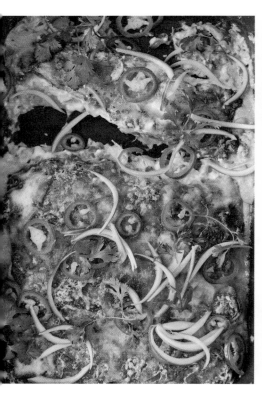

CREAM CHEESE CHICKEN ENCHILADAS

When my sister-in-law, Anna, was about to give birth to her second kiddo, I went through the custom of asking her what hotdishes she was into, or if there were any foods she was craving that I could try turning into casserole form. Because the best thing about having a pregnant family member—other than the imminent arrival of a small new human to love—is delivering a casserole. Her answer was the cream-cheese-covered chicken chimichanga from the Mexican Village in Fargo, which sounded like the subject of a pregnancy fever dream, but no, it's real, and it's real good.

I am generally opposed to pairing cheese with chicken because I find that it either makes chicken look bad and dry since cheese is so rich and tasty, or, in the case of a very good flavorful juicy chicken, it diverts too much attention. It's rare to find a productive cheese and chicken relationship. But here, the chicken is basically a vehicle for a cream cheese béchamel, which has just enough personality to be delicious, but not so much that you're forced to ask why chicken is even at the party. You don't have to worry about the chicken being dry because it's covered in that béchamel. When it's eaten between the folds of a flour tortilla, oh, you really can't stop.

SERVES 4 TO 6

8 ounces (226 grams) cream cheese

2 tablespoons (28 grams) unsalted butter

1½ tablespoons (12 grams) all-purpose flour

1½ cups (360 grams) whole or 2% milk

Kosher salt

3 cups shredded cooked chicken breast (from about 18 ounces/509 grams boneless, skinless chicken breasts)

One 10-ounce (283-gram) jar green enchilada sauce

Two 4-ounce (113-gram) cans diced green chiles

6 scallions, thinly sliced

Freshly ground black pepper

Eight 8-inch flour tortillas

1 cup (4 ounces/113 grams) shredded Swiss, mozzarella, or Oaxaca cheese

Pickled red onions, for topping

Handful of cilantro leaves, for topping

1 jalapeño, thinly sliced, for topping

PREHEAT the oven to 375°F. Set the cream cheese on the counter to take the chill off while you make the béchamel.

TO make the béchamel, heat a medium saucepan over medium heat and melt the butter. Whisk in the flour and continue to whisk for 2 minutes. Add the milk very gradually, in 3 or 4 additions, whisking continuously and allowing the mixture to thicken before each addition. Increase the heat and continue whisking frequently until it just begins to simmer, then reduce the heat to low and simmer very gently for 5 minutes, whisking occasionally. Stir in the cream cheese, a few plops at a time, making sure each addition is melted and incorporated before adding more. Add a pinch of salt, taste, and add more salt, if desired. Remove from the heat. In a big bowl, combine the chicken, ½ cup of the cream cheese sauce, 6 ounces of the enchilada sauce (you can eyeball this, just add a little more than half of the jar), the green chiles, the scallions, a few turns of black pepper, and salt to taste.

SPREAD the remaining enchilada sauce all over the bottom of a 9 x 13-inch casserole dish. Roll up each of the tortillas with about ½ cup of the chicken mixture and nestle them in the dish, seam side down. Cover the enchiladas with the remaining cream cheese sauce and sprinkle with the shredded cheese. Bake until golden brown on top; begin checking for doneness at 30 minutes. Top with the pickled red onions, cilantro, and jalapeño and enjoy!

MOO SHU CHICKEN

My love for moo shu chicken is strong but conflicted. On one hand, I want to eat it every day of my life. On the other hand, the version I know and love is about as Chinese as orange chicken samples at the shopping mall food court. In its traditional form, moo shu is made with wood ear mushrooms, enokitake mushrooms, lily buds, cucumbers, pork, and egg. And it's served with rice, not wrapped in pancakes. Since my grandma never made it and since my biggest source of inspiration was Chinese restaurants that have sections on their menus for hot dogs and cheeseburgers, I go the Americanized Chinese food route. Americanized Chinese food is indeed its own cuisine that's different from authentic Chinese food, but, hey, I love eating it. When I make moo shu, I use chicken, egg, coleslaw mix, a sauce that smacks you on the face with flavor, and extra pancakes, sometimes tortillas. Etymologically, I consider myself in the clear because the name moo shu refers to a yellow and white flower that alludes to the yellow and white egg. So as long as there's egg, we're good??

SERVES 4

¼ cup (80 grams) hoisin sauce

2 tablespoons (30 grams) rice vinegar

2 tablespoons (30 grams) soy sauce

1 tablespoon (12 grams) toasted sesame oil

1 tablespoon (19 grams) oyster sauce

4 garlic cloves, finely chopped

Freshly ground black pepper

2 tablespoons (25 grams) neutral oil, divided

2 large eggs, beaten with a splash of water

1 pound (454 grams) boneless, skinless chicken breasts, cut into very thin, 1- to 2-inch-long strips

One 14-ounce (396-gram) bag coleslaw mix

4 scallions, cut into 1-inch slices

Mandarin Pancakes (page 185) or flour tortillas, warmed, for serving

Sambal oelek or sriracha, for serving

IN a medium bowl or large measuring cup, whisk together the hoisin sauce, rice vinegar, soy sauce, sesame oil, oyster sauce, garlic, and loads of black pepper and set aside.

HEAT a large skillet over medium-high heat and add 1 tablespoon (13 grams) of the oil. Add the eggs, and swirl around so they're in one even layer. Let them cook fully, undisturbed, then slide them onto a cutting board. Chop into very thin strips and set aside.

INCREASE the heat to high and add the remaining tablespoon (13 grams) of oil. Add the chicken and cook, tossing occasionally, until browned on the outside but not yet fully cooked on the inside, 3 to 5 minutes. Fold in the coleslaw mix and cook until wilted, another few minutes. Add the sauce and cook, stirring and scraping the bottom of the pan with a spatula, for another few minutes, until enough of the moisture has evaporated that the mixture is saucy, not soggy. Remove from the heat, stir in the egg and scallions, and serve with Mandarin Pancakes and sambal oelek or sriracha.

MANDARIN PANCAKES

I have to tell you about how cool these pancakes are; you make *two at once*. It's efficiency at its finest, and an easy way to get paper-thin pancakes without any special tools. The boiling water in the dough helps to result in a smooth, sturdy, deliciously chewy pancake that works with you when you're rolling it out.

MAKES 16 PANCAKES, TO SERVE 4 TO 6

3 cups (390 grams) all-purpose flour, plus more for dusting

1½ teaspoons kosher salt

½ cup (120 grams) boiling water

½ cup (120 grams) cold water

About 2 tablespoons (25 grams) neutral oil or toasted sesame oil

IN a large bowl, combine the flour and salt and create a well in the middle. Add the boiling water, mix it in with a rubber spatula, then incorporate with your hands until you have a mealy, shaggy mixture. Mix in the cold water with a spatula and bring everything together into a dough. Turn it out onto a work surface and knead for 7 to 10 minutes, adding more flour if it gets too sticky to work with, until you have a smooth and slightly sticky dough. Cover loosely with plastic wrap or a damp towel and let rest for 10 minutes.

HEAT a large skillet over medium-high heat. Divide the dough into 16 equal balls and keep them covered when you're not working with them. Use your palms to smash 2 balls of dough into equal-size discs, about 2 to 3 inches in diameter. Brush the top of 1 disc with a thin layer of oil and stack the other disc on top of it to create 1 thick disc. Using a rolling pin, roll the disc into about an 8-inch pancake, dusting your work surface and rolling pin with flour if needed to prevent sticking. (If the dough is fighting you when you try to roll it out, cover it back up and let rest for 10 more minutes.)

PLACE the pancake in the dry skillet and cook for about a minute on each side, until splotchy with brown marks. Transfer to a plate and cover with a towel. Repeat with the remaining dough, stacking the cooked pancakes on top of one another and keeping them covered so that they steam. When they're cool enough to handle, peel the 2 halves of each pancake apart so that you have 2 very thin pancakes (*nifty, huh?!*) and enjoy while they're still warm. Store leftovers in an airtight container in the fridge for up to a few days. Reheat in the microwave covered by a damp paper towel.

CHICKEN SHAWARMA MEATBALLS

This is my hack for reliving the Foodstand Friday chicken and rice lunches of my New York college years without having to fly back to New York or marinate meat, two things I really don't have time for when the craving strikes. I've mixed my go-to shawarma spice blend into some meatballs for a quick and satisfying focal point. They get plopped on a bed of yellow spiced rice next to the customary crisp cooling lettuce and tomatoes that really don't care if it's tomato season or not. They're then splattered with the requisite creamy tangy white sauce and just enough hot sauce to party. It's a flavor mosh pit, and we're all back in college, protein-loading for a wild Friday night ahead.

SERVES 3 TO 4

Meatballs

2 tablespoons (25 grams) neutral oil or extra virgin olive oil, plus more for cooking the meatballs

½ medium yellow onion, finely chopped

Kosher salt

2 garlic cloves, finely chopped

¾ teaspoon garam masala

¾ teaspoon curry powder

2 teaspoons coriander seeds, crushed in a mortar and pestle

1 large egg

½ cup (30 grams) panko breadcrumbs

1 pound (454 grams) ground chicken

Freshly ground black pepper

½ bunch (about 20 grams) cilantro, finely chopped

Rice

2 tablespoons (25 grams) extra virgin olive oil

½ teaspoon ground turmeric

1 teaspoon garam masala

1½ cups (270 grams) basmati rice, rinsed

2½ cups (600 grams) low-sodium chicken stock

Kosher salt

Sauce

½ cup (120 grams) plain Greek yogurt (whole milk, 2%, or nonfat)

¼ cup (52 grams) mayonnaise

1 garlic clove, finely chopped or grated with a fine zester

Juice of half a lemon

Kosher salt and freshly ground black pepper

Accessories

4 ounces (113 grams) shredded iceberg lettuce

1 medium tomato, sliced into half moons

½ medium yellow onion, thinly sliced

Lemon wedges

Hot sauce

PREHEAT the oven to 425°F.

HEAT a large oven-safe skillet over medium heat and add the oil. Add the onion and a pinch of salt and cook, stirring, until soft, 5 to 7 minutes. Add the garlic, garam masala, curry powder, and coriander seeds and cook, stirring, for another minute, until fragrant. Remove from the heat and let cool slightly.

MEANWHILE, in a large bowl, combine the egg and breadcrumbs. Add the chicken and spread it out to increase the surface area, which will help the seasoning distribute. Sprinkle evenly with 1 teaspoon salt, a few turns of black pepper, the cilantro, and the slightly cooled onion mixture. Use your hands to combine; don't overmix.

WIPE out the skillet and return to medium-high heat. Heat a drizzle of oil and then form a small tester patty of the chicken mixture and brown it for a few minutes on each side until cooked through. Taste it for seasoning (depending on the freshness of your spices, you may want to add more). Adjust the spices accordingly, then shape the meatballs, forming the mixture into balls slightly smaller than golf balls. Heat a thin layer of oil in the pan and then, working in batches so as to not overcrowd the pan, brown the balls all over to create a tasty crust. Add more oil to the pan if it ever seems dry. When all the meatballs are browned, return them to the skillet and stick the skillet in the oven until the meatballs are cooked through and have an internal temperature of 165°F; begin checking for doneness at 7 minutes.

TO make the rice, heat a pot over medium heat and add the oil. Add the turmeric and garam masala, and toast, stirring, until fragrant, about a minute. Stir in the rice, stock, and ¾ teaspoon salt and increase the heat to bring to a boil. Reduce the heat to a simmer, cover, and cook for 15 minutes. Turn off the heat and let steam with the lid on for an additional 15 minutes. Fluff with a fork, taste, and add more salt, if desired.

TO make the sauce, stir the yogurt, mayonnaise, garlic, and lemon juice together until smooth and season with salt and pepper to taste.

TO serve, spread the rice out in a large shallow bowl and pile the meatballs on half. On the other half, pile the lettuce, tomato, and onion and garnish with lemon wedges. Drizzle the meatballs and veggies with half of the white sauce and serve the remaining sauce at the table along with the hot sauce. These meatballs are also great in pita!

PICKLE CHICKEN WITH TOUM

My ideal winter weekend afternoon smells like chicken, sounds like Hallmark Christmas movies, feels like an oversize sweater, is dark because the sun went down at four o'clock, and ends with this small colorful feast. At the center is pickle chicken (!) which is hard to write without an exclamation point after it because it's so fun to say. It's essentially just a great juicy roasted chicken all dressed up with the flavors of garlic dill pickle brine. It comes together easily and makes the house smell extra cozy. My favorite way to eat this is with hot fresh chewy laffa (or pita), pickles for snappiness, a simple crunchy romaine salad, and an addictive Lebanese condiment, toum.

Toum is kind of like a fluffier mayonnaise that is loaded with garlic and lemon. It's incredible on *so* many things, but I extra like it with this. For our family, I typically make the small batch that's written here using a mortar and pestle, and it's very rewarding to see it come together. But if you'd like to use a food processor, you can do that if you make a quadruple batch. (Leftovers will keep in the fridge for weeks.) Last, the biggest takeaway I want you to get from this recipe is that letting your chicken sit *uncovered* in your fridge for at least an hour will give you crispy skin. That's all!

SERVES 2 TO 4

Chicken

2 teaspoons kosher salt

2 teaspoons dried dill

1 teaspoon ground black pepper

½ teaspoon ground ginger

½ teaspoon ground allspice

½ teaspoon ground coriander

One 4- to 5-pound (1.8- to 2.3-kilogram) roasting chicken

¼ cup (56 grams) unsalted butter, melted

or sub extra virgin olive oil

¼ cup (60 grams) garlic dill pickle brine

1 garlic head, halved crosswise

Handful of flat-leaf parsley sprigs, plus chopped parsley for serving

Toum

6 large garlic cloves, germ removed and coarsely chopped

Kosher salt

6 tablespoons (75 grams) neutral oil

Juice of half a large lemon, plus more to taste if desired

Accessories

Buttermilk Laffa (page 252) or pita

Garlic dill pickles

FOR the chicken, combine the salt, dill, pepper, ginger, allspice, and coriander in a small bowl. Pat the chicken dry and season all over (including inside) with the spice mixture, rubbing it in well. Place the chicken in a metal or cast-iron roasting pan and refrigerate uncovered for at least an hour, up to overnight, so that the skin will dry out and get extra crispy.

MEANWHILE, make the toum: In a mortar and pestle, smash the garlic with ½ teaspoon salt until it's broken down and pasty. Don't rush this step! Or any of these steps. Toum demands toddler-parent-level patience. Incorporate the oil, drizzling in 1 teaspoon at a time, smashing/mixing (smixing? smashxing?) in each one fully before adding the next. The mixture should begin to take on a thick and fluffy texture and, as it does, make sure that it returns back to that texture after each addition of oil before adding more. If this is your first time making this, you might think you're doing something wrong for those first few oil additions, because it's kind of hard to imagine how it all comes together into a beautiful dollop-y sauce. But it's okay! You're doing great! Just keep on taking your time, otherwise it could break. Once you've added all the oil, gradually drizzle in the lemon juice while stirring with the pestle. Taste and add more lemon juice or salt as desired. Refrigerate until ready to serve. (If using a food processor, blend the mixture instead of smashing it and stop very frequently to scrape down the sides and bottom of the processor with a rubber spatula to ensure that each bit of oil is incorporated before adding more.)

PREHEAT the oven to 400°F.

IN a small bowl, stir together the melted butter and pickle brine. Stuff the halved garlic and parsley in the cavity of the chicken and tuck the wings under. Brush with half of the pickle mixture. Roast for 45 minutes. Brush with the remaining pickle mixture and with some of the pan juices as well. Roast until the skin is very crisp and deep golden and the internal temperature in the deepest part of the thigh is 165°F; begin checking after another 30 minutes. Let the chicken rest for at least 15 minutes before carving. Sprinkle the carved chicken with chopped parsley.

SERVE with the toum on the side, laffa or pita, and garlic dill pickles.

TURKEY SPINACH MEATBALLS
A.K.A. THE FAMILY MEATBALL

Anatomy of a perfect meatball:

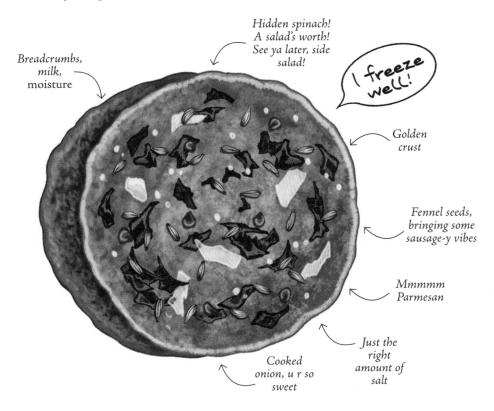

Hidden spinach! A salad's worth! See ya later, side salad!

Breadcrumbs, milk, moisture

I freeze well!

Golden crust

Fennel seeds, bringing some sausage-y vibes

Mmmmm Parmesan

Just the right amount of salt

Cooked onion, u r so sweet

SERVES 4

2 tablespoons (25 grams) extra virgin olive oil, plus more for cooking the meatballs

1 small yellow onion, finely chopped

Kosher salt

2 garlic cloves, finely chopped

1 teaspoon fennel seeds

5 ounces (142 grams) fresh baby spinach, chopped, or frozen spinach, thawed and drained

¼ cup (60 grams) whole milk

½ cup (30 grams) panko breadcrumbs

1 large egg

1 pound (454 grams) ground turkey, 93% lean

½ cup (60 grams) grated Parmesan

Freshly ground black pepper

Crushed red pepper

PREHEAT the oven to 425°F.

HEAT a large oven-safe skillet over medium heat and add the oil. Add the onion and a pinch of salt and cook, stirring, until soft, 5 to 7 minutes. Add the garlic and fennel and cook, stirring, for another minute, until fragrant. If using fresh spinach, add it in batches with a pinch of salt, stirring until wilted. (If using frozen spinach, sit tight, we'll get to that!) Remove from the heat and let cool slightly.

MEANWHILE, in a large bowl, combine the milk and breadcrumbs and let sit for a couple of minutes so the breadcrumbs absorb the milk. Add the egg and turkey and spread out the turkey to increase the surface area, which will help the seasoning distribute. Sprinkle evenly with 1 teaspoon salt, the Parmesan, a bunch of turns of pepper, a couple of good pinches of crushed red pepper, and the slightly cooled spinach mixture (or, if using frozen spinach, add the onion mixture and the thawed drained spinach). Use your hands to combine. Don't overmix; that could create a tough texture. Roll into 1½-inch balls, to yield about 20 to 22 balls.

WIPE out the skillet and return to medium-high heat. Heat a thin layer of olive oil, then, working in batches so as to not overcrowd the pan, brown the balls all over to create a tasty crust. Add more oil to the pan if it ever seems dry. When all the meatballs are browned, return them to the skillet and stick the skillet in the oven until the meatballs are cooked through and have an internal temperature of 165°F; begin checking for doneness at 7 minutes. (Alternatively, you can finish these by simmering them in a big pot of red sauce until they're cooked through and have an internal temperature of 165°F.) Serve over spaghetti or polenta, in a hoagie, or, our favorite, in biscuits (see next page)!!

FAVE THING ABOUT MEATBALLS

They freeze so well. Cooked meatballs (not in sauce) can be cooled and stored in an airtight container in the freezer for up to 3 months. To reheat, plop into simmering red sauce and cook until heated through, about 15 minutes, or place on a rimmed sheet pan and cover with foil and bake at 350°F for 15 to 20 minutes, until heated through.

MEATBALLS IN BISCUITS!

MAKES 16 BISCUITS

Two 16-ounce (454-gram) cans refrigerated buttermilk biscuits (8 biscuits in each can)

8 thick deli slices mozzarella, cut in half

16 Turkey Spinach Meatballs (page 194; see Note), prepared through the browning step

2 tablespoons (28 grams) unsalted butter

1 tablespoon (13 grams) extra virgin olive oil

4 garlic cloves, finely chopped

Crushed red pepper

Handful of flat-leaf parsley, finely chopped

2 tablespoons (15 grams) grated Parmesan

Flaky salt

Marinara sauce, warmed, for serving

NOTE: *Since the Turkey Spinach Meatball recipe makes 20 to 22 balls and you only need 16 for this, you will have some meatballs left over for snacking or another use. Be sure to complete their cooking process as directed in the meatball recipe, since the browning step only cooks the outside. Don't be tempted to avoid leftovers by making larger meatballs; they'll be too big for the biscuits and pan! But if you definitely want to avoid leftover meatballs, make them a touch smaller to get 24 balls and then multiply the rest of the biscuit ingredients by 1½ to make a 9 x 13-inch pan, increasing the baking time by a few minutes.*

PREHEAT the oven to 375°F.

FLATTEN each biscuit with your palm to about 4 inches in diameter. Place a half piece of mozzarella on each biscuit, and top it with a meatball. Wrap the dough up around the meatball and pinch the edges of the dough to seal. Place seam side down in a 9-inch square baking dish. Bake until lightly browned, about 30 minutes.

MEANWHILE, heat the butter and oil in a small saucepan over medium-low heat. Add the garlic and a pinch of crushed red pepper and cook for 2 minutes, swirling occasionally. Brush the biscuits with the butter mixture, sprinkle with the parsley, Parmesan, and a pinch of flaky salt, and continue to bake until golden and cooked through (the meatballs should have an internal temperature of 165°F); begin checking for doneness at 5 minutes. Let cool slightly and serve with marinara for dunking.

CRISPY SKIN SALMON WITH SALSA VERDE

Somewhere between my weird face mole scare of 2017 and having a child, I decided that we should really listen to all the articles on the internet that say you'll live longer if you have fish once a week. So I worked up a back-pocket recipe for a simple punched-up version of the seared salmon and vegetables that Nick and his parents order every single time we go out to eat at those restaurants where you get to order two sides with your protein—you know the ones. A quick cooking time is one of the most convenient perks of fish, but it's also potentially its greatest downfall, because fish can overcook in seconds. I find that the most vital step in cooking fish isn't to "find the freshest most high-quality fish possible" (although that's a good idea); it's actually to not trust your husband when he calls to say that it will only take five minutes to finish up the wheat harvest for the day. Because if you cook the fish right then, it will either be overcooked or ice-cold by the time he actually gets home half an hour later. (Do you see why hotdishes are so popular on farms?) Instead, get going on the salsa verde, and allow ample time for your fish to come to room temperature. When you hear mud-caked boots coming up the steps, fire that fish! Our favorite pick-two sides to this meal are buttery brown rice or oily angel hair and some simple sautéed broccoli. Cover your whole plate with the salsa verde.

SERVES 4

Salsa verde

¼ cup (10 grams) coarsely chopped flat-leaf parsley

¼ cup (10 grams) coarsely chopped cilantro

1 large garlic clove, peeled

Zest and juice of half a large lemon

⅓ cup (67 grams) extra virgin olive oil

Kosher salt and freshly ground black pepper

Salmon

Four 5- to 6-ounce (142- to 170-gram) skin-on salmon fillets, brought to room temperature for 15 minutes and patted very dry

Kosher salt and freshly ground black pepper

1 tablespoon (13 grams) extra virgin olive oil

1 tablespoon (14 grams) unsalted butter

IN a food processor, combine the parsley, cilantro, garlic, lemon zest and juice, olive oil, a good pinch of salt, and a bunch of turns of black pepper and blend to the consistency of pesto, scraping the sides every so often. (Alternatively, you can chop the herbs and garlic very finely and mix everything together in a bowl.) Taste and adjust as desired. Set aside.

HEAT a large cast-iron or stainless steel skillet over medium-high heat for at least a couple of minutes, so you're sure it's hot. Use this time to season the salmon all over with ¾ teaspoon salt and a bunch of black pepper. Add the oil and butter to the pan, swirling it around, and once it's hot, add a salmon fillet skin side down, pressing with a fish spatula for a few seconds so that the skin makes full contact with the skillet before adding and pressing the second fillet (allow at least an inch in between each fillet, cooking in batches if necessary). Continue going around the pan, pressing each fillet down for a few seconds at a time, so that the skin keeps on getting crispy, until an instant-read thermometer stuck halfway into the thickest part of the fillet reads 120°F (for medium rare); start checking for doneness at 5 minutes and continue to check frequently, as salmon can overcook very quickly. Also check visually by peeking at the side of the fish: as it cooks, it'll turn opaque, and it's ready to flip when most of the thickest part of the flesh is opaque. Depending on the thickness of the fish, it could take up to 8 minutes or so. At this point, the skin should release easily from the pan. Carefully lift the fillets, flip, and cook the other side until cooked through; this is quick, just around 30 seconds. Serve immediately, skin side up, passing the salsa verde at the table.

KNOEPHLA, SAUSAGE, AND SAUERKRAUT SKILLET

Bernie has two best friends, two identical stuffed bunnies named Bungee and Other Bungee. Other Bungee was never supposed to be part of the equation; she was supposed to stay hidden in the closet in case, heaven forbid, Bernie ever lost Bungee on the family summer road trip to Bemidji and needed a replacement. But somehow Bernie found Other Bungee, and now when we tuck her into bed, we are to nestle Bungee in one armpit nook and Other Bungee in the other armpit nook. Even though I cannot tell them apart, my heart always goes out to Other Bungee. Imagine your whole identity being that you are just another something else. One day we'll discover that Other Bungee has some unique traits, like being an extra good tea party conversationalist . . . or making delicious *Other Knoephla . . .*

Knoephla (NEH-fla) are tiny German dumplings that sort of resemble gnocchi, but they're chewier and are most commonly found around here in creamy potato soup. This soup is one of my all-time favorite foods (you can find recipes on my blog and in *Molly on the Range*) and I can't *not* order it at a restaurant if it's ever their soup of the day. Mention "knoephla" to a local, and pretty much everyone assumes you're talking about this soup. But what also deserves our love and affection is: Other Knoephla! It's the less common but just as delightful skillet in which the dumplings are sautéed in a pan with sauerkraut and smoked sausage. Typically this skillet contains potatoes, which I don't love because they look too similar to the dumplings and eating a big forkful of potatoes when you're expecting chewy dumplings is disappointing. So I add brussels sprouts in their place, which go especially great with the smoked sausage. And then the sauerkraut makes this thing go into my mouth on turbo speed because it brightens up an otherwise hefty supper.

SERVES 4

Knoephla
Feel free to substitute 2 cups (12 ounces/ 340 grams) store-bought frozen knoephla!

Kosher salt

1½ cups (195 grams) all-purpose flour, plus more for dusting

¾ teaspoon baking powder

Freshly ground black pepper

⅛ teaspoon freshly grated nutmeg

¼ cup (10 grams) finely chopped flat-leaf parsley, plus more for serving

⅓ cup (80 grams) water

1 large egg

Assembly

Neutral oil

12 ounces (340 grams) brussels sprouts, quartered

Kosher salt

12 ounces (340 grams) German smoked sausage, thinly sliced

1 pound (454 grams) sauerkraut, drained

1 tablespoon (14 grams) unsalted butter

2 tablespoons (30 grams) heavy cream

Freshly ground black pepper

TO make the knoephla, bring a large pot of water to a boil and season with a small handful (about a heaping tablespoon) of salt. In a medium bowl, whisk together the flour, baking powder, ½ teaspoon salt, a few turns of pepper, the nutmeg, and the parsley. Stir in the water and egg and mix to form a shaggy dough. Turn it out onto a clean work surface and knead it for a few minutes, adding flour as needed to prevent sticking, until you have a smooth and stiff dough. Cover loosely with plastic wrap or a damp towel and let sit for 10 minutes. (This is a perfect time to chop your brussels sprouts and sausage if you haven't already!)

ROLL the dough out into a ½-inch-thick blob and cut into ½- to ¾-inch squares, dusting with flour so they don't stick together. Boil for 8 to 10 minutes, until cooked through. (If using store-bought frozen knoephla, boil for the same amount of time; no need to thaw before boiling.) Drain and set aside.

MEANWHILE, heat a large skillet over medium-high heat and add a drizzle of oil. Add the brussels sprouts and a pinch of salt and cook undisturbed until crisp on one side, 6 to 8 minutes. Toss, add the sausage, and cook for another 5 to 7 minutes or so, tossing occasionally, until the sausage has some nice brown marks and the brussels sprouts' texture is just shy of where you'd like it to be. If the pan looks dry, add another drizzle of oil. Add in the knoephla and cook for a few minutes, tossing occasionally, to get a little brown color on them. Reduce the heat to medium low, fold in the sauerkraut, and cook until warm. Finish with the butter and cream. Season with black pepper and, if needed, salt. Top with parsley and enjoy!

RED-COOKED SHORT RIBS

If my dad was a publicist for food, he would be both fantastic and terrible at it. Fantastic because he transforms into a confetti-spitting disco ball ray of light when you get him talking about foods he loves (which is every food except for goat cheese). Terrible because as soon as you express interest in trying whatever food he's talking about, he reaches into his backpack and pulls out a broken Styrofoam container of half-eaten meat that's been in his backpack since he was at my grandma's house . . . which is in LA . . . which is a twelve-hour journey to Grand Forks . . . and he expects me to try it. And it's like, *How are you not dead of salmonella yet?*

This is only a slight exaggeration of a real-life thing that happened the last time my grandma made my dad's favorite tepong pork (red-cooked pork shoulder). I had never had it before, probably because these days when we visit her we go out for Chinese food, and tepong pork is not a typical restaurant menu item. It's an at-home thing, and the "red" refers to the red tint of a braise that's a classic Chinese preparation. Eventually my dad's excitement about it got me curious enough to call up my grandma for the recipe: an entire pork shoulder braised with star anise, cloves, loads of sherry vinegar, and soy sauce. At first bite, I realized why my dad was so enthusiastic about this. It has that same comforting nostalgic quality that my mom's braised brisket evokes. It is so flavorful, juicy, and tender, and the cloves and anise give it a cozy energy that just makes you want to cuddle up with it.

When I red-cook at home now, I do it with short ribs, because short ribs rock and they're more user-friendly than a whole honkin' pork shoulder. This recipe is a special one, but the prep is not a heavy lift, and it makes the house smell insane.

My dad will tell you sternly to never skip the eggs, and he's right! They're called lu dan, which translates to soy eggs, and they soak up the braising liquid, becoming cute and creamy sidekicks. Eat this over rice, and for a veggie, sautéed bok choy or garlicky spinach is the way to go.

4 pounds (1.8 kilograms) bone-in beef short ribs, cut English style

Kosher salt and freshly ground black pepper

2 tablespoons (25 grams) neutral oil

2 medium yellow onions, peeled and quartered

4 garlic cloves, peeled and smashed

2 tablespoons (18 grams) finely chopped fresh ginger (from about a 2-inch piece)

6 whole star anise pods

10 whole cloves

3 tablespoons (38 grams) packed dark brown sugar

¾ cup (180 grams) soy sauce

¾ cup (180 grams) sherry vinegar

6 large eggs

White or brown rice, for serving

Sliced scallions, for serving

PREHEAT the oven to 350°F.

SEASON the ribs lightly with salt and pepper. Heat a large Dutch oven over medium-high heat and add the oil. Sear the ribs, in batches if needed, until browned all over, 6 to 8 minutes. Remove from the pot and set aside. Reduce the heat to medium, add the onions and garlic, and cook, stirring occasionally, until the onions start to soften, 4 to 5 minutes. Add the ginger, star anise, and cloves and cook, stirring, for another minute, until fragrant.

STIR in the sugar and cook, stirring frequently, until melted, 1 to 2 minutes. Pour in the soy sauce and vinegar and stir to combine. Return the ribs to the pot and add 4 cups (960 grams) cold water. Cover the pot and increase the heat to bring the mixture to a boil.

TRANSFER to the oven and bake until the short ribs are tender and pulling away from the bones; begin checking at 1½ hours.

MEANWHILE, place the eggs in a medium pot and cover with cold water. Bring the water to a boil, then turn off the heat and let the eggs sit in the hot water for 4 minutes. Drain the water, then submerge the eggs in an ice bath to stop the cooking. Peel the eggs and cut small slits into the white parts. Refrigerate the eggs until needed.

REMOVE the ribs from the pot and turn the heat to high. Bring the liquid left in the pot to a boil and cook for 5 minutes. Add the eggs and cook for 5 to 7 more minutes, until the sauce has thickened.

STRAIN the sauce into a bowl or gravy strainer and skim off the fat.

SERVE the short ribs over the rice and spoon the sauce on top. Garnish with sliced scallions and serve with the eggs on the side.

SLOW COOKER VERSION

BROWN the ribs and sauté the onion, garlic, and ginger with the cloves and star anise as opposite. Arrange the short ribs in one layer in the slow cooker, bones facing up. Add the brown sugar, soy sauce, and vinegar and 1 cup (240 grams) water. Cover the slow cooker and cook on low for 6 to 8 hours, until tender.

REMOVE the ribs and bring the cooking liquid to a simmer in the slow cooker on high.

MIX 1 tablespoon (8 grams) cornstarch with a few tablespoons water and whisk this slurry into the simmering sauce. (Alternatively, if you don't mind dirtying up another pot, you can transfer the liquid to a pot and heat as opposite.) Add the eggs as opposite. Strain the sauce into a bowl or gravy strainer and skim off the fat. Serve as opposite.

HANDHELDS
IDEAL FOR HARVEST!

A few years ago I filed the motion to formally take over the harvest lunch-making reins from Nick's mom, who had been doing it ever since she took it over from his grandma in the early 2000s. I was so excited because after experiencing four harvests I finally felt like I understood what was required to fuel such a physically demanding job and had come to terms with the fact that cute, colorful bento boxes of dainty DIY Lunchables would have to wait until Bernie started kindergarten. I would make hearty manly food! It would be sturdy, it would contain *meat*, it'd be packed in ugly containers that could be tossed around a tractor, and it would enable Nick to harvest the heck out of his beets. I was so ready and in the mindset. I went to the grocery store and stocked up on nuts, energy bars, nut butter packets (I had to add *some* cuteness), turmeric shots, wellness dust, ingredients for dense, seedy sandwich bread, cheese, meat, carrots, apples, jerky, and more freakin' meat. I made notes on my phone devoted to Venn diagramming Nick's to-go meals and my at-home meals in order to increase efficiency, and lined up all of the silicone sandwich bags, like army men ready for a battle. If premiums on beets were calculated based on the quality of snacks that a farmer eats while harvesting those beets, Nick could have gone right into early retirement.

But do you know what happened that year?

Did word get out about the harvest of '19??

It never happened. The beets stayed in the ground.

The fields flooded, the snow came, the rain came, the beets froze, and then more snow came. In all of Nick's dad's years of farming, he had never seen anything like it. It was one lightning bolt away from locusts and frogs falling from the sky. Farms were tested that year, and it was really, really

awful. Nick likened it to filming an entire season of *Girl Meets Farm* and then accidentally destroying the memory cards in the laundry. It took some time to recover, both physically and emotionally, but Nick and his dad powered on, did what they could to save the fields, and looked ahead to the following year. I hid the nut butter packets in the back of the pantry and drank all the energy shots so we could just forget about that year and my false start as field lunch maker. The expiration dates on the nut butter packets would last us to the following harvest.

And then do you know what happened the next year???

Did you hear about the harvest of '20?????

?!!??1?!!!???

They harvested so effing fast I could barely get a batch of pasties out of the oven before they were done. The skies were sunny, the temperature just right, I tell ya, it was *rude*. I never got to pack a lunch. We actually got to sit down at a table in broad daylight and eat those pasties *together*.

So I've had a couple of dress rehearsals for my role as lunch maker, and you know what they say about a bad dress rehearsal . . .

CORNISH PASTIES

The winter before Bernie was born, Nick and I did something we'd wanted to do for a while that no small child would ever have the patience for: drive back home from visiting my family in Chicago the long way, looping around the northern end of Lake Michigan and through the Upper Peninsula, using only paper maps and restaurants that specialized in Cornish pasties as our guides. It was a snowy adventure, fit for a pregnant lady. I just sat in the passenger's seat the whole time, legs elevated on the dashboard, belly catching all the buttery flaky crumbs from the pasty crusts.

Cornish pasties, which hail from England and are now an attraction of the Upper Peninsula, are a meat-and-potatoes meal in handheld form, as everything is encased in a rich sturdy dough. They typically include the underrated root vegetable rutabaga, and they're best with spicy ketchup or gravy or both. Most convenient of all, however, is that the filling requires no precooking. You just pile a bunch of raw stuff into dough—store-bought for busy nights, homemade for weekends—bake, and let the house smell like you've put in way more effort than you actually have. The way the flavors cozy up with one another inside of their buttery blanket makes them irresistible. The original purpose for pasties in the Upper Peninsula was to be a full, hearty handheld meal for coal miners, and you know who else requires a full, hearty handheld meal? Nick during harvest! So this is a beet harvest slam dunk.

Don't feel like you have to make both the spicy ketchup and the gravy. Make one of them, and if you find yourself with the extra time and desire, make the other!

MAKES 6 PASTIES

Pastry

2½ cups (325 grams) all-purpose flour, plus more as needed

1 teaspoon sugar

1 teaspoon kosher salt

¾ cup (170 grams) cold unsalted butter, cut into ½-inch cubes

1 large egg yolk

1 tablespoon (15 grams) apple cider vinegar

½ cup (120 grams) ice water, plus more as needed

NOTE: *Don't feel like making homemade crust? Use 1½ pounds (680 grams) store-bought refrigerated pie dough, smooshed into a fat log.*

Filling and assembly

12 ounces (340 grams) lean boneless sirloin steak, small diced

1 cup (144 grams) small-diced russet potato (from about 1 small potato)

1 cup (144 grams) small-diced rutabaga (from about 1 small rutabaga)

1 cup (126 grams) small-diced yellow onion (from about 1 small onion)

¾ cup (96 grams) small-diced carrot (from about 1 medium carrot)

2 teaspoons fresh thyme leaves

1 teaspoon kosher salt

1 egg, beaten with a splash of water, for egg wash

Flaky salt

Spicy ketchup

½ cup (140 grams) ketchup

2 tablespoons (24 grams) chopped pickled jalapeño, plus 2 teaspoons brine

1 tablespoon (17 grams) prepared horseradish

1 teaspoon Worcestershire sauce

Gravy

2 tablespoons (28 grams) unsalted butter

2 tablespoons (16 grams) all-purpose flour

1 teaspoon fresh thyme leaves

¼ cup (60 grams) dry white wine

1 cup (240 grams) low-sodium beef stock

1 tablespoon (15 grams) heavy cream

1 teaspoon Worcestershire sauce

Kosher salt and freshly ground black pepper

FOR the pastry, combine the flour, sugar, and salt in a food processor and pulse to combine. Add the butter and pulse until the butter is pea size. In a medium measuring cup, whisk together the egg yolk, vinegar, and ice water. Drizzle over the flour mixture and pulse until the dough comes together. (If the dough is too crumbly to come together, add a little more water or, if it appears too sticky to work with, more flour.) Roll it into a fat log and wrap in plastic wrap. Chill until firm, about 1 hour.

FOR the filling, in a large bowl, combine the beef, potato, rutabaga, onion, carrot, thyme, and salt and mix well.

PREHEAT the oven to 400°F. Line a sheet pan with parchment paper and set aside. This pan will eventually go in the freezer, so if you don't have the freezer space for a large sheet pan, use 2 smaller pans.

TO form the pasties, cut the chilled dough (or store-bought pie dough, if using) into 6 equal pieces. On a floured surface, roll each piece into a 6-by-8-inch oval. Pack a scant cup of the filling in a measuring cup and invert near the bottom of each oval to make a high mound of filling. Brush the edges of the pastries with the egg wash. Fold the tops of the pastries over the filling and press the dough to make a big circular mound of filling in the center of each. Crimp the edges of the pastries and cut 2 air vents in the top of each. Place on the prepared sheet pan, brush with egg wash, and sprinkle with a pinch of flaky salt. Freeze for 30 minutes (or longer! See below for freezing directions).

BAKE the pasties for 15 minutes, then reduce the oven temperature to 350°F and continue to bake until deep golden and cooked through; begin checking at 30 minutes.

FOR the spicy ketchup, combine the ketchup, jalapeño, brine, horseradish, and Worcestershire in a small bowl. Chill until ready to serve.

FOR the gravy, melt the butter in a small saucepan over medium-low heat. Add the flour and cook, whisking, for 2 minutes. Add the thyme and wine and whisk until thickened. Whisk in the beef stock and bring to a simmer. Simmer until thickened enough to coat the back of a spoon, 2 to 3 minutes. Whisk in the cream and Worcestershire and season to taste with salt and pepper.

SERVE the pasties with the spicy ketchup and/or gravy.

TO FREEZE: Unbaked pasties can be frozen in an airtight container for up to 3 months. Bake at 400°F for 15 minutes, then at 350°F for about 50 minutes, until golden brown and cooked through.

KIMCHI CHEDDAR JUCY LUCIES

A Jucy Lucy is a burger with cheese *inside* of the meat, and I am proud to report that it was invented here in Minnesota. It's like a dumpling where the meat is the wrapper and the filling is just straight-up melty cheese! I think Jucy Lucies are brilliant because they put more emphasis on the cheese than your typical cheeseburger, where all too often the cheese gets lost among the lettuce. The cheese gets the attention it deserves here. Kimchi is my topping of choice for three reasons: (1) kimchi and cheddar go together like peanut butter and jelly; (2) kimchi's brininess cuts the richness of this so-called meat-cheese dumpling; (3) kimchi is healthy!

Minnesota summers are terribly mosquito-y, but grilling up a stack of these ladies makes braving the outside worth it.

1½ pounds (680 grams) ground beef, 80% lean

1 tablespoon (15 grams) sambal oelek or sriracha, plus more if desired

2 scallions, thinly sliced

Kosher salt and freshly ground black pepper

1 cup (4 ounces/113 grams) shredded sharp cheddar

Neutral oil, for grilling

4 brioche or potato buns

Mayonnaise, ideally Kewpie

Ketchup

1 cup (200 grams) chopped cabbage kimchi

IN a large bowl, combine the beef, sambal oelek or sriracha (more if you're feeling spicy), scallions, 1 teaspoon salt, and a few good turns of pepper. Use your hands to combine, being careful not to overmix. Divide into 4 parts, roll into balls, and create a large divot in the center of each. Divide the cheese evenly among the divots. Pull the meat over the cheese to seal the cheese inside, then press into roughly 4-inch patties. If you're forming these in advance, place them on a parchment-lined plate or quarter sheet pan, cover with plastic wrap, and refrigerate until ready to cook.

SEASON both sides of the patties with salt and pepper. Heat a cast-iron pan or grill over medium-high heat and lightly oil it. Grill the burgers to desired doneness, 4 to 5 minutes on each side for medium rare.

DRIZZLE the cut surfaces of the buns with oil and grill until golden brown, 1 to 2 minutes.

DRIZZLE mayo and ketchup (and more hot sauce, if desired) on each half of the buns and stack up the burgers with a pile of kimchi. Get the napkins ready.

FALAFEL TURKEY BURGERS

My love for the '90s knows no end (#TeamBackstreetBoys), but if that decade had one major screwup, it was turkey burgers, or more broadly, an aversion to fat. (SnackWell's? Really??) My mom was and still is a great cook, but I am scarred by all the dry-as-summertime-soil ground turkey versions of foods that should have been made with fattier meats. So scarred that when the *Girl Meets Farm* showrunner, Jenny, suggested that we make a turkey burger for a New Year's healthy episode, I almost gagged. The prospect of making a turkey burger taste good seemed impossible, based on everything that had been ingrained in me since childhood. Turkey burgers were meant to be terrible, I thought, like elevator music and beer at college parties, and we just ate them because other people were.

I don't know whose idea a falafel-spiced turkey burger was (Jenny, was it you??), but the mention of that combination coaxed me into the kitchen, because I've always felt like the flavor profile of a coriander-heavy falafel would look great on a piece of meat. When I got experimenting, I learned that giving turkey the meatball treatment—that is, mixing it in with a bunch of breadcrumbs and an egg—and loading it up with fresh herbs and toasty seeds, made it something worth obsessing over. This thing was Juicy Couture juicy and filled with enough flavor to retroactively make up for all the bad turkey burgers of my youth. What's more, I actually find it more manageable on a weeknight than falafel because it doesn't require soaking beans, pulling out the food processor, or frying.

MAKES 4 BURGERS

Patties

2 tablespoons (25 grams) extra virgin olive oil, plus more for cooking the patties

½ medium yellow onion, finely chopped

Kosher salt

2 large garlic cloves, finely chopped

1 tablespoon (5 grams) coriander seeds

2 teaspoons cumin seeds

½ teaspoon ground cinnamon

1 large egg

½ cup (30 grams) panko breadcrumbs

1 pound (454 grams) ground turkey, 93% lean

Freshly ground black pepper

Pinch of crushed red pepper

1 bunch (about 40 grams) cilantro, finely chopped

Sauce

½ cup (120 grams) plain Greek yogurt (whole milk, 2%, or nonfat)

2 tablespoons (28 grams) good-quality tahini (see page xxi)

1 garlic clove, finely chopped or grated with a fine zester

Zest and juice of half a lemon

2 tablespoons (3 grams) finely chopped mint

Kosher salt and freshly ground black pepper

Assembly

4 brioche buns, potato buns, or pitas

¼ medium red onion, thinly sliced

4 romaine leaves, torn in half

¼ cup (6 grams) torn mint leaves

Hot sauce, optional

TO make the patties, heat a large skillet over medium heat and add the oil. Add the onion and a pinch of salt and cook, stirring, until soft, 5 to 7 minutes. Add the garlic, coriander, cumin, and cinnamon and cook, stirring, until fragrant, another minute. Remove from the heat and let cool slightly.

MEANWHILE, in a large bowl, combine the egg and breadcrumbs. Add the turkey and spread it out to increase the surface area, which will help the seasoning distribute. Sprinkle evenly with ¾ teaspoon salt, a few turns of black pepper, the crushed red pepper, cilantro, and cooled onion mixture and use your hands to combine. Do not overmix; that could create a tough texture. Form into 4 balls, then flatten the balls into patties (make the patties bigger in diameter than you ultimately want them, since they'll shrink while cooking—about 4 inches is good). If you're forming these in advance, place them on a parchment-lined plate or quarter sheet pan, cover with plastic wrap, and refrigerate until ready to cook.

SEASON both sides of the patties with salt and pepper. Heat a large skillet over medium-high heat and add a thin layer of olive oil. Cook until the patties are browned and have an internal temperature of 165°F, about 5 minutes on each side.

TO make the sauce, in a small bowl, stir together the yogurt, tahini, garlic, lemon zest and juice until smooth and spreadable. Stir in the mint and season with salt and pepper to taste.

TO serve, toast the buns in the skillet used for the patties, adding a little more olive oil as needed, until they are lightly browned and crisp around the edges. Assemble each burger with a slathering of the sauce, a little pile of onion, a leaf of romaine, a couple of torn fresh mint leaves, and a few shakes of hot sauce, if desired.

SLOPPY JOE PITAS

Growing up I was extremely neutral about sloppy Joes, but I was inspired to revisit the concept after watching *It Takes Two* for the hundredth time, in which the rich Olsen twin takes her first bite of one at summer camp and loses her dang mind.

Like most things that will allow it, I gave it the shakshuka treatment. That is, I projected the flavors of my go-to shakshuka onto this format, and, well, a star was born. She will *not* answer to Slop-Shuka, and her artist rider consists of funky preserved lemon, salty feta, sour pickles, and the much less sloppy vessel of a thick, fluffy pita pocket.

SERVES 6 TO 8

2 tablespoons (25 grams) extra virgin olive oil

1 medium yellow onion, finely chopped

1 red bell pepper, finely chopped

1 jalapeño, seeded and finely chopped

Kosher salt

4 garlic cloves, finely chopped

1 tablespoon (6 grams) ground cumin

1 teaspoon smoked paprika

2 tablespoons (32 grams) harissa paste or (12 grams) dried harissa

2 tablespoons (30 grams) tomato paste

2 pounds (908 grams) ground turkey, 93% lean

One 14-ounce (396-gram) can crushed tomatoes

2 teaspoons packed light brown sugar

2 tablespoons (30 grams) red wine vinegar

1 tablespoon (16 grams) rinsed and finely chopped preserved lemon rind (or sub the zest and juice of half a lemon)

8 thick pita pockets
Homemade is ideal! Store-bought is okay—see Note.

Accessories

Sliced pickles

Crumbled feta

Chopped flat-leaf parsley

Lemon wedges, for serving

NOTE: *My go-to pita recipe can be found in* Molly on the Range *or on my website!*

HEAT a large pot over medium-high heat and add the olive oil. Add the onion, bell pepper, jalapeño, and a pinch of salt and cook, stirring, until soft, about 7 minutes. Add the garlic, cumin, and paprika and cook, stirring, until fragrant, another minute. Add the harissa and tomato paste and cook for another minute. Add the turkey and season with 1½ teaspoons kosher salt. Cook, breaking up with a wooden spoon or spatula, until browned all the way through. Stir in the tomatoes and brown sugar and simmer, covered, over medium-low heat for 20 minutes, stirring occasionally, to allow the flavors to meld. Stir in the vinegar and preserved lemon. Taste and adjust the seasoning as desired.

TO serve, stack the pitas, wrap in foil, and heat in a warm oven for a few minutes. Cut the tops off and fill with the turkey mixture. Top with pickles, feta, and parsley and serve with lemon wedges.

PICKLE DIP GRILLED CHEESE

This is the grandchild of my favorite drunk food in town, the fried cheesy pickles at the Toasted Frog. Those pickles are completely addictive, and not just because they have deep-fried cheese, but also because their combination of the Havarti, the pickle, and that dunk-in sriracha-spiked ranch is like a raging unsupervised party for my taste buds. A while ago I started making a dip that combines all of those flavors and then, in a pimiento-grilled-cheese-like move suggested by my brilliant friend Heather, it ended up between two slices of bread. It's so convenient because the cream cheese and ranch mean the center gets melty at lightning speed, and the pickles add that brininess that keeps you coming back for more.

MAKES 1 GRILLED CHEESE, EASILY MULTIPLIABLE

2 slices seedy or white bread

Pickle Dip (recipe follows)

Mayonnaise

HEAT a skillet over medium heat.

SPREAD one slice of bread with a thick layer of Pickle Dip and sandwich on the other slice of bread. Spread the outsides with a thin layer of mayo. Grill on each side for a few minutes until the bread is golden brown and the cheese is melty. Cut in half and enjoy!

PICKLE DIP

MAKES ENOUGH FOR 4 GRILLED CHEESES (ABOUT 1 ⅓ CUPS)

4 ounces (113 grams) cream cheese, softened

2 tablespoons (30 grams) ranch

2 teaspoons sriracha, or more if desired

1 cup (4 ounces/113 grams) shredded aged Havarti

¾ cup (100 grams) finely chopped kosher dill pickles, plus brine if desired

1 tablespoon (3 grams) chopped dill

IN a medium bowl, mash together all the ingredients except for the pickle brine. Taste, and if you'd like it saltier and more pickle-y, mix in a teaspoon or two of pickle brine. Use immediately or store in an airtight container in the fridge for up to 3 days.

NOTE: *To make it more of a party dip for veggies or crackers, add another ¼ to ½ cup (60 to 120 grams) of ranch to reach your desired dippable consistency.*

KALE GIARDINIERA MELTS

Kale has it good in this one: a thick mattress of sourdough, a duvet of Swiss, and . . . Somewhere here there is a giardiniera metaphor about spicing things up in kale's bedroom, but we're not going there! Giardiniera has this ability to effortlessly add life to anything that it touches, and kale is no exception. It delivers on the acidity that kale requires while also imparting some peppery heat and major Chicago flair. This simple little open-faced sandwich is light on the labor but big on the flavor.

MAKES 4 SANDWICHES

½ cup (112 grams) oil-packed giardiniera (I prefer mild because I'm a wimp), scooped out of the jar with a fork so that most of the excess oil drains off

2 garlic cloves, finely chopped

6 ounces (170 grams) chopped kale

Kosher salt

4 thick slices sourdough or other crusty bread

OPTIONAL PROTEINS: chopped salami, ham, other cooked meat, or white beans

Freshly ground black pepper

4 deli slices Swiss cheese *or mozzarella or cheddar!*

Hot sauce

Flaky salt, optional

PREHEAT the oven to 450°F.

HEAT a large skillet over medium heat. Add the giardiniera and garlic and cook for a minute or two, until fragrant. Add the kale, in batches if needed, and 2 pinches of salt and cook, tossing occasionally, until wilted, 5 to 7 minutes.

WHILE the kale cooks, arrange the bread on a sheet pan and stick it in the oven for a few minutes until it reaches your preferred toastiness.

FOLD any desired proteins into the kale mixture, then season with salt and pepper to taste.

PILE the kale onto the bread and top with cheese. Stick in the oven and cook until the cheese is melty, about 5 minutes. Top with hot sauce, black pepper, and a pinch of flaky salt, if desired, and buckle up.

WALLEYE TACOS

In the past few years, it's become one of my favorite springtime traditions to serve deep-fried walleye at the local Catholic school's fish fry. It's definitely a minor plot twist in my life as a Jew who until recently didn't really love fish other than lox on a bagel, but it's a blast! Nick and I glove up and stand in front of a mountain of golden crispy fish, visiting with the community and topping their plates with fillets before they flock off to find a seat in the bustling gymnasium. Every Friday during Lent, the line forms early and doesn't stop for hours; it's the most hoppin' place in town. By the end of the night, when our hand muscles are achy from using the tongs and our face muscles are sore from saying hello more times in one night than we have in the past six months, nothing, *nothing*, tastes better than that hot flaky fish, squeezed with lemon, *coverrrrrrred* in tartar sauce, and pounded into my mouth via a soft slice of bread in the car on the five-minute drive home. I've never considered converting to Catholicism, but I see why people do.

Here is all of that in taco form. (But sandwiched between two slices of white bread is a good move too.)

MAKES EIGHT 6-INCH TACOS

Sauce

¼ cup (52 grams) mayonnaise

½ cup (120 grams) plain Greek yogurt (whole milk, 2%, or nonfat)

1 tablespoon (15 grams) grainy mustard

2 teaspoons sweet pickle relish

1 tablespoon (3 grams) chopped dill, plus more for topping

Kosher salt and freshly ground black pepper

Slaw

½ teaspoon kosher salt

1 teaspoon sugar

Freshly ground black pepper

Juice of half a lemon

1 tablespoon (15 grams) apple cider vinegar

2 tablespoons (25 grams) neutral oil

One 10-ounce (283-gram) bag coleslaw mix

Walleye

½ cup (65 grams) all-purpose flour

Kosher salt and freshly ground black pepper

2 large eggs

1½ cups (90 grams) panko breadcrumbs

1 teaspoon sweet paprika

½ teaspoon onion powder

¼ teaspoon garlic powder

1½ pounds (680 grams) walleye fillets, skin removed, cut in half crosswise so they're not so long
Other flaky whitefish would work too!

Neutral oil, for cooking

Eight 6-inch flour tortillas

Lemon wedges

TO make the sauce, in a medium bowl, mix together the mayo, yogurt, mustard, relish, dill, and salt and pepper to taste. Set aside.

TO make the slaw, in a large bowl, whisk together the salt, sugar, a few turns of pepper, the lemon juice, vinegar, and oil. Add the coleslaw mix and fold to combine. Set aside.

TO make the walleye, set up a dredging station with 3 wide shallow bowls. In the first bowl, combine the flour, ¼ teaspoon kosher salt, and a few turns of pepper. In the second bowl, beat the eggs with 2 splashes of water. And in the third bowl, combine the panko, paprika, onion powder, garlic powder, ¼ teaspoon kosher salt, and a few turns of pepper. Coat each piece of walleye in the flour, then the egg, and then the panko mixture. Heat a large skillet over medium-high heat and add enough oil to generously coat the bottom. Heat the oil until a breadcrumb dropped into it sizzles. Working in batches so as not to crowd the pan, cook the walleye until the crust is golden and the fish is opaque all the way through, 3 to 5 minutes per side. Add more oil to the pan if it ever seems dry. Transfer the walleye to a wire rack or plate lined with a paper towel and season with another pinch of salt. Once all the walleye is cooked, slice it into strips.

TO assemble, warm the tortillas in a dry skillet and top each with a few walleye strips, a couple of dollops of sauce, a pile of slaw, and a sprinkle of fresh dill. Serve with lemon wedges and enjoy!

TURKEY, BRIE, AND CORNICHON SANDWICH

The five deli sandwiches that I dream about regularly are:

1. The Gobbler from the Millburn Deli in New Jersey
2. The Turkey and Brie from La Sandwicherie in Miami
3. The Leslie B with no sprouts from Loeb's Foodtown in Lenox, Massachusetts
4. The Vito from Jimmy John's
5. Salami and butter on white bread

Out of those five, the one I get most excited about re-creating at home is the Sandwicherie sandwich, because it's both totally unique and fully achievable. (1 and 3 are "you just kinda have to be there" sandwiches, 4 is available almost everywhere, and 5 is, well, I just gave you the recipe for it.) The Sandwicherie sandwich is a giant croissant (or baguette, but go for the croissant) filled with sane amounts of meat and cheese and basically a pile of salad, so it meets my requirements for perfect balance. The crisp crunchy veggies are punctuated with briny cornichons (Order extra! It's the pro move.) and rather than doubling down on the creaminess of the Brie with mayonnaise, the sandwich is brought together with a sharp mustard vinaigrette that is its sparkly pizzazz, its daily glow serum. Between my time spent at the South Beach Wine and Food Festival, auditioning for (and not making) the New World Symphony, and plotting my future as a retired Jewish grandma living in Boca Raton, I have eaten—and plan to eat—many turkey and Brie sandwiches from La Sandwicherie in my lifetime, and I will never tire of them. So when I'm not exploring future retirement communities, I re-create these sandwiches at home, which allows the option of warming them up and getting the Brie melty. Since it's a lot of toppings, I prep enough for a bunch of sandwiches at once to keep in the fridge so that we can have deliciousness at a moment's notice. When I'm feeling extra Miami, I inflate Bernie's kiddie pool so I can have a pool to sit by while I eat.

NOTE: *Since croissant and baguette (and appetite) sizes can vary, and since it's kinda annoying to measure a million toppings when you're just building a sandwich, and since this thing will be delicious no matter what, there are no real measurements for the toppings. Just keep in mind that because there are a lot of different toppings, you don't need too much of one thing, except the lettuce (do a big pile).*

MAKES 1 GREAT BIG SAMMY, EASILY MULTIPLIABLE

1 croissant or demi baguette

Thick slices of Brie

Sliced deli turkey
also great with prosciutto!

Thinly sliced tomato

Thinly sliced red or yellow onion

Thinly sliced green bell pepper

Shredded romaine lettuce

Sliced black olives or kalamata olives

Thinly sliced pickled peppers

Cornichons

Vinaigrette (recipe follows)

PREHEAT the oven to 350°F.

SLICE open the croissant or baguette and place it on a sheet pan. Top half with a layer of Brie and the other half with turkey. Stick it in the oven until the bread is toasty and the cheese is melty, about 5 minutes. Transfer to a serving plate and top with tomato, onion, bell pepper, a big pile of lettuce, olives, pickled peppers, cornichons, and more cornichons, and drizzle liberally with vinaigrette. Sandwich together and voilà!

VINAIGRETTE

MAKES ABOUT 1 CUP, ENOUGH FOR A GOOD FEW SANDWICHES

1 medium shallot, very finely chopped

3 tablespoons (45 grams) white wine vinegar

1 tablespoon (15 grams) Dijon mustard

½ cup (100 grams) extra virgin olive oil

Kosher salt and freshly ground black pepper

IN a large measuring cup, combine the shallot and vinegar and let it sit for a few minutes so the shallot can mellow out. Whisk in the mustard, then drizzle in the olive oil while whisking continuously so that it emulsifies. Season to taste with salt and pepper.

SWEET POTATO AND BLACK BEAN FREEZER BURRITOS

After stocking our four (4!) freezers with meals in anticipation of Bernie's arrival, these burritos were the first things to get eaten. They're packed with veggies, protein, all that good stuff, but they're also aggressively crave-able thanks to tortilla folds and a giant pile of salty queso fresco. I purposely call for only eight ounces of queso fresco here even though my grocery sells it in ten-ounce blocks so that we can all have a little left over to nosh on while we cook. (You're welcome!)

MAKES 8 BURRITOS

1 pound (454 grams) sweet potatoes, unpeeled and chopped into ½-inch cubes

3 tablespoons (38 grams) extra virgin olive oil, divided

Kosher salt

½ medium yellow onion, chopped

1 jalapeño, seeded and finely chopped

2 garlic cloves, finely chopped

1 tablespoon (15 grams) tomato paste

1 tablespoon (8 grams) chili powder

½ teaspoon dried oregano

One 15-ounce (425-gram) can black beans, drained and rinsed

One 14.5-ounce (410-gram) can chopped tomatoes

3 ounces (85 grams/2 cups) baby spinach

8 ounces (226 grams) queso fresco, crumbled

Handful of chopped cilantro

Freshly ground black pepper

Hot sauce

Juice of half a lime

Eight 10-inch whole wheat tortillas

PREHEAT the oven to 425°F.

TOSS the sweet potatoes in 1 tablespoon (13 grams) olive oil and spread them out on a parchment-lined rimmed sheet pan. Season with a couple of good pinches of salt and roast for 10 minutes. Give them a toss and continue roasting until browned on the outside; begin checking at 6 minutes. You'll want them to still have a bit of a bite because when you reheat the burritos, the potatoes will continue to cook. (If you want to eat the burritos now and not freeze them, roast for a few more minutes, until the potatoes are tender.)

HEAT a large skillet over medium-high heat and add the remaining 2 tablespoons (25 grams) olive oil. Add the onion, jalapeño, and a pinch of salt and cook, stirring occasionally, until soft, 5 to 7 minutes. Add the garlic, tomato paste, chili powder, and oregano and cook, stirring, until fragrant, another minute. Add the black beans, tomatoes, and spinach and simmer for about 7 to 10 minutes, stirring occasionally, until the spinach has wilted and most of the liquid has cooked off. Add the sweet potato, queso fresco, cilantro, a few turns of black pepper, a few shakes of hot sauce, and the lime juice. Taste and adjust as desired. Remove from the heat. Lay out a tortilla and mound about ¾ cup of filling in the center. Fold the bottom of the tortilla over the filling, fold in the wings, and roll it up to finish. Wrap with plastic wrap or foil, then repeat with the rest of the burritos. Freeze for up to 3 months.

TO reheat, remove the plastic wrap or foil and wrap in a paper towel or parchment. Microwave for 2½ to 3 minutes, flipping once, until heated through. Let cool slightly before eating. If you want to bring these to the next level, heat a thin layer of oil in a skillet and cook the (fully heated) burritos on each side until browned and crisp.

SNACKS + BREADS

COOKING WITH A TODDLER

Bernie's artistic medium of choice is egg wash on challah dough, and I take full responsibility for and pride in this. Since day two, I've had so much fun getting Bernie involved in the kitchen, sticking pieces of bread and herbs under her nose so she could familiarize herself with the great smells of the world and, over time, introducing more and more about food and its preparation. It's not just so that I can claim her as my sous chef before Nick tries to put her to work harvesting beets; it's also because she's usually way more interested in eating food that she helped prepare (as long as there's lots of bread and/or cheese involved). Each new milestone in her development has opened up ways for her to help out in the kitchen, and it's so messy but, barring any freak run-ins between the new bag of flour and the floor, so worth it. I can't handle the squishiness of her little hands reaching for spoonfuls of sugar and seeing her reaction to her first bites of steamed buns. It makes me completely verklempt. Here are a few things I've learned in my years of cooking with Bernie and her friends:

1. Make sure they're on your level. Bring ingredients down to their little tables or the floor, or consider investing in a toddler tower so they can stand at counter height.
2. Use tiny tools and utensils. Little cookie cutters, whisks, spatulas, spoons, and measuring spoons will fit more comfortably in their hands.
3. But mix stuff in big bowls to minimize splashing.

4. Pour sprinkles into a separate bowl in controlled quantities so that when they inevitably dump the whole bowl onto the cake you still have some left in the jar.

5. If you are neurotic about potentially harmful cooties like I am, consider using heat-treated flour and flax eggs or pasteurized eggs instead of raw flour (which can contain harmful bacteria) and regular eggs when making things like cookie dough that they'll be tempted to pop into their mouth. Heat-treated flour can be purchased online, or you can make your own by microwaving or baking it until it reaches 165°F.

6. Use a scale and weights instead of measuring cups, which are prone to being half filled or half dumped on the floor. It's way easier to make correct ingredient measurements this way.

7. Try some of Bernie's favorite tasks: putting muffin liners in muffin tins, spreading peanut butter on toast, brushing vegetables with olive oil and doughs with egg wash, washing potatoes in a big bowl of water, pouring premeasured ingredients, cutting soft things like bananas and avocados with an age-appropriate cutter, rolling out dough, scooping things from one bowl to another, decorating cakes, and, of course, taste-testing.

8. Mise en place and clean as you go! Start 'em young!

9. Don't make something that's going to be a gift for someone outside of your immediate family. Making little ones wash their hands every time they pick their nose is just too much energy.

10. Embrace the rustic aesthetic.

11. Buy a really pretty broom and dustpan set. When the nonpareils go all over the floor, you can actually look forward to using it!

I obviously feel way the heck better about Bernie taste-testing flax-seed-packed rugbrød one million times than I do about her taste-testing cookie dough. So welcome to the world of breads and snacks that we love eating, making, and hoarding in big batches as delicious defenses against hanger!

POTATO CHALLAH

As a member of the Jewish food blogging world, I take my job seriously in the unspoken race every holiday to think up the craziest, most outrageous variations on classic Jewish dishes. On Purim, it's about hamantaschen (should we make them savory this year?); Passover is about macaroons (but can they be deep-fried??); and babkas are a whole genre by themselves (Chanie Apfelbaum wins for salami babka). Toward the end of the summer, as Rosh Hashanah draws near, we dust off our challah-braiding hands and get to work, stuffing halva into the dough, dyeing the strands all the colors of the rainbow, covering the entire surface with sprinkles—you name it, the Jewish food bloggers have done it.

But the loaf that I return to again and again—all year round, not just at Rosh Hashanah—grew out of a way to use up our garden potatoes. Mashed potatoes, it turns out, take an already super-soft bread to mega fluffy cloud status. I was instantly obsessed, but found that the extra steps of peeling, boiling, and mashing potatoes took too much time and effort. My solution is the same as my lefse secret ingredient: potato flour! A scoopful of it in the dough yields the same fluff in half the amount of time, like magic. So while this challah might not look all that flashy, one bite of it is enough to be convincing. Sometimes I add a sprinkle of turmeric for a gorgeous color and notes that I find are reminiscent of rosemary. And beyond a braided loaf, I turn to this dough often as a go-to for sandwich bread, handheld pizzas, kuchen, pigs in blankets—the options are endless.

MAKES 2 MEDIUM BRAIDED LOAVES OR 1 PULLMAN SANDWICH LOAF

4 cups (520 grams) bread flour or all-purpose flour, plus more as needed

⅓ cup (60 grams) potato flour

2 tablespoons (25 grams) sugar

2¼ teaspoons (1 packet) instant yeast

1½ teaspoons kosher salt

1 teaspoon ground turmeric and a few cracks of black pepper, optional

1 cup (240 grams) warm water (105°F to 110°F)

2 large eggs

½ cup (100 grams) neutral oil, plus a little more for the bowl

For braided loaves only

1 egg, beaten with a splash of water, for egg wash

Flaky salt and/or various seeds for topping

IN a large bowl or the bowl of a stand mixer, whisk together the flours, sugar, yeast, salt, and turmeric and pepper, if using. In a medium bowl or large measuring cup, whisk together the water, eggs, and oil. Add the wet ingredients to the dry ingredients and use a stiff rubber spatula or wooden spoon to mostly combine into a shaggy dough. It may seem dry at first, but it will come together as you knead it. Knead, either on a work surface or with the stand mixer fitted with a dough hook on medium, adding more flour if the dough is too sticky to work with, until the dough is smooth and slightly sticky, 10 to 15 minutes.

STRETCH the dough into a ball, pinching the ends under to form a taut surface, and transfer to an oiled bowl (or simply oil the bowl you used to mix the dough if it isn't too covered in dough), turning to coat the dough fully in a thin layer of oil. Cover with plastic wrap or a towel and let rise in a draft-free place until doubled in size, 1 to 2 hours.

PREHEAT the oven to 375°F and line 2 sheet pans with parchment paper (for braided loaves) or grease a 4 x 13-inch pullman loaf pan with a cover and set aside.

IF braiding loaves, turn the dough out onto a clean surface and divide it in half. Divide each half into 3 equal pieces and roll each into a log that is tapered at the ends. Braid 3 logs together, pinching the ends so they adhere, and transfer the loaf to a prepared sheet pan. Repeat to make a second braided loaf. Cover loosely with plastic wrap or towels and let rise in a draft-free place until puffy and risen by half, 30 to 45 minutes.

IF making a pullman loaf, stretch the dough into a fat cylinder and place it in the pan. Grease the cover and slide it on. Let rise in a draft-free place until puffy and risen by half, 30 to 45 minutes.

BRUSH the braided loaves with a thin layer of egg wash and sprinkle with your toppings of choice (omit the egg wash and toppings on a pullman loaf). Bake until golden brown with an internal temperature of 190°F; begin checking for doneness at 18 minutes for braided loaves and 30 minutes for a pullman loaf. When baking braided loaves, switch racks and rotate 180 degrees about halfway through the baking time. Let cool slightly and tear into it because nothing is better than hot (buttered) challah.

LEFTOVERS, stored in an airtight container at room temperature, are best eaten within a couple of days and then after that make French toast. They can also be sliced and frozen in an airtight container for up to a few months. Reheat in a toaster or skillet.

CRISPY BOTTOM VEGGIE BUNS

Veggie buns and dumplings are all too often viewed as the sad underachieving siblings of their meaty superstar counterparts. And not without reason; I've had lifeless, blandly cabbagey vegetable fillings often enough that I assume they're typically only on a menu to keep vegetarians from feeling excluded. So when my sister helped me create this filling for *Girl Meets Farm*, I couldn't believe my taste buds. It was the best bun filling I'd ever had, period. It milks vegetables for all their flavor by roasting them first and reaches celebrity status from a combination of fresh basil and red Thai chile, creating a gold standard of vegetable fillings that makes up for years of boring buns. A quick crisp on the bottom of the buns post-steam fills the textural void that's left when you don't have something bulky and meaty in the filling, and optional peanuts or eggs tossed in lend a protein boost that makes accidentally eating too many and ruining your dinner a really clutch, nonregrettable move.

Dough

2 cups (260 grams) all-purpose flour, plus more for dusting

1 cup (128 grams) cake flour

6 tablespoons (75 grams) sugar

2¼ teaspoons (1 packet) instant yeast

¾ teaspoon kosher salt

1 cup (240 grams) warm water (105° to 110°F)

2 tablespoons (25 grams) neutral oil, plus more for the bowl and crisping the buns

Filling

1 small white onion, thinly sliced

8 ounces (226 grams) bok choy or baby bok choy, thinly sliced

4 scallions, thinly sliced

½ small red cabbage, cored and thinly sliced

1 red Thai chile (or Thai bird chile) pepper, thinly sliced

2 garlic cloves, finely chopped

1 tablespoon (9 grams) peeled and finely chopped fresh ginger (from about a 1-inch piece)

1 tablespoon (13 grams) neutral oil

Kosher salt and freshly ground black pepper

¼ cup (10 grams) Thai basil leaves, chopped or torn (regular basil is great too)

1 teaspoon toasted sesame oil

1 teaspoon soy sauce, plus more for serving

1 teaspoon unseasoned rice vinegar

OPTIONAL: ½ cup (72 grams) roasted salted peanuts (see page xviii), chopped, or 3 scrambled eggs, seasoned with salt and pepper and chopped

Black vinegar (or more unseasoned rice vinegar), for serving

IN a large bowl or the bowl of a stand mixer, whisk together the flours, sugar, yeast, and salt. Add the water and oil and use a stiff rubber spatula or wooden spoon to mostly combine into a shaggy dough. Knead, either on a work surface or with the stand mixer fitted with a dough hook on medium, adding more flour if the dough is too sticky to work with, until the dough is smooth and slightly sticky, 7 to 10 minutes. Stretch the dough into a ball, pinching the ends under to form a taut surface, and transfer to an oiled bowl (or simply oil the bowl you used to mix the dough if it isn't too covered in dough), turning to coat the dough fully in a thin layer of oil. Cover with plastic wrap or a towel and let rise in a draft-free place until doubled in size, 1 to 2 hours. While the dough is rising, prepare the filling.

PREHEAT the oven to 425°F. Spread the onion, bok choy, scallions, red cabbage, chile pepper, garlic, and ginger in an even layer on a parchment-lined rimmed sheet pan. Drizzle with the oil and season with a good pinch of salt and a few turns of pepper. Stick in the oven for 45 minutes, until cooked down and roasty. Transfer to a mixing bowl, add the basil, sesame oil, soy sauce, rice vinegar, and peanuts or eggs (if using), and toss to combine. Taste and adjust the seasoning as desired. Refrigerate until you are ready to form buns.

TO make the buns, cut sixteen 3-inch parchment squares. Turn the risen dough out onto a clean work surface and divide it into 16 balls. Keep the dough balls covered when you're not working with them. Working with 1 ball at a time, roll out to a 4- to 5-inch circle, making the outside edges a little thinner than the center, and dusting with flour if needed to prevent sticking. Spoon 2 heaping tablespoons of filling in the center of the dough circle. Stretch the dough up over the filling and pinch the edges shut firmly to seal well. Place the bun on a parchment square, pinched end up. Repeat to make the rest of the buns.

SET the buns (on their parchment squares) in a bamboo or metal steamer, 1½ to 2 inches apart. (If your steamer doesn't fit all the buns at once, keep the remaining buns covered on the counter or a sheet pan and steam in batches.) Cover and let sit 30 to 40 more minutes, until slightly risen and puffy. If any seams break open in their second rise, pinch them back together.

BRING a large pot of water to a boil over high heat (the water should come up high enough in the pot so that it is close to the steamer). Reduce the heat to medium high, place the steamer over the pot, and steam the buns until light and fluffy, about 20 minutes.

REMOVE the buns from the heat. Heat a large skillet over medium-high heat and add a thin layer of neutral oil. When the oil is hot, peel the parchment from the buns, add them to the pan, and cook until the bottoms are golden, just about a minute or two. Check them frequently, since they can burn easily, and cook in batches so as to not overcrowd the pan. Add more oil if the pan ever gets dry.

REMOVE the buns to a paper towel to soak up any excess oil and serve with a dipping sauce of 1 part black vinegar or rice vinegar and 1 part soy sauce.

LEFTOVER cooked and crisped (and fully cooled) buns can be frozen in an airtight container for up to 3 months and reheated in the microwave.

RUGBRØD

After our town bakery closed and good fresh rye bread became impossible to buy locally, I began this habit of bringing a gigantic half-empty suitcase with me on my work trips and stopping at bakeries on my way home in order to stock up on loaves, which I'd promptly slice and stick in our freezer. We'd enjoy them until my next trip. Somehow this was just easier to wrap my head around than trying to keep a sourdough starter alive and make my own. But when the pandemic hit and I had no access to these special out-of-town bakeries, I started to really miss that dense, seedy, *your-suitcase-is-overweight* Danish rye bread, or rugbrød. So here is a loaf that I started making that combines the wheat berries that Nick harvests, beer, and buttermilk for gorgeous dark depth. If you don't have a wheat farmer spouse, take a trip to your local bulk or health food section for these seeds. While this recipe does take time, it requires no starter or kneading. Also, the bang for your buck is truly worth it, since it tastes even better on the second and third days, and it's so filling that one loaf lasts for a while, even in my bread-obsessed household.

MAKES 1 LOAF

Pre-ferment

½ cup (120 grams) dark beer or ½ cup (120 grams) buttermilk

¼ cup (60 grams) buttermilk

1 cup (130 grams) rye flour, preferably stone-ground

¼ teaspoon active dry or instant yeast

Grains

½ cup (100 grams) cracked rye or wheat berries

or rye or wheat berries coarsely ground in a spice grinder or high-powered blender such as a Vitamix

⅓ cup (56 grams) flaxseeds

⅓ cup (46 grams) hulled, unsalted raw sunflower seeds

Bread

Softened butter, for the pan

3 tablespoons (54 grams) unsulphured molasses

1½ cups (195 grams) rye flour, preferably stone-ground

½ cup (65 grams) bread flour

2 teaspoons kosher salt

2 teaspoons unsweetened cocoa powder

¾ teaspoon active dry or instant yeast

Sunflower seeds, flaxseeds, and old-fashioned oats, optional, for topping

THE night before you want to bake the bread, make the pre-ferment: in a large bowl, stir together the beer, buttermilk, rye flour, and yeast to make a thick paste. Cover and let sit at room temperature overnight, until bubbly.

THE same night, combine the cracked rye or wheat berries, flaxseeds, and sunflower seeds in a medium bowl or lidded container. Add water to cover by 2 inches. Cover and let sit at room temperature overnight.

THE next day, butter a 4 x 9-inch pullman loaf pan or a 5 x 9-inch loaf pan and set aside. Drain the seeds well over a large measuring cup to reserve ½ cup (120 grams) of the soaking water (if you don't have enough for ½ cup, fill in with additional tap water). Put the seeds in the bowl with the pre-ferment. Add the molasses and soaking water and stir to combine. Add the rye flour, bread flour, salt, cocoa, and yeast and stir to make a thick, sticky batter.

TRANSFER the batter to the prepared loaf pan and spread in an even layer. Cover and let sit until risen by about a third, about 2 hours (if using a 5 x 9-inch pan, cover with greased plastic to avoid sticking since the dough will come close to the top).

PREHEAT the oven to 450°F. Brush the top of the loaf lightly with water (to help the seeds stick). Sprinkle the top with the sunflower and flaxseeds and oats, if using. Bake for 10 minutes, then reduce the oven temperature to 350°F. Bake until a tester inserted in the middle of the bread comes out clean and the internal temperature is 210°F; begin checking for doneness at 1 hour 40 minutes but be prepared to bake for up to 20 or 30 minutes more because those last few degrees can really make you wait for 'em. Cover loosely with foil if the top ever appears to be getting too dark for your liking. Toss a kitchen towel over the pan and cool on a rack for 30 minutes, then unmold and cool *completely*. I know it's always tempting to slice into warm bread, but in this case, it's really important to let it cool completely. Otherwise it'll be weirdly gooey and hard to slice.

THIS bread is delicious the day it is made but even better the next day. Store in a bread box or paper bag at room temperature for up to a few days or in an airtight container (sliced or unsliced) in the freezer for up to a few months. Thaw at room temperature or reheat individual slices in a toaster or skillet.

WEEKNIGHT LEFSE

Lefse is a thin Norwegian pancake that looks like a tortilla but is much more tender due to a large amount of riced potato in the dough. It's traditionally rolled up with butter and sugar (and maybe cinnamon) and served on holiday tables all over this region. Making it is a multiday process that requires a long stick (preferably one that you got on your wedding day or that has been in your family for generations), a special griddle, and either a large group of helpers in a church basement or your therapist on speed dial. Because making it is almost as difficult as what I imagine homesteading this region was when there was no central heating or broad-spectrum sunscreen.

In my experience, lefse is the type of thing you make once a holiday season in a big batch so that you can keep a stack in your freezer, right next to the rhubarb, for the coming months. But what do you do if you've used up your stash and offended all the church ladies because they found out you tried to make sweet potato lefse?

Here's a solution that requires no special tools and no advance prep—just the secret ingredient of potato flour. It's easy enough to make on a weeknight for tacos or wraps or even a snack. What it lacks in tidiness (you'll use kind of a lot of flour on the counter) it makes up for in time, because this dough does not require kneading, resting, or even that much energy to roll.

I have no business telling you to replace your family's lefse recipe with this one, but I can tell you that you no longer need to stress out about hoarding your special freezer stash, because if you run out, you can make these in a pinch.

MAKES EIGHT 6-INCH LEFSE

¾ cup (98 grams) all-purpose flour, plus a lot more for dusting

¼ cup (45 grams) potato flour

½ teaspoon kosher salt

2 teaspoons sugar

¼ cup (56 grams) unsalted butter

¾ cup (180 grams) whole milk

SERVING SUGGESTIONS: rolled up with butter and cinnamon sugar, rolled up with ham and mustard, rolled around a hot dog, in breakfast tacos (page 56), or to replace tortillas in walleye tacos (page 225)!

IN a medium bowl, whisk together the flours, salt, and sugar.

IN a microwaveable bowl or saucepan, combine the butter and milk and heat gently, in 30-second increments in the microwave or on the stove over

medium-low heat, until the butter is just melted, stirring occasionally. Don't let the milk boil.

ADD the butter and milk to the dry ingredients and fold together with a rubber spatula. Continue folding a few more times until combined and thickened into a sticky dough. Flour a work surface and scrape the dough onto the surface. Form it into a log, dusting with flour if needed, and cut into 8 equal pieces.

ON a floured surface, with a floured rolling pin, gently roll out each piece of dough into a thin round, about 6 inches in diameter. Flip and rotate the rounds as you roll to ensure that they aren't sticking to the counter and, if they are (or if they're sticking to your rolling pin), dust with more flour. This is a delicate process, but don't be afraid to use as much flour as necessary to help you through it. If your rounds are consistently tearing no matter how gently you handle them, knead in a little more flour. (The answer to any of your lefse problems is most likely flour.)

HEAT a large skillet over medium-high heat. Cook the lefse in the dry skillet for a minute or two on each side, until splotchy with brown marks. Transfer to a plate, stacking the lefse on top of one another, and keep them covered with a towel until ready to serve.

I like these best the day they're made, but leftovers can be stored in an airtight container in the fridge for up to a few days or in the freezer for up to a few months. Thaw at room temperature and/or reheat in the microwave before serving.

ZINGY NAVY BEAN DIP

In our first few years here, Nick was farming navy beans and soybeans in addition to sugar beets and wheat. Contrary to what would have been awesome, he did not ride around on his tractor whistling, *Beans, beans, the musical fruit. The more you eat, the more you toot.* I had never knowingly tried a navy bean before moving here, but when I started experimenting with them, I was pleasantly surprised at their creaminess. This simple dip is as bright as the nine p.m. summer sun (stunningly bright) and quick to whiz up with staple ingredients. It's great piled onto toast or pizza (see the Pan-Fried Garden Pizza on page 128) or nestled into a snack board.

MAKES 1 HEAPING CUP

2 large garlic cloves, peeled and smashed

Juice of half a lemon

One 15-ounce (425-gram) can navy beans, drained and rinsed

6 tablespoons (75 grams) extra virgin olive oil

¼ teaspoon smoked paprika

Kosher salt and freshly ground black pepper

IN a small bowl, cover the garlic with the lemon juice and let sit for 5 minutes to mellow.

IN a food processor, combine the beans, olive oil, smoked paprika, a big pinch of salt, a bunch of turns of pepper, and the garlic and lemon juice and blend until very smooth, a full 2 to 3 minutes.

TASTE and adjust the seasoning as desired.

STORE leftovers with a thin layer of olive oil on top so it doesn't dry out and keep in an airtight container in the fridge for up to 3 days.

CHEESE-AND-OLIVE-STUFFED PITA

Bosco Sticks (heroes of the school cafeteria, essentially breadsticks stuffed with cheese and dunked in marinara sauce) balanced out by a green Naked Juice were my lunch almost every day in high school for a while, enjoyed in the secret dining space, the marching band locker room, which was exactly as dorky as it sounds. Just like me, Bosco Sticks will always lose the popularity contest to deep-fried mozzarella sticks, but the very soft, texturally homogenous nature of the breadstick coating on a Bosco Stick understood me on a much deeper level than a crunchy mozzarella stick coating. I love eating them both, but I definitely see more of myself in a Bosco Stick.

Now that I'm an adult, I make Bosco Sticks from scratch in the form of stuffed pita, because I make pita on a regular basis to keep in the freezer and also because "stuffed pita" sounds better than "Bosco Stick bun knockoff thing." I also find myself inhaling olives to make up the time I lost as an olive hater in my youth, so I throw them in too. The result is a melty, bready ball of wonder made only better with a dip into matbucha (page 251) as a nod to the classic marinara.

MAKES 12 PITAS

Pita

3¾ cups (488 grams) bread flour, plus more for dusting (all-purpose is OK too)

2¼ teaspoons (1 packet) instant yeast

1½ tablespoons (19 grams) sugar

1½ teaspoons kosher salt

1½ cups (360 grams) warm water (105° to 110°F)

3 tablespoons (38 grams) extra virgin olive oil, plus a little more for the bowl

Filling

9 deli slices mozzarella (6 ounces/170 grams), cut or torn into quarters

¾ cup (144 grams) finely chopped kalamata olives

Marinara sauce or Matbucha (page 251), for serving

Optional garlic oil topping

1 tablespoon (14 grams) unsalted butter

2 tablespoons (25 grams) extra virgin olive oil

2 garlic cloves, finely chopped

Pinch of crushed red pepper

2 tablespoons (15 grams) grated Parmesan

Handful of flat-leaf parsley, finely chopped

IN a large bowl or the bowl of a stand mixer, whisk together the flour, yeast, sugar, and salt. Add the water and oil and use a stiff rubber spatula or wooden spoon to mostly combine into a shaggy dough. Knead, either on a work surface or with the stand mixer fitted with a dough hook on medium, adding more flour if the dough is too sticky to work with, until the dough is smooth and slightly sticky, 7 to 10 minutes. Stretch the dough into a ball, pinching the ends under to form a taut surface, and transfer to an oiled bowl (or simply oil the bowl you used to mix the dough if it isn't too covered in dough), turning to coat the dough fully in a thin layer of oil. Cover with plastic wrap or a towel and let rise in a draft-free place until doubled in size, 1 to 2 hours.

ARRANGE oven racks in the upper middle and lower middle positions and preheat the oven to 500°F. Line 2 rimmed sheet pans with parchment paper and set aside.

TURN the dough onto a clean work surface and divide it into 12 equal balls. Place them 1 inch apart on the sheet pans, cover them loosely with plastic wrap or a towel, and let rise for 30 minutes.

ROLL each ball of dough into about a 5-inch circle and top with 3 quarters of a slice of cheese and 1 tablespoon (12 grams) chopped olives. Gather the edges of the dough and pinch them to seal, then gently flatten the dough with your palm into 3- to 4-inch circles. Place seam side down on the sheet pans and bake until puffy and lightly browned in spots; begin checking for doneness at 5 minutes. The pan on the lower rack may need a little longer; feel free to move it to the upper rack once the top pan comes out. Let cool slightly and serve with marinara or matbucha for dunking.

IF you're planning to make the garlic oil topping, heat the butter and oil in a small saucepan over medium-low heat. Add the garlic and crushed red pepper and simmer lightly, swirling occasionally, for 2 minutes. Brush over the warm pitas and top with the Parmesan and parsley.

STORE leftovers in an airtight container in the freezer for up to a few months. To reheat, microwave for 45 to 60 seconds, then crisp up the exterior in a toaster oven or hot skillet. Or you can wrap in foil and stick in a 350°F oven until heated through; begin checking at 25 minutes.

Cheese-and-Olive-
Stuffed Pita

Zingy Navy
Bean Dip

Matbucha

MATBUCHA

In my most disheveled state, emerging from a week of hotdish and doughnut testing and not showering only to realize that all the vegetables in the fridge have gone bad and my hair hurts from being in the same bun for three days, here is what I like to make. Matbucha is a dish with Maghrebi origins whose name translates to "cooked salad" in Arabic. It consists of tomatoes and peppers, cooked down with loads of garlic and some heat until the tomatoes and peppers get dreamy and sweet. I fell in love with it in my travels to Israel, where it is extremely popular, and these days no matter how bare the fridge is, I always have canned tomatoes and jarred roasted red peppers to crank out this any-season version. (In the summer when your garden is overflowing with tomatoes, you should 10,000 percent use those!) The key here is simply to give it enough time for the flavors to really develop and sweeten, so don't try to rush it.

Matbucha is my go-to dipping sauce whenever I make Cheese-and-Olive-Stuffed Pita (page 248); I also love it on toast with a plop of yogurt or sprinkle of feta, or on a great big snack board for dinner with pickles, bean dip, hard-boiled eggs, cheese, and bread.

MAKES 3 CUPS

2 tablespoons (25 grams) extra virgin olive oil

2 large garlic cloves, finely chopped

1 tablespoon (6 grams) sweet paprika

One 16-ounce (462-gram) jar or 2 large roasted red peppers, coarsely chopped

One 28-ounce (794-gram) can chopped tomatoes, or 2 pounds (908 grams, about 3 large) fresh tomatoes, peeled, seeded, and chopped

1 teaspoon sugar

Kosher salt and freshly ground black pepper

HEAT a large nonreactive pot over medium heat and add the oil. Add the garlic and paprika and cook, stirring, until fragrant, 1 to 2 minutes. Add the red peppers, tomatoes, sugar, 2 good pinches of salt, and a bunch of turns of pepper and bring to a simmer. Simmer, uncovered, for 35 to 45 minutes, until thickened and dreamily sweet, stirring occasionally and reducing the heat if it gets too spitty and violent. Taste and adjust the seasoning as desired. Enjoy hot or at room temperature. Store leftovers in an airtight container in the fridge for up to 3 days.

BUTTERMILK LAFFA

If freshly made pita is the ideal sleeping bag of breads, then laffa is the comforter. Laffa is a flatbread of Iraqi origin that is like a bigger, flatter pita. Its size and floppiness make it perfect for wrapping around falafel or meats (see Pickle Chicken with Toum on page 190!) or swiping up hummus and other dips. It's best when baked right on a pizza stone, making it a low-risk way to practice using a pizza peel, because there are no toppings.

Buttermilk in the dough lends a hint of sourness and makes for a slightly more tender texture, but if you're all out or prefer to keep it dairy-free, you can sub in the same amount of water.

MAKES 6 LAFFA

3¾ cups (488 grams) bread flour, plus more for dusting

2¼ teaspoons (1 packet) instant yeast

1½ tablespoons (19 grams) sugar

1½ teaspoons kosher salt

¾ cup (180 grams) warm water (105° to 110°F)

¾ cup (180 grams) buttermilk *or plain Greek yogurt*

3 tablespoons (38 grams) extra virgin olive oil, plus a little more for the bowl

IN a large bowl or the bowl of a stand mixer, whisk together the flour, yeast, sugar, and salt. Add the water, buttermilk, and oil and use a stiff rubber spatula or wooden spoon to mostly combine into a shaggy dough. Knead, either on a work surface or with the stand mixer fitted with a dough hook on medium, adding more flour if the dough is too sticky to work with, until the dough is smooth and slightly sticky, 7 to 10 minutes. Stretch the dough into a ball, pinching the ends under to form a taut surface, and transfer to an oiled bowl (or simply oil the bowl you used to mix the dough and use that if it isn't too covered in dough), turning to coat the dough fully in a thin layer of oil. Cover with plastic wrap or a towel and let rise in a draft-free place until doubled in size, 1 to 2 hours.

PREHEAT the oven to 500°F with a pizza stone inside if you have one (or a rimless baking sheet if you don't).

TURN the dough onto a clean work surface and divide it into 6 equal pieces. Mold each piece into a ball by stretching the top and tucking the edges under. Place the balls 1 inch apart on your counter or a large parchment-lined sheet pan, cover them loosely with plastic wrap or a towel, and let rise for 30 minutes.

WITH a rolling pin on a floured surface, roll out the balls of dough into 8- to 10-inch circles, dusting with more flour as needed. Bake one at a time: slide onto the pizza stone and bake until puffy and lightly browned on the bottom; start checking at 2 to 3 minutes. (If they're not puffing up, fear not; they'll still be good. But also try cranking the heat higher on your oven and waiting a few minutes before cooking the next laffa to let the oven heat back up again after losing heat from the last time you opened the door.) Stack the finished laffa on top of one another and cover with a towel so they steam slightly and get all soft.

STORE leftovers in an airtight container at room temperature for up to a few days or in the freezer for up to a few months. Thaw at room temperature and/or reheat in the microwave or a skillet.

SMOKY SQUASH HUMMUS

Since my first trip to Israel about ten years ago, I have been snobbier about my hummus than anything else in my life—turning my nose up at any hummus that isn't made with freshly cooked chickpeas and very good tahini, feeling sorry for any party spread that has dry carrots and celery with a tiny cold cup of store-bought, and using a bunch of barf emojis at any mention of a "cake batter hummus" (OMG what on earth?!). Freshly made hummus, still warm from cooking the chickpeas, is a beautiful centerpiece of a meal that's worth the hours of preparation involved and needs no flavoring beyond lemon juice, garlic, and maybe some cumin.

But I have one exception, and it's holding me back from fully campaigning for chairwoman of the hummus snob society: *squash hummus*. It's one of my favorite recipes I've ever made on *Girl Meets Farm*. A roasted squash chucked into the food processor (with canned chickpeas (!!)) adds sweetness and a hidden serving of vegetables, but honestly what really does it for me is the chipotle chile the squash brings as its plus-one. The smoky, spicy notes at the front and center are balanced by the nutty tahini, sweet squash, and hit of lemon, which come together for a performance that is—and I don't use this term lightly—game changing. My favorite way to eat this is by turning it into a meal with a tangle of salad on top and some crusty bread or fresh pita.

(And for anyone who is here for a follow-up to the hummus story in *Molly on the Range*, the update is that Nick has still never farted in front of me.)

MAKES ABOUT 2 CUPS

½ small (1½- to 2-pound/680- to 908-gram) butternut squash, seeds removed

¼ cup (50 grams) extra virgin olive oil, plus more for brushing

Kosher salt

One 15-ounce (425-gram) can chickpeas, drained and rinsed

¼ cup (56 grams) good-quality tahini (see page xxi)

Juice of half a lemon

1 to 2 tablespoons (20 to 40 grams) canned chipotle chile in adobo and juice, depending on how spicy you'd like it

Pita or crusty bread, for serving

PREHEAT the oven to 400°F.

BRUSH the squash with a thin layer of olive oil and season with ¼ teaspoon salt. Place on a parchment-lined sheet pan, cut side down. Roast until tender when pierced with a fork; begin checking at 30 minutes. Set aside until cool enough to handle.

SCOOP the flesh of the squash into a food processor, discarding the skin. Add the chickpeas, tahini, lemon juice, chipotle, and ¾ teaspoon salt. Process until mostly smooth. With the machine running, drizzle in the olive oil and process until very smooth and creamy, about 1 minute. Taste and blend in more salt and/or chipotle, if desired. Serve with pita or crusty bread and enjoy!

TO serve with a little salad on top (my favorite way to turn this into a meal), spread a thick layer at the bottom of a shallow bowl and top with a handful of mixed greens, olives or cornichons or both, sliced tomatoes, a sprinkle of crumbled feta, a drizzle of olive oil, and a pinch of flaky salt.

STORE leftovers with a thin layer of olive oil on top so it doesn't dry out and keep in an airtight container in the fridge for up to 3 days.

BAKED EGG ROLLS

About once a year, my friend Nile hosts an egg roll night at her house, during which our friends Heather and Mollie and I sit and eat the best egg rolls of our lives, paired with crispy pork and white rice, as we catch up on what I take pleasure in calling "town gossip." I am completely powerless against these egg rolls, and when Nile wraps up leftovers for me to bring home to Nick, I promptly hide them in the back of our fridge so that I can eat them for breakfast the next morning. (Sorry, Nick.)

When I finally begged Nile for her recipe, I was delighted by how few ingredients it required and learned that the magic was loads of garlic and a heavy shot of apple cider vinegar. The vinegar adds that punch that puts you in the position where you actually have to announce out loud that *this is your last bite, you promise* in order to finally quit eating them.

Since inviting myself over to Nile's for a weekly egg roll feast would be weird for both our friendship and my waistline, I fiddled with a baked version that, unlike other baked versions of fried things, is definitely not a ghost of its true fried self. Texturally it is different, but it has some legitimate legs and can stand on its own. This egg roll takes a cue from flautas and uses flour tortillas brushed with a little oil for the wrapper, and the result is crispy in some places, chewy in other places, and straight-up glorious all around.

These are awesome to keep in the freezer to heat up for easy peasy noshes. So go ahead and make a double batch.

MAKES 12 ROLLS

1 tablespoon (13 grams) neutral oil, plus more for brushing

1 small yellow onion, finely chopped

1 large celery stalk, finely chopped

Pinch of kosher salt

4 garlic cloves, finely chopped

1 pound (454 grams) ground beef, 85% lean

One 10-ounce (283-gram) bag coleslaw mix

2 tablespoons (30 grams) soy sauce, plus more for serving

1 tablespoon apple cider vinegar

Freshly ground black pepper

Twelve 6-inch flour tortillas

Rice vinegar, for serving

PREHEAT the oven to 425°F. Line a rimmed sheet pan with parchment paper and set aside.

HEAT a large skillet over medium heat and add the oil. Add the onion, celery, and salt and cook, stirring occasionally, until soft, 5 to 7 minutes. Add the garlic and cook, stirring, for another minute. Add the beef and cook, breaking up with a spoon, until browned. Turn off the heat and stir in the coleslaw mix, stirring for a minute or two so that the cabbage wilts slightly. Add the soy sauce, apple cider vinegar, and loads of black pepper and mix to combine.

SCOOP ½ cup of the mixture in a line across the equator of a tortilla, roll it up, and place it seam side down on the prepared sheet pan. Repeat with the remaining tortillas and filling, spacing them out evenly on the sheet pan. Brush the tops with a thin layer of oil and bake until lightly golden; begin checking for doneness at 14 minutes. Let cool slightly and cut in half.

SERVE with a dipping sauce of 1 part rice vinegar and 1 part soy sauce.

TO FREEZE: When the rolls come out of the oven, let them cool completely, then freeze in an airtight container for up to 3 months. Reheat in the microwave for a minute or two or in the oven at 350°F until hot; begin checking at 15 minutes.

SPICY RANCH SNACK MIX

Nick's vice is oyster crackers. Not beer or sports or the occasional bong hit, just the boringest cracker ever to be invented. I don't want to hypothesize that it stems from his textbook Calvinistic aversion to any kind of self-indulgence out of fear of offending a whole people, but I also don't want to *not* hypothesize it because I'm pretty positive I'm right (and also he told me I could say that). In his defense, the fact that oyster crackers are boring doesn't mean that they don't taste good. I, too, love an overflowing handful of the crunchy, floury things. But when I'm in need of a flavor-blasted moment, I take inspiration from a popular move around here: dumping a packet of Hidden Valley ranch seasoning all over a bag of crackers. This is a homemade version woken up with sriracha and a rotating selection of other crunchy snacks.

.

3 tablespoons (30 grams) buttermilk powder

2 teaspoons dried parsley

2 teaspoons dried chives

1 teaspoon dried dill

1 teaspoon dry mustard

½ teaspoon cayenne

½ teaspoon garlic powder

½ teaspoon onion powder

6 tablespoons (84 grams) unsalted butter, melted

1 tablespoon (15 grams) sriracha

5 cups (one 9-ounce/255-gram bag) oyster crackers

5 cups of a mix of other crunchy snacks (our favorites: pretzel snaps, cheddar bunnies, almonds, sriracha peas, or just another bag of oyster crackers)

6 tablespoons (45 grams) grated Parmesan

PREHEAT the oven to 250°F. Line a rimmed sheet pan with parchment paper and set aside.

IN a small bowl, stir together the buttermilk powder, parsley, chives, dill, mustard, cayenne, garlic powder, and onion powder.

IN a large bowl, combine the butter and sriracha. Add the oyster crackers and other snacks and toss to coat thoroughly. Sprinkle on the seasoning mix and Parmesan and toss to combine. Spread on the prepared sheet pan and bake, tossing once or twice, until everything is dry and toasted; begin checking for doneness at 25 minutes. Let cool on the sheet pan.

STORE in an airtight container at room temperature for up to a few weeks.

SWEETS

THE SWEETEST THING I EVER BAKED

The day I first started feeling pregnant with Bernie was a Sunday in the summer. Sundays in the summer used to be prime baking times because the summer is Nick's busy farming season. So whenever he'd work on a Sunday, I'd bake purely for relaxation (no work-related recipe testing allowed), spending hours getting my frosting color palette just right, piping buttercream roses all afternoon, thinking for minutes before placing individual gold dragées with tweezers, and even sometimes getting so absorbed that I'd forget to eat (?!) until my tweezer hands got shaky. I felt like a sculptor, building physical creations that satisfied me on a spiritual level. This particular Sunday, though, I was so tired that I had only enough energy to sit on the couch and watch *BoJack Horseman* over and over. Cake and sprinkles would have to wait; this was some next-level exhaustion. A few days later we learned that, oh, a tiny baby poppy-seed-size Bernie was sprouting! And that was the beginning of our Elmo-filled lives.

A few weeks later I got my energy back, as well as my ability to stomach food beyond white bread and matzo and other bland things. That's when I learned that everything tastes better when you're pregnant. Especially Korean barbecue, and pineapple, and Sonic tots, and my friend Nile's sour cream pasta, which is basically just sour cream mixed with pasta and Parmesan, and grocery store chocolate doughnuts, and huge hotel brunch buffets with stacks of macadamia nut pancakes. Man, I really came to understand where all those pregnant stereotypes come from. And filming a food show, it turns out, is a pregnant person's *dream*.

I remember during the really, really pregnant season (season 3), there was this breakfast sandwich episode that consisted of homemade potato

bagels and cheesy baked eggs. It was kind of an involved recipe because they required a bunch of steps to make and we also wanted to show how to freeze and reheat them. So between all the swap outs and beauty bagels, there were what felt like *hundreds* of breakfast sandwiches lying around. Everywhere I looked there was another breakfast sandwich for me to eat, and I didn't care if it was still frozen in some parts or accidentally microwaved for too long, it went into my mouth. They should really change "kid in a candy store" to "pregnant lady on a food TV show set."

As a whole, my pregnancy was thankfully uneventful. I ate a lot of matzo, a lot of bagels, and a lot of tots from Sonic, and dreamt every night about big fat Italian subs. Two days before my due date, I spent my day testing Thanksgiving recipes for *Girl Meets Farm*, tying up all the loose ends I could. It felt kind of silly to be testing Thanksgiving recipes in March, but when you combine maternity leave with pre- and postproduction time and count backward from November, it all makes sense. I had just made a batch of sweet corn cupcakes with cranberry sauce in their bellies, and they were some of my favorite cakes that I'd ever made (a variation on the Official Family Cake on page 308). So soft and moist, and good enough to forget that everything about them was out of season. I covered the leftovers and put them on the counter thinking how nice it would be if I went into labor within a day or two so that these cupcakes could still be moist enough to gift to the labor and delivery nurses.

Bernie must have understood the urgency to give those cupcakes away while they were still fresh, because sure enough, my water broke that night and it was time to go to the hospital. But not before I could fold up a pink bakery box and pack up those cupcakes! This absolutely horrified Nick, because he was worried that the more time I wasted, the higher the chances were that he'd have to deliver a baby by the side of the road. Luckily for everyone, we got to the hospital safe and sound with the cupcakes, just in time for a super-chill twenty-five hours of labor.

Shortly after midnight on her due date, Bernie came strolling out, all hairy and cuddly, sticking her tongue out just like this emoji ☺, and I knew instantly we'd get along.

Baking days go a little differently now. They're either crammed into nap time or done with the assistance of you-know-who standing in her toddler tower. Food coloring is chosen swiftly before the bottles walk off into the living room, sprinkles are applied by the small sticky handful, and I suddenly understand why my mom felt the need to shellac and frame the gross piece of matzo that I bit into the shape of a heart when I was twelve. It's all so beautiful!!! I cherish everything that Bernie helps me make more than any cake I ever made pre-Bernie, and I take approximately five thousand photos of it before allowing anyone to dig in. I never imagined that baking could possibly take on more meaning in my life, especially when buttercream roses weren't involved, but somehow it has, and it's a lot more delicious because of it.

This chapter contains casual sweets that are generally low-maintenance to both make and keep around. Most are convenient to whip up no matter what (or who) you're juggling, and everything here does pretty well in a cookie jar or the fridge or the freezer for at least a good few days, so you don't have to worry about feeling like you need to throw a party or share it before it loses its freshness. These recipes come together straightforwardly, use one bowl whenever possible, and don't require too many steps. They're meant to satisfy your daily sweet tooth, simple as that.

TAHINI MONSTER COOKIES

Don't tell Bernie, but my favorite monster isn't Elmo; it's this cookie. Is it because this cookie doesn't have a theme song that keeps me up at four a.m. when I can't get it out of my head? Off the record, *yeah*. On the record, it's because this cookie is chewy and achieves flavor for days without having to soften butter or chill dough. It's a take on the classic monster cookie, which hails from Michigan and traditionally contains oats (no flour!) and peanut butter, which I obviously subbed with tahini because . . . do you know me?? Since tahini pairs so nicely with coconut and pistachios, I threw those in as well to make a monster variation that would be kind of like Elmo's Middle Eastern pen pal. I wouldn't be mad if you also added chopped halva. And you can easily make these vegan by swapping the eggs for flax eggs.

MAKES ABOUT 15 LARGE COOKIES

½ cup (100 grams) unrefined coconut oil, melted but not hot

¾ cup (168 grams) good-quality tahini (see page xxi), room temperature

¾ teaspoon kosher salt

1 teaspoon ground cinnamon

2 teaspoons pure vanilla extract

⅔ cup (132 grams) packed light brown sugar

⅓ cup (67 grams) granulated sugar

2 large eggs

½ cup (45 grams) shredded sweetened coconut

¾ cup (96 grams) roasted salted pistachios (see page xviii), whole or chopped

1 cup (180 grams) candy-coated chocolates (M&M's or similar), plus more for topping

3½ cups (315 grams) quick-cooking oats

1 teaspoon baking soda

Flaky salt, optional

ARRANGE oven racks in the upper middle and lower middle positions and preheat the oven to 350°F. Line 2 sheet pans with parchment paper and set aside.

IN a large bowl, whisk together the coconut oil, tahini, salt, cinnamon, vanilla, and sugars until combined and creamy. Add the eggs one at a time, whisking well after each addition. Switch to a rubber spatula and fold in the coconut, pistachios, and candy-coated chocolates. Sprinkle the oats, and then the baking soda over the top of the batter, dispersing them as evenly as possible. Mix to combine.

SCOOP ¼-cup balls of dough (about the size of a plum) onto the prepared sheet pans, 2 inches apart. Press a few additional candy-coated chocolates into the tops and sprinkle each with a pinch of flaky salt, if desired.

BAKE for 8 minutes, switch the racks and rotate the pans 180 degrees, and bake until lightly browned and just set in the center; begin checking at 7 minutes.

THESE have a tendency to spread into uneven blob shapes in the oven, so I like to shape them back into circles as soon as they come out of the oven by inverting a small bowl on top of the cookies and gently swirling the bowl around to curve the edges back into alignment. Let cool on the pan completely (well, eat one or two while they're still warm, but then let the rest cool on the pan).

STORE in a cookie jar or airtight container at room temperature for up to a week, or even longer if you haven't eaten them all by then.

MARZIPAN CHOCOLATE CHIP COOKIES

Do you ever feel like your brain is going to melt out of your head and into a puddle on the floor and then you're like, "How am I going to clean this up?" and then you're like, "Oh, I should get a dog"? (And then you're like, "Ew, gross, just kidding and sorry, to this imaginary dog.") That is what I went through to bring you this CCC. I don't take it lightly that if you Google "chocolate chip cookie recipe" 122 *million* results come up. Between Levain's and Birdbath's and Jacques's and this uh-mazing local Minnesota cookie company called T-Rex, there's seriously no reason to put another chocolate chip cookie recipe into the world. Unless . . . there's marzipan.

MAKES ABOUT 12 LARGE COOKIES

½ cup (113 grams) unsalted butter, melted but not hot

¾ cup (150 grams) packed light brown sugar

¼ cup (50 grams) granulated sugar

1 large egg

½ teaspoon instant espresso powder

1½ teaspoons pure vanilla extract

¼ teaspoon pure almond extract

4 ounces (113 grams) almond paste (see Note), torn into almond-size crumbles

3 ounces (a heaping ½ cup/ 85 grams) roasted almonds (see page xviii), coarsely chopped

salted or unsalted

4 ounces (113 grams) good-quality dark (70% to 85%) chocolate, coarsely chopped

I prefer Valrhona feves for this

1½ cups (195 grams) all-purpose flour

¾ teaspoon kosher salt

½ teaspoon baking soda

½ teaspoon baking powder

Flaky salt, optional

NOTE: *Almond paste is less sweet than marzipan, providing more almond flavor and better balance in this cookie. When it comes together with the rest of the sugar in the cookie dough, you get more of a marzipan vibe (hence the name!).*

ARRANGE oven racks in the upper middle and lower middle positions and preheat the oven to 350°F. Line 2 sheet pans with parchment paper and set aside.

IN a large bowl, whisk together the butter and sugars to combine. Whisk in the egg, then the espresso powder and extracts. Switch to a stiff rubber spatula and mix in the almond paste, smashing it a little as you mix but allowing most of the chunks to stay intact, because that will be tasty, and fold in the almonds and chocolate, shards and all, reserving some chocolate pieces for the top. Sprinkle the flour evenly over the surface of the mixture, followed by the salt, baking soda, and baking powder. Give the dry ingredients a rough little mix to combine before incorporating into the rest of the batter.

SCOOP ¼-cup balls of dough (about the size of a plum) onto the prepared sheet pans, 2 inches apart. Top with the reserved chocolate and a little flaky salt, if desired.

BAKE for 6 minutes, switch the racks and rotate the pans 180 degrees, and continue to bake until lightly browned and the centers are puffy; begin checking for doneness at 6 minutes. If you have an instant-read thermometer handy, aim for an internal temperature in the range of 175° to 185°F. Let cool completely on the pans and enjoy.

STORE in a cookie jar or airtight container at room temperature. These are best within a few days of baking. After that they'll be okay for a few more days, *but* if you anticipate that you won't finish the batch in that time, I'd recommend freezing unbaked balls of dough and baking one or two at a time whenever the craving strikes. Unbaked balls of dough can be frozen in an airtight container for up to 3 months. Bake from frozen and add a few minutes onto the baking time.

THE OFFICIAL FAMILY SUGAR COOKIE

Welcome to our family's sugar cookie recipe! This is our go-to Christmas cookie, Hanukkah cookie, Halloween cat cookie, Valentine's Day heart cookie, the cookie I'll make with Bernie to bring to school on her birthday, and passport-shaped cookie for the event in which I have to try to bribe someone at the passport office in order to get mine renewed the day before I'm supposed to fly to Korea for the Olympics. (It turns out government officials can't accept cookie bribes. *But* they did renew my passport in time, and I did fly to Korea, and I *did* watch Mirai land that triple axel in real life!!!)

What's awesome about these cookies is that they're super thick, really soft, and you don't have to refrigerate the dough. The combination of almond and lemon makes them taste like the bakery cookies of my youth, and some almond flour in the dough gives them a loaded dense texture. The tricks to achieving the best texture are to roll out the dough really thick and take them out of the oven when they are just starting to *think* about turning brown but haven't yet.

Cookies

3⅓ cups (433 grams) all-purpose flour, plus more for dusting

1⅓ cups (149 grams) almond flour

Not a fan of almonds? Sub any ground nut! Hazelnuts are my other fave, especially with some orange zest.

1 teaspoon kosher salt

1 teaspoon baking powder

1 cup (226 grams) unsalted butter, room temperature

⅔ cup (133 grams) granulated sugar

⅔ cup (80 grams) powdered sugar

Zest of half a lemon, optional

2 large eggs

2 teaspoons pure vanilla extract (or 1 teaspoon vanilla and 1 teaspoon LorAnn Princess Emulsion, on the off chance you have it)

¾ teaspoon pure almond extract

Frosting and decorating

½ cup (113 grams) unsalted butter, room temperature

1½ cups (180 grams) powdered sugar

Pinch of kosher salt

½ teaspoon pure vanilla extract

½ teaspoon pure almond extract

3 tablespoons (45 grams) heavy cream or 2 tablespoons (30 grams) whole milk

Food coloring, optional

Sprinkles, encouraged

IF you plan to bake the cookies immediately, arrange oven racks in the upper middle and lower middle positions and preheat the oven to 350°F. Line 2 sheet pans with parchment paper and set aside. (Alternatively, you can make the dough up to 2 days in advance.)

TO make the cookies, in a medium bowl, whisk together the all-purpose flour, almond flour, salt, and baking powder and set aside. In a stand mixer fitted with a paddle, cream together the butter, sugars, and lemon zest (if using) on medium high until pale and fluffy, 3 to 4 minutes, occasionally scraping down the sides of the bowl with a spatula. Add the eggs, one at a time, beating well after each addition, then add the extracts.

REDUCE the speed to low and add the flour mixture, mixing until just combined, occasionally scraping down the sides to help everything combine evenly. At this point you can pat the dough into a disk, wrap tightly in plastic wrap, and refrigerate for 1 hour or up to 2 days, or you can make your cookies immediately.

ROLL out the dough on a lightly floured surface to a scant ½-inch thickness (use your kitchen ruler!), dusting with a little more flour as needed to prevent sticking. Cut out your shapes as desired and transfer them to the prepared sheet pans, 1 inch apart. Reroll the scraps and cut out more shapes.

BAKE for 6 minutes, switch the racks and rotate the pans 180 degrees, and continue to bake until the cookies are just thinking about starting to turn brown. They should be set around the edges but still soft in the center; begin checking larger cookies for doneness at 6 minutes and smaller cookies at 4 minutes. If they need more time, check frequently so that they don't overbake—every 30 seconds or so. Let cool on the sheet pans for 5 minutes, then carefully transfer to a wire rack to cool completely.

TO make the frosting, combine the butter, sugar, and salt in a stand mixer fitted with a paddle and mix on low until you're confident that sugar won't fly everywhere, then increase the speed to medium and continue to mix until smooth. (It will seem like there's too much sugar at first, but keep on mixing!) Add the extracts, heavy cream, and food coloring, if using; increase the speed to medium high, and continue to mix for a few more seconds, until combined and fluffy. Scrape down the sides of the bowl if necessary to ensure that everything combines evenly.

SPREAD or pipe the frosting onto the cookies and decorate with sprinkles as desired and enjoy!

STORE in a cookie jar or airtight container at room temperature for 4 to 5 days. Frosted cookies can also be stored in an airtight container in the freezer for up to a few months; thaw at room temperature.

OLIVE OIL MANDEL BREAD

Mandel bread is the ideal cookie jar cookie because it lasts forever, looks good in a glass jar, and does the job in the afternoon when you need something to gnaw on with your post-lunch decaf. It's basically Jewish biscotti in that it's twice-baked and crispy, and it's typically flecked with almonds. ("Mandel" is "almond" in Yiddish.) I appreciate a bright, chewy element to break up the crispness, so I throw in a handful of dried cranberries or sometimes cherries, as well as some mini chocolate chips because they make everything better. Olive oil lends some rad undertones, but coconut oil or a neutral oil would also work. These cookies are not flashy or trying to prove anything, they're just there for you whenever you need them.

MAKES ABOUT 50 COOKIES

1 cup (200 grams) plus 4 teaspoons (17 grams) sugar, divided

1 cup (200 grams) extra virgin olive oil

3 large eggs

2 teaspoons pure vanilla extract

½ teaspoon pure almond extract

½ cup (72 grams) raw or roasted almonds (see page xviii)

½ cup (72 grams) raw or roasted hazelnuts (see page xviii)

¾ cup (90 grams) dried cranberries

½ cup (120 grams) semisweet mini chocolate chips

3½ cups (455 grams) all-purpose flour, plus more for dusting as needed

¾ teaspoon kosher salt

1 teaspoon baking powder

ARRANGE oven racks in the upper middle and lower middle positions and preheat the oven to 350°F. Line 2 sheet pans with parchment paper and set aside.

IN a large bowl, whisk together the 1 cup (200 grams) sugar and the olive oil until combined. Whisk in the eggs, one at a time, then whisk in the vanilla and almond extracts. With a rubber spatula, fold in the nuts, cranberries, and chocolate chips. Sprinkle the flour evenly over the surface of the mixture, followed by the salt and baking powder. Give the dry ingredients a rough little mix to combine, then incorporate into the rest of the ingredients to form a sticky dough. Divide into 4 equal parts, place 2 on each sheet pan, and shape the dough into skinny logs, about 13 inches long, spaced 3 to 4 inches apart. The dough should be quite sticky, but if it's too sticky to work with, dust your hands with flour. Flatten the logs slightly, and sprinkle the tops with the remaining 4 teaspoons sugar. Bake for 12 minutes, switch the racks and rotate the pans 180 degrees, and continue to bake until lightly browned; begin checking for doneness at 12 minutes.

REMOVE from the oven and reduce the heat to 250°F.

WHEN the mandel bread is just cool enough to handle, carefully transfer the logs to a cutting board and use a sharp serrated knife to cut them on the bias into 1-inch cookies. Turn the cookies on their cut side, transfer them back to the sheet pans, and bake until dry and crisp; begin checking at 30 minutes.

LET cool on the pans and dunk in coffee, hot chocolate, or tea.

STORE in a cookie jar or airtight container at room temperature for up to several weeks.

CARDAMOM COFFEE CHOCOLATE SHORTBREAD

A crisp chocolate cookie is important to have on standby for potential needs that range from icebox cakes to tea parties to homemade Oreos. One of these cardamom'd babies is a tiny personal party to have anytime you need to eat chocolate or get a microscopic caffeine buzz.

MAKES ABOUT 42 COOKIES

1½ cups (195 grams) all-purpose flour

½ cup (40 grams) good-quality unsweetened cocoa powder

1½ teaspoons instant espresso powder

¾ teaspoon kosher salt

¼ teaspoon ground cardamom

1 cup (225 grams) unsalted butter, room temperature

½ cup (100 grams) sugar

¼ cup (38 grams) sesame seeds

IN a medium bowl, whisk together the flour, cocoa powder, espresso powder, salt, and cardamom. In the bowl of a stand mixer fitted with a paddle, cream together the butter and sugar on medium high until pale and fluffy, 2 to 3 minutes. Scrape down the sides of the bowl with a spatula and add the dry ingredients. Mix on low until all the dry ingredients are incorporated, increasing the speed if necessary.

SCRAPE the dough out onto a work surface and gather it all together with your hands. Divide in half and roll each half into a log that's a little thicker than 1½ inches across. Spread the sesame seeds out on a plate and roll the logs in the sesame seeds to coat completely (as you roll, the logs will get a little skinnier; aim for 1½-inch thickness). Wrap the logs in parchment paper or plastic wrap and refrigerate until firm, 2 hours or overnight.

WHEN ready to bake, arrange oven racks in the upper middle and lower middle positions and preheat the oven to 325°F. Line 2 sheet pans with parchment paper. Slice the logs into ¼-inch discs and place them on the sheet pans 1 inch apart (they will spread a little). Bake for 8 minutes, switch the racks and rotate the pans 180 degrees, and continue to bake until no longer shiny; begin checking for doneness at 8 minutes. Let cool on the pans and enjoy!

STORE in a cookie jar or airtight container at room temperature for up to a week.

HOME IS WHERE THE EGGS ARE

OPTIONAL AND STRONGLY ENCOURAGED: *Sandwich two cookies together with tahini filling in the center. For the filling, cream together ½ cup (113 grams) softened unsalted butter, ¼ cup (56 grams) tahini, 1½ cups (180 grams) powdered sugar, a good pinch of kosher salt, and a good pinch of cinnamon until smooth. Store in an airtight container in the fridge for up to a few weeks.*

JAM-FILLED SPRINKLE COOKIES

The inspiration for these cookies came from two notable cookies of my youth. One, a puffy green Christmas tree from my kindergarten friend James, the other filled with jam from my favorite summertime sandwich counter at Loeb's Foodtown in Lenox, Massachusetts. These cookies shared a distinct sourness that amplified their flavor far above and beyond any other sugar cookie I'd known, making me crave them even decades later. The path to get to that sourness, it turns out, is cream cheese in the dough. Because in the same way that you need the acidity of lemon, lime, vinegar, wine, and pickle brine to balance out the flavors in your cooking, a bit of acid will turbocharge even the simplest of cookies.

MAKES ABOUT 22 COOKIES

3 cups (390 grams) all-purpose flour

¾ teaspoon kosher salt

1 teaspoon baking powder

¾ cup (168 grams) unsalted butter, room temperature

4 ounces (113 grams) cream cheese, room temperature

1 cup (200 grams) sugar

1 large egg

1½ teaspoons pure vanilla extract

½ teaspoon pure almond extract

1¼ cups (210 grams) sprinkles (classic cylinders)

About ½ cup (160 grams) strawberry or raspberry jam

ARRANGE oven racks in the upper middle and lower middle positions and preheat the oven to 375°F. Line 2 sheet pans with parchment paper and set aside. These pans will eventually (ideally) chill in the fridge for a bit, so if you don't have the fridge space for large sheet pans, feel free to use smaller pans (baking in batches, if necessary).

IN a medium bowl, whisk together the flour, salt, and baking powder. In the bowl of a stand mixer fitted with a paddle, cream together the butter, cream cheese, and sugar on medium high until pale and fluffy, 3 to 4 minutes, scraping the sides occasionally with a spatula. Add the egg and mix until combined, followed by the vanilla and almond extracts. Reduce the speed to low, add the dry ingredients, and mix until combined.

PLACE the sprinkles in a bowl and have them standing by.

NOW, before we get shaping: the dough is quite soft, but it should not be too sticky to work with. If it's really giving you a hard time, stick it in the fridge for just 15 to 20 minutes, and resist the urge to dust with flour because that will prevent the sprinkles from sticking. Pinch off a small piece of dough (about 2 tablespoons), roll it into a ball, and flatten it in your palm into a circle a little smaller than 3 inches in diameter and with a slightly thicker center. Add a scant teaspoon of jam to the center, fold the dough over, pinch the edges to seal in the jam, and roll the little dumpling back into a nice round ball. Make sure there's no jam peeking out of the center. If there is, you can patch it up with another little piece of dough. Roll the ball all over in the sprinkles and place it on a prepared sheet pan. Gently flatten to a healthy ½-inch thickness (these won't really spread in the oven). Repeat with the rest of the dough, placing the cookies an inch apart.

IF you have time, chill the cookies on the sheet pans for at least 30 minutes and up to overnight to help prevent jam leakage in the oven. But if you want to bake now, that's okay too. Some might leak, but they will still be very tasty. Bake for 6 minutes, switch the racks and rotate the pans 180 degrees, and continue to bake until very lightly browned on the bottom; begin checking for doneness at 5 minutes. Let cool slightly, transfer to a wire rack to cool completely, and enjoy!

STORE in a cookie jar or airtight container at room temperature. These honestly get softer and better after a day or two. If you anticipate that you won't finish the batch in 5 days or so, I'd recommend freezing unbaked cookies and baking one or two at a time whenever the craving strikes. Unbaked cookies can be frozen in an airtight container for up to a few months. Bake from frozen and add a few minutes onto the baking time.

PISTACHIO COOKIE BARS

My sister-in-law Anna has this habit of introducing me to foods that make me raise my eyebrows so far up they almost fall off my head. They're classic recipes from family archives that she and Nick grew up with, and over time, I've realized how common they are around here. I like to think that I'm generally open to these new foods, but how can you not be totally shocked at hearing the words "candy bar salad" for the first time? (Or *hey*, "popcorn salad"? ☺) This happened with the inspiration for these here cookies—the originals were made with a box of Jell-O pudding mix poured right into the dough. Jell-O pudding!

Once I finally put my eyebrows back in place, I realized how delicious they were and had no choice but to tinker with homemade versions of them. The original cookies have this great, soft chewy quality, which I figured was from the gelatin or cornstarch from the pudding packet, but it turns out that with a combination of cream cheese and paying close attention to avoid overbaking, you can get a texture that is every bit as worthy.

MAKES 16 BARS

Cookie bars

½ cup (113 grams) unsalted butter, room temperature

4 ounces (113 grams) cream cheese, room temperature

¾ cup (150 grams) sugar

½ teaspoon kosher salt

Zest of half a lemon

Few drops of green food coloring, optional

I like AmeriColor's moss, juniper, or cypress.

1 large egg

1 teaspoon pure vanilla extract

½ teaspoon pure almond extract

1 cup (130 grams) all-purpose flour

½ cup (64 grams) roasted pistachios (see page xviii), coarsely chopped, plus more for topping

If you're using unsalted nuts, add another pinch of salt to the batter.

Frosting

½ cup (113 grams) unsalted butter, room temperature

1½ cups (180 grams) powdered sugar

Pinch of kosher salt

½ teaspoon pure vanilla extract

¼ teaspoon pure almond extract

2 tablespoons (30 grams) heavy cream (or 1 tablespoon (15 grams) whole milk)

PREHEAT the oven to 350°F. Grease an 8-inch square metal baking pan and line with enough parchment paper to allow for 1-inch wings on opposite sides. (If you only have a glass or ceramic pan, that's okay; just prepare to bake these a little longer!)

IN a stand mixer fitted with a paddle, beat together the butter, cream cheese, sugar, salt, lemon zest, and food coloring (if using) on medium-high speed until pale and fluffy, 2 to 3 minutes, occasionally scraping down the sides of the bowl to ensure that everything combines evenly. Add the egg, beat to combine, then mix in the vanilla and almond extracts. Reduce the speed to low and mix in the flour and pistachios until just combined. Scrape the batter into the pan and spread it out evenly. (It's easiest to use a small offset spatula for this, but a rubber spatula or spoon will work too.)

BAKE until a toothpick inserted into the center comes out with a few crumbs, and try your darnedest not to overbake; begin checking for doneness at 22 minutes. Let cool fully in the pan.

TO make the frosting, combine the butter, sugar, and salt in a stand mixer fitted with a paddle and mix on low until you're confident that sugar won't fly everywhere, then increase the speed to medium and continue to mix until smooth. Add the extracts and heavy cream, increase the speed to medium high, and continue to mix for a few more seconds, until combined and fluffy. Scrape down the sides of the bowl if necessary to ensure that everything combines evenly.

REMOVE the cookie from the pan, if desired, spread the frosting over the whole thing, and sprinkle with additional pistachios. Cut immediately or, to get very clean cuts, stick it in the fridge for about 30 minutes so the frosting firms up, then use a sharp knife to slice into 16 squares.

STORE in an airtight container at room temperature for 4 to 5 days or in the fridge for a week.

PINE NUT BLONDIES

I can still remember the look on my friend Lily's face when she had her first bite of the pine nut blondie at Lodge Bread Company in Los Angeles and announced notes of orange blossom. If there is one thing that Lily and I share a deep appreciation for (other than bizarre autocorrects of Hebrew greetings), it's orange blossom. And let me tell you, what orange blossom does to a blondie is like what a good night's sleep does for a new mom: it wakes it up, gives it new life, and makes it think that anything and everything is possible. The pine nuts were the cherry on top, providing buttery crunch and a striking appearance. Everything in this bite worked so well. Here is my ode to that blondie.

MAKES 16 BLONDIES

⅔ cup (92 grams) pine nuts

1 large egg

½ cup (100 grams) extra virgin olive oil

1 cup (200 grams) packed light brown sugar

Zest of half an orange

½ teaspoon kosher salt

1 teaspoon orange blossom water

1 teaspoon pure vanilla extract

1 cup (130 grams) all-purpose flour

Flaky salt

PREHEAT the oven to 350°F. Grease an 8-inch square metal baking pan and line with enough parchment paper to allow 1-inch wings on opposite sides. (A glass or ceramic pan is okay; just prepare to bake a little longer!)

SCATTER the pine nuts on a rimmed sheet pan and toast until very lightly browned; begin checking at 5 minutes.

IN a large bowl, whisk together the egg, olive oil, brown sugar, orange zest, salt, orange blossom water, and vanilla until smooth. Switch to a rubber spatula and stir in the flour. Scrape the batter into the prepared pan and spread it out evenly. Scatter the pine nuts over the surface, pressing lightly so they stick, and sprinkle with a good pinch of flaky salt.

BAKE until golden around the edges and set on top; begin checking for doneness at 22 minutes. Let cool completely in the pan, carefully lift the blondies out, and slice into 16 squares. Store in an airtight container in the fridge for up to a week. (Storing at room temperature is fine too, up to 5 days, but I can't resist the chewiness of a cold blondie.)

RHUBARB PIE BARS WITH COCONUT CRUMBLE

Routine dictates that when the rhubarb patch sprouts, we make rhubarb jam (page 15). But when the stalks popped up just weeks after Bernie was born, the idea of making jam with a newborn around was positively terrifying, even if Nick was holding her in the next room. What if a hot splatter leapt across ten feet of air and landed on her? What if she needed me before the jam was at its ready temperature? Could I trust Nick to stir it while I tended to her? There were too many unanswered questions, and I hadn't had enough sleep to process them effectively.

So I made rhubarb bars—just a pile of rhubarb sandwiched between a coconut-butter mixture that plays double duty as the crust and crumble. A multitasking crust like the multitasking mom I was. All of rhubarb's best friends are at this party: pistachio, coconut, rosewater, cinnamon, cardamom, and lemon. *I mean.* So while they look like just an average pie bar, they are in fact way the heck fancier.

MAKES 16 BARS

Crust/crumble

2 cups (260 grams) all-purpose flour

½ teaspoon kosher salt

½ teaspoon ground cinnamon

¼ teaspoon ground cardamom

1 cup (226 grams) unsalted butter, room temperature

⅔ cup (133 grams) sugar

1 teaspoon pure vanilla extract

½ cup (45 grams) shredded sweetened coconut

¼ cup (32 grams) chopped roasted pistachios (see page xviii), optional
salted or unsalted

Filling

3 cups (340 grams) ¼-inch-sliced rhubarb

Juice of half a lemon

1 tablespoon (15 grams) rosewater

2 tablespoons (16 grams) all-purpose flour

⅔ cup (133 grams) sugar

¼ teaspoon kosher salt

PREHEAT the oven to 350°F. Grease an 8-inch square metal baking pan and line with enough parchment paper to allow 1-inch wings on opposite sides. (If you have only a glass or ceramic pan, that's okay; just prepare to bake these a little longer!)

IN a small bowl, combine the flour, salt, cinnamon, and cardamom. In a stand mixer fitted with a paddle, combine the butter, sugar, and vanilla and beat on medium until creamy and combined. Reduce to low, add the flour mixture, and mix to combine.

PRESS about three-quarters of the mixture into the pan, spreading it out so that it covers the bottom. Bake until lightly browned around the edges; begin checking at 15 minutes.

WHILE the crust bakes, make the crumble and filling. Add the coconut and pistachios (if using) to the remaining crust mixture and combine with your hands into a coarse, crumbly mixture.

TO make the filling, in a large bowl, toss the rhubarb with the lemon juice and rosewater. Sprinkle in the flour, sugar, and salt and toss to combine. Arrange evenly on top of the par-baked crust. Top with the crumble and bake until the crumble is browned; begin checking for doneness at 40 minutes.

LET cool completely in the pan, loosen the edges with a butter knife or offset spatula, carefully lift it out, and slice into 16 squares (see Note).

STORE in an airtight container in the fridge for 4 to 5 days.

NOTE: *Chilling these for a few hours will help them slice more cleanly, so have a messy slice for yourself right out of the pan and stick the remainder in the fridge before slicing the rest.*

CHOCOLATE PEANUT BUTTER BROWNIES

Brownies too often bury their lede, which is that they're one of the lowest-maintenance baked goods out there. They don't require you to soften butter or use a stand mixer or chill anything or even cool fully before receiving their blanket of glaze. You can make them in one bowl and keep them for a while in the fridge. Any brownie craving can be cured start to finish well within nap time, even allowing ample time for the chocolate smell to dissipate while you clean up all the evidence so that you-know-who doesn't demand a post-nap brownie that will definitely ruin her dinner. This is the recipe I grew up with, it's the only one I need, and it produces rich fudgy squares that get the job done in a few little bites. The peanut butter glaze is there because no one will ever tire of chocolate and peanut butter, but you know I'll support you if you want to sub the peanut butter for tahini or almond butter or even *errrrmmg* pistachio butter.

MAKES 16 BROWNIES

½ cup (113 grams) unsalted butter

1 cup (200 grams) sugar

⅓ cup (27 grams) unsweetened cocoa powder

¼ teaspoon kosher salt

½ teaspoon instant espresso powder

1 teaspoon pure vanilla extract

2 large eggs

½ cup (65 grams) all-purpose flour

¼ teaspoon baking powder

¼ cup (45 grams) semisweet or bittersweet chocolate chips

Glaze and decoration

¼ cup (64 grams) unsweetened peanut butter

¼ cup (60 grams) heavy cream

1 teaspoon pure vanilla extract

½ cup (60 grams) powdered sugar

Kosher salt, if needed

Sprinkles, for decorating

PREHEAT the oven to 350°F. Grease an 8-inch square metal baking pan and line with enough parchment paper to allow 1-inch wings on opposite sides. (If you have only a glass or ceramic pan, that's okay; just prepare to bake these a little longer!)

IN a large saucepan, melt the butter over medium-low heat, stirring until *just* melted. Remove from the heat, add the sugar, cocoa powder, salt, espresso powder, and vanilla, and whisk until smooth. At this point the mixture shouldn't be too hot (you don't want it cooking the eggs that you're about to crack in), so if it feels pretty hot, whisk a little longer until it cools slightly. Add the eggs and whisk until combined. Sprinkle the flour and baking powder evenly over the top of the batter, then mix until just combined. Pour the batter into the pan, spread it out (it will be a thin layer), and scatter the chocolate chips on top.

BAKE until the center is set and the top is no longer glossy; begin checking for doneness at 24 minutes. Let cool for at least 10 minutes in the pan before glazing.

TO make the glaze, in a medium bowl, whisk together the peanut butter, heavy cream, vanilla, and powdered sugar until very smooth. Add salt to taste (if your peanut butter is salty, you might not need to add any).

TOP the warm brownies with the glaze, nudging it all the way to the edge with a small spatula or butter knife, and sprinkle with sprinkles. Lop off a sloppily cut brownie to enjoy while it's still warm, then let the remainder cool completely. This will allow you to get cleaner cuts. Slice into squares.

STORE in an airtight container in the fridge for up to a week. (Storing at room temperature is fine too, up to 4 to 5 days, but I can't resist the chewiness of a cold brownie.)

BAMBA MARSHMALLOW SQUARES

After learning that the peanut allergy rate in Israeli babies is really low, thanks to their national bestselling snack, Bamba, which is basically a Cheeto but peanut butter flavored, I bought out the entire supply in the Target kosher section. Bernie goes nuts for it, and I do too. When I saw this idea for Rice Krispies Treats made from Bamba posted on Instagram by a friend of a friend, @diasporadinners, I had to re-create them immediately. The result wasn't what I expected, though. They were much airier than standard Rice Krispies Treats and had an almost stale-like quality. But over the following few days, they totally grew on me and I came to majorly appreciate both the airy quality, which allows you to eat a giant wedge without feeling weighed down, and that weird stale-like chew. It was oddly addicting. I can't tell if I'm selling them well or not, but honestly Bamba is one of those IYKYK things, so if you're in the know, you've probably stopped reading by now and are already melting marshmallows.

MAKES 20 SQUARES

¼ cup (56 grams) unsalted butter

One 10-ounce (283-gram) bag mini marshmallows

2 teaspoons pure vanilla extract

Two 3.5-ounce (100-gram) bags Bamba

1 cup (180 grams) bittersweet chocolate chips

Flaky salt

GREASE a 9 x 13-inch pan and line with enough parchment paper to allow 1-inch wings on opposite sides.

IN a large pot, melt the butter over medium heat. Add the marshmallows and stir until melted. Stir in the vanilla extract, remove from the heat, and fold in the Bamba. Quickly fold in the chocolate chips and then scrape the mixture into the prepared pan and spread it out evenly. Place a piece of parchment paper on top and use your hands to pack the mixture as firmly and evenly as you can without crushing the Bamba. Uncover and sprinkle with a few pinches of flaky salt. Let set at room temperature for at least an hour, until firm. Cut into squares and have at 'em. Store in an airtight container in the fridge for up to a week (or even longer if you haven't eaten them all by then).

HALVA BUCKEYES

Sometimes it blows my mind that the old tree-lined streets of the Chicago suburbs where I grew up, the flatlands where I live now whose closest big city is Winnipeg (IN CANADA), and a state that can practically reach out and touch New York are all technically part of the same region. I mean, the cookie salad Norwegian culture of the North could not be more different from the Juicy Couture/Kate Spade/body glittered culture of my upbringing. And Ohio is *so* far away that the only reason I'm talking about it is because I've been meaning to ask you, have you ever had a buckeye? The chocolate things, not the tree. Holy buckets, they are everything you've ever wanted out of a Reese's peanut butter cup but couldn't ask for because you didn't have a direct line to the Reese's peanut butter cup office. I'm talking about a better ratio of filling to chocolate, where the emphasis is more rightly on that filling, and a cute spherical shape! I am the buckeye's number one out-of-state fan! Typically they are made with peanut butter to give you that creamy Reese's experience, but of course I tried subbing tahini, and the result is like a buttery, creamier version of halva that is also *wayyy easier* to make than halva. *I love these so much*. There are no bad days when there's a stock of them in your fridge.

½ cup (112 grams) good-quality tahini (see page xxi), room temperature

¼ cup (56 grams) unsalted butter, room temperature

2 big pinches of kosher salt

2 shakes of ground cinnamon

¼ teaspoon pure vanilla extract

1½ cups (180 grams) powdered sugar

4 ounces (113 grams) semisweet or bittersweet chocolate, chopped

2 teaspoons refined coconut oil

Flaky salt, optional

LINE a rimmed quarter (9½ x 13-inch) sheet pan (or any pan of a similar size that will fit comfortably in your freezer and fridge) with parchment paper and set it aside.

IN a stand mixer fitted with a paddle, combine the tahini, butter, salt, cinnamon, and vanilla and beat on medium for a couple of minutes until smooth and creamy. Stop the mixer, scrape down the sides with a rubber spatula, add the powdered sugar, and turn the mixer back on low to incorporate it. When you're reasonably confident that powdered sugar won't fly everywhere, you can increase the speed to medium and continue mixing, scraping down the sides of the bowl as needed, until everything is combined and you have a soft dough.

ROLL the dough into very smooth 1-inch balls and place them on the prepared sheet pan. Freeze for 20 minutes.

IN a small bowl or mug, combine the chocolate and coconut oil and microwave in 30-second increments, stirring after each, until smooth and melted. You can also melt this in a double boiler. Working one at a time, pick up the halva balls by poking the tops with a toothpick or wooden skewer and dip them into the chocolate about three-quarters of the way, leaving the top exposed. Scrape any excess chocolate off the bottom, transfer back to the sheet pan, take the toothpick out, and smooth over the toothpick hole with a knife. Sprinkle with flaky salt, if desired. Let set in the fridge and enjoy!

STORE in an airtight container in the fridge for up to a few weeks.

CHERRIES AND WHIPPED CREAM POPS

Bern's asleep, we're in that middle-of-summer lull when the farm work pulls back on intensity and just kind of coasts, and we've found a new show we like. At the crossroads of this is Nick, getting a very specific decision-making look on his face. He's analyzing whether his dinner was healthy enough, his physical activity was plentiful enough, and his work that day was quality enough to deserve one of two things: a miniature glass of red wine or one ice pop. (You ask how he stays so svelte with all my food around? Well, this very modest interpretation of "deserve" is how.) Our go-tos are inspired by our favorite JonnyPops, which have so few ingredients that the flavors of the fruit and cream shine right through; they feel almost old-timey. This homemade version takes the principle of no-churn ice cream, which typically involves folding sweetened condensed milk into whipped cream and freezing, but subs out the condensed milk for a milky jam. These pops have a fluffy light texture (which makes molding them in Dixie cups necessary, since they'll stick to traditional ice pop molds, and who can ever find their ice pop molds, anyway?), but their flavor is rich, and the chocolate coating adds that extra bite to drive home that special desserty mood.

MAKES 8 POPS

1 pound (454 grams) fresh or frozen pitted cherries, quartered if you like larger cherry chunks, or chopped smaller if desired

1 cup (240 grams) whole milk

¼ cup (50 grams) sugar

Pinch of kosher salt

½ teaspoon pure vanilla extract

1 cup (240 grams) heavy cream

4 ounces (113 grams) chopped semisweet, bittersweet, or dark chocolate

2 tablespoons (25 grams) unrefined coconut oil

IN a medium saucepan, combine the cherries, milk, sugar, and salt and heat over medium-high heat, stirring and scraping the bottom of the pan with a spatula frequently, until thickened to a jam-like consistency, 25 to 30 minutes. Don't be alarmed if curdles appear; they will cook away. Stir in the vanilla and set aside to cool completely. This can be made up to a day in advance and kept covered in the fridge.

IN a large bowl with a whisk or stand mixer fitted with a whisk, beat the heavy cream to medium peaks, then stir in the cooled jam mixture until evenly combined. The mixture will be speckled. Distribute evenly among eight 3- or 5-ounce Dixie cups, tap the bottoms on the counter to even it out, and smooth the tops. Stick wooden ice pop sticks in the centers and freeze for 6 hours, or until solid.

IN a medium bowl, combine the chocolate and coconut oil and microwave in 30-second increments, stirring after each one, until smooth and melted. You can also use a double boiler. Let cool for a few minutes until the mixture is no longer hot. Line a plate with parchment paper. Working with one or two pops at a time, rip the Dixie cups off, dip the pops into the chocolate, twirling to coat most of the way, let the excess chocolate drip off, and place the pops on the plate. Let firm up in the freezer for a few minutes before enjoying.

STORE in an airtight container in the freezer for up to a few months.

CHOCOLATE-COVERED GRAPES

This is the simplest-ever recipe, but I wanted to tell you about it because chocolate-covered grapes aren't nearly as common as they should be. Between their thin, crisp chocolate shell and juicy, sweet innards (hello, Gushers vibes!), they're the perfect sweet bite to keep in the fridge for when you need some after-dinner chocolate but you ate too much pasta. I am partial to cotton candy variety grapes because they're a flavor explosion, but any grape will work.

MAKES 12 OUNCES OF GRAPES

12 ounces (340 grams/about 2 heaping cups) grapes, rinsed and dried *very* well, stems removed

3 ounces (85 grams) semisweet chocolate, chopped

1 tablespoon (13 grams) refined or unrefined coconut oil

Flaky salt, optional

LINE a rimmed quarter (9½ x 13-inch) sheet pan (or any pan of a similar size that will fit comfortably in your fridge) with parchment paper. Place the grapes in a large bowl and have a large rubber spatula standing by.

IN a small bowl, combine the chocolate and coconut oil and microwave in 30-second increments, stirring after each one, until smooth and melted. You can also use a double boiler. Dump the chocolate mixture over the grapes and, using the rubber spatula, quickly fold it in to coat the grapes. Dump the grapes onto the prepared sheet pan and spread them out. Don't worry about getting every grape perfectly coated; this is supposed to be casual. Sprinkle with a pinch of flaky salt, if desired.

SET the sheet pan in the fridge and let the grapes set until the chocolate is firm, about 20 minutes.

STORE in an airtight container in the fridge for up to 5 days or in the freezer for a few months. Eat straight from the fridge or freezer, whenever you need the teensiest sweet bite!

PRESERVED LEMON YOGURT LOAF CAKE

Throughout that nightmare pandemic lockdown, one thing I desperately wanted to do was go to the grocery store with Bernie. I fantasized about plopping her down in a grocery cart, weaving slowly through the aisles as we perused the fun snacks together, and eventually swinging by the bakery section to get a box of lemon poppy seed mini muffins and sneaking one into those chubby little hands reaching out for a nosh, just like my mom did with me when I was Bernie's age. I so vividly remember the flavor and feel of those mini muffins, right down to the undertones of dish soap.

Lemon poppy seed remains one of my favorite cakes of all time, only these days I swap out that artificial lemon soap funk for another kind of groovier funk, that of preserved lemon. It's a staple in Moroccan cooking, and while I'd only ever used it in savory dishes, but my friend Hetty McKinnon mentioned adding it to a cake one day, and I knew I needed to try it. The result was depth for days and a lemon poppy seed version that felt so cool and grown-up.

This one-bowl cake stays moist for*ever*, and the flavor gets better with time (it's what my friend Natasha calls a "brisket cake," better on the second day). The crumb is dense as can be, with added textural power from almond flour, and a slightly crunchy armor. I loaf this loaf.

MAKES 1 LOAF

1¼ cups (250 grams) plus 1 tablespoon (13 grams) sugar, divided

¾ cup (150 grams) extra virgin olive oil

2 large eggs

¾ cup (180 grams) plain whole milk Greek yogurt

Zest of 1 lemon

¼ cup (64 grams) lemon juice (from 1 to 2 lemons)

1 teaspoon pure almond extract

2 tablespoons (20 grams) poppy seeds

2 tablespoons (32 grams) *verrrry* finely chopped well-rinsed preserved lemon rinds or preserved lemon paste

Fresh out of preserved lemons? Omit them and increase the salt amount to ¾ teaspoon.

½ cup (56 grams) almond flour

1½ cups (195 grams) all-purpose flour

¼ teaspoon kosher salt

¼ teaspoon baking soda

1 teaspoon baking powder

Heaping ½ cup (3 ounces/85 grams) fresh or frozen raspberries and/or blackberries, dusted with a little flour, optional, for topping

PREHEAT the oven to 350°F. Grease a 4 x 9-inch pullman loaf pan or 5 x 9-inch metal loaf pan and line with enough parchment paper to come all the way up on the long sides and allow 1-inch wings.

IN a large bowl, whisk the 1¼ cups (250 grams) sugar and the olive oil to combine. Add the eggs, one at a time, whisking to fully combine after each. Whisk in the yogurt, lemon zest, lemon juice, almond extract, poppy seeds, preserved lemon, and almond flour. Sprinkle the all-purpose flour, salt, baking soda, and baking powder evenly over the top of the batter and give the dry ingredients a rough little whisk before incorporating into the batter. Whisk until just combined. Pour into the loaf pan, scatter on the berries (if using), and sprinkle evenly with the remaining tablespoon (13 grams) of sugar. Bake until a toothpick inserted into the center comes out clean and the top is golden; begin checking for doneness at 1 hour (it will need a few more minutes if using berries).

LET cool in the pan for 15 minutes and then use the parchment wings to lift the loaf out of the pan and transfer it to a wire rack to cool completely.

THIS will keep covered at room temperature for 4 to 5 days.

ONE! CHOCOLATE! CUPCAKE!

Well, sometimes you just need one cupcake! And a real bona fide Kristen Wiig in *Bridesmaids* cupcake, not a dang microwaved mug cake (but I'm sure there's a time and place for those too?). The plan here is for you to mix up a big batch of homemade cake mix and keep it on hand for cake emergencies. When you have your cake emergency, spoon a little of it out and mix it with some coffee and the secret ingredient, mayonnaise, which, c'mon, is way easier than telling you to add one eighth of an egg, *and* it contributes enough moisture and structure to make this cake very forgiving. That's it! The whole thing bakes in the amount of time that a tiny pat of butter for your frosting takes to soften. Make the frosting that matches your mood, slather it on, and eat it immediately. It's everything you want in a chocolate cupcake (sweet, soft, dense, moist) and nothing you don't (the annoying temptation to eat another because, guess what, you didn't make another!).

FIRST, make your cake mix! Combine the following ingredients in an airtight container. This will make enough for 12 cupcakes, which you can bake individually whenever you want. Keep it with your other baking dry goods and it should be good for months.

¾ cup (150 grams) sugar

1½ cups (195 grams) all-purpose flour

¼ cup (20 grams) unsweetened cocoa powder

½ teaspoon kosher salt

1½ teaspoons baking soda

TO make one cupcake, preheat the oven to 350°F. Line 1 cupcake tin with a cupcake liner and set aside. (This is also a good time to get out 1 tablespoon (14 grams) butter for your frosting and place it in the sun or next to the oven so it can soften quickly.)

IN a measuring cup, whisk together 3 tablespoons (30 grams) of your cake mix, 1 tablespoon (13 grams) mayonnaise, and 1 tablespoon (15 grams) hot coffee or water. Pour the batter into the pan and bake until a toothpick stuck into the center comes out clean; begin checking for doneness at 12 minutes. Let cool for a couple of minutes in the pan, then remove to a plate or rack to cool completely before frosting. Or fine, don't let it cool and eat it while it's hot, because it's *your cupcake* and you can do what you want.

FROSTING FOR 1 CUPCAKE

1 tablespoon (14 grams) unsalted butter, softened

2 tablespoons (15 grams) powdered sugar

¼ teaspoon milk

Tiny pinch of kosher salt

IN a small bowl, mush around the butter with a small rubber spatula so it gets creamy. Add the powdered sugar, milk, and salt, and mix vigorously until smooth and combined. Add any additional mix-ins you desire (ideas opposite). Frost your cooled cupcake and don't share it.

FROSTING VARIATION IDEAS

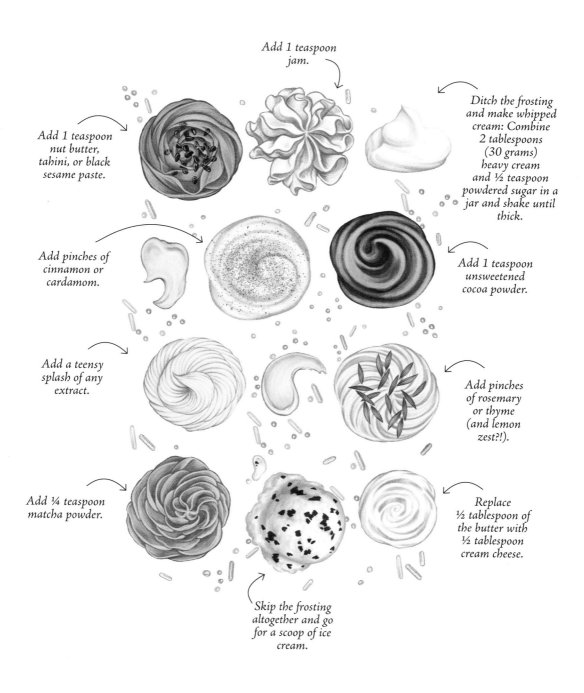

Add 1 teaspoon jam.

Add 1 teaspoon nut butter, tahini, or black sesame paste.

Ditch the frosting and make whipped cream: Combine 2 tablespoons (30 grams) heavy cream and ½ teaspoon powdered sugar in a jar and shake until thick.

Add pinches of cinnamon or cardamom.

Add 1 teaspoon unsweetened cocoa powder.

Add a teensy splash of any extract.

Add pinches of rosemary or thyme (and lemon zest?!).

Add ¼ teaspoon matcha powder.

Replace ½ tablespoon of the butter with ½ tablespoon cream cheese.

Skip the frosting altogether and go for a scoop of ice cream.

PLUM KUCHEN

If I ever find myself in a German-speaking country for more than three days, I can eventually recall enough of my four years of high school German class to politely order a slice of cake. And, boy, do I love German cake. So imagine my delight when I moved to Grand Forks and saw how popular kuchen is here! "Kuchen," the German word for "cake," refers to all kinds of tasty treats: streusel-topped coffee cakes, pancakes, gingerbread, even pies. But in this region, it refers to a very specific "Dakota-style" cake that was brought over by German-Russian immigrants. It consists of a yeasted base with a custard on top and optional fruit. Some of our local grocery stores have it in the frozen section, and you'll also find it at parties and weddings. I love the way the yeastiness shines through as a central mood and how it's not too sweet.

Because Dakota-style kuchen can be slightly labor-intensive, I have taken to piggybacking my kuchen-making onto other recipes that require yeasted dough. So on Fridays when I make challah or pizza or both, I'll reserve some of the dough for a very nontraditional shortcut. (And, yeah, I'll totally use store-bought pizza dough for this!) My go-to custard could not be simpler, and my favorite fruit choice by far is dark, slightly sour plums.

1 pound (454 grams) pizza dough or challah dough completed through the first rising, room temperature

A half batch of the potato challah dough on page 236 is perfect.

Custard

½ cup (120 grams) heavy cream

¼ cup (50 grams) sugar

2 large eggs, separated

Pinch of kosher salt

½ teaspoon pure vanilla extract

Assembly

2 plums, sliced into thin wedges (peeled if desired, but I don't)

2 tablespoons (25 grams) turbinado sugar

½ teaspoon ground cinnamon

DIVIDE the dough into 4 balls, place a few inches apart on 2 parchment-lined sheet pans, and cover loosely with plastic wrap or a towel. Let sit at room temperature for 30 minutes.

ARRANGE oven racks in the upper middle and lower middle positions and preheat the oven to 350°F.

MAKE the custard: in a medium saucepan, whisk together the cream, sugar, egg yolks (reserve the whites for the egg wash), and salt until smooth. Place the saucepan over medium-high heat and cook, whisking vigorously and continuously, until the mixture is thick enough to coat the back of a spoon, 5 to 10 minutes. Remove from the heat but continue to whisk for another minute or two so that the residual heat from the pan doesn't curdle the mixture. Whisk in the vanilla and set aside to cool slightly while you shape the dough.

TO shape the kuchen, roll or pat out the dough into 5- to 6-inch circles and create a rim around the edge that will function as a barrier to hold in the custard. Fill with custard and top evenly with the plums. Beat the reserved egg whites with a splash of water and brush it onto the crust. Sprinkle all over with the turbinado sugar and cinnamon.

BAKE for 8 minutes, switch the racks and rotate the pans 180 degrees, and continue to bake until the custard is set and the bottoms of the crusts are browned; begin checking for doneness at 7 minutes. Let cool slightly and enjoy!

STORE leftovers in an airtight container in the freezer for up to a few months and reheat in the microwave or a 350°F oven.

A NUTTY LITTLE CAKE

Say hi to the ideal snack cake! It just hangs out under the cake dome, minding its own business, ready to provide a bite of glee whenever the moment calls for it. A post-workday treat, a reward for doing the dishes, a boredom activity—this cake doesn't judge, and it also doesn't threaten to go bad if you don't eat it immediately. This one-bowl, few-ingredient wonder has a texture that's slightly chewier than your typical cake, hinting at some possible blondie ancestry. And as the name specifies, it's a little cake, but the dense quality from the nut flour ensures that even the tiniest bites really mean it.

NOTE: *If getting out your electric mixer takes more energy than you'd like to exert for a little cake, go ahead and double this recipe, make two cakes, and freeze one for later.*

MAKES 1 SHORT 8-INCH CAKE

½ cup (113 grams) unsalted butter, room temperature

¾ cup (150 grams) sugar

Zest of half an orange

2 large eggs, room temperature

1 cup (112 grams) hazelnut flour

½ teaspoon kosher salt

¼ cup (33 grams) all-purpose flour (or gluten free all-purpose flour)

ACCESSORY OPTIONS: powdered sugar to dust, whipped cream to plop, melted chocolate or ganache (see Note opposite) to spread (with a pinch of flaky salt to sprinkle)

PREHEAT the oven to 350°F. Grease an 8-inch round cake pan, line the bottom with parchment paper, and set it aside.

IN a stand mixer fitted with a paddle, beat the butter, sugar, and orange zest on medium high until pale and fluffy, 3 to 4 minutes, scraping the sides of the bowl occasionally to ensure that all the ingredients combine evenly. Add the eggs, one at a time, beating well and scraping the sides of the bowl after each addition. Reduce the speed to low and mix in the hazelnut flour and salt until combined. Mix in the all-purpose flour until just combined. If necessary, finish up with a couple of stirs by hand with your spatula to ensure that everything is incorporated. Scrape the batter into the cake pan and spread it out evenly with a small offset spatula or spoon.

BAKE until a toothpick stuck into the center comes out clean and the edges are lightly browned; begin checking for doneness at 23 minutes. Let cool in

the pan for 15 minutes, loosen the edges with a butter knife or offset spatula if needed, and turn onto a wire rack to cool completely.

IF dusting with powdered sugar or topping with chocolate (and flaky salt) you can do that now and keep this under the cake dome for up to 5 days. If topping with whipped cream, add plops to individual slices as you enjoy them, keeping the whipped cream in the fridge.

NOTE: *The ganache I use for this is dead simple and on the thicker side: combine 3 ounces (85 grams) chopped bittersweet or dark chocolate with 3 tablespoons (45 grams) heavy cream in a microwaveable bowl and microwave for about 15 seconds or so, until the cream just begins to bubble. Mix with a whisk or little rubber spatula until smooth and spread over the cake before sprinkling with flaky salt.*

VARIATIONS

THIS is also delicious with almond flour or pistachio flour in the place of hazelnut flour. For either of these options, swap out the orange zest for the zest of a quarter of a lemon and add ¼ teaspoon almond extract after the eggs. I wouldn't be mad if you also added ½ teaspoon rosewater.

THE OFFICIAL FAMILY CAKE

Do you ever have those moments where you're like, *Hmmm, I've been getting really good sleep . . . too good, in fact, I've gotten too comfortable, and I'd like to have something to keep me up in the middle of the night??* You could try to have another child, but what if they're a really good sleeper? Here's a more reliable way to lose sleep: get *really* particular about your cake preferences and then develop! that! cake!

Welcome to the Official Family Cake, and congratulations on whatever you're celebrating, even if what you're celebrating is just . . . Wednesday.

Developing this cake was a long, winding, sleepless journey, if you can imagine a version of *Homeward Bound* in which the mountains are actually piles of half-eaten almost-moist-enough cake. It's seen close to fifty variations over the years, all in the name of finding the kind of hefty cake we need up here in the North. I'm talking a cake that could survive the -40°F temps. A parka, not a jacket. The complete and total opposite of an angel food cake. What would happen if a vanilla cake ate another vanilla cake and then had to squeeze itself into skinny jeans. It's gotta be mega dense and so drastically far from the definition of dry that everyone stops caring about "moist" being a gross word so they can tell their friends about it.

The name of the game in this development process was cramming fat into every possible orifice of this thing without deflating it. Too much fat will destroy a cake's structure, and it will deflate. But, of course, not enough fat will make it dry.

So I collected all the fats:

- butter, for flavor—and ideally European-style butter (which has 2 percent more fat than traditional butter, *cha-ching*)
- coconut oil, for additional moisture*
- heavy cream, for fat and liquid**
- sour cream, for more richness***

---

* Since the coconut oil is solid at room temperature, it gives the cake more structure than a liquid oil. I recommend unrefined for a subtle hint of coconut flavor that simply adds a glow to the vanilla flavor on the forefront.

** Heavy cream adds tons of fat and richness, which is what we're going for, but it adds so much fat that it can take the structure to the edge of stability. So handle these layers with care.

*** I wouldn't make you clear out the dairy aisle if it weren't for a good reason. The difference that sour cream makes in this cake is like the difference between the flannel-lined duck boots and the shearling-lined duck boots. You are reading the book of a shearling-lined duck boot owner.

And put them in with flour (all-purpose, not cake flour, because it doesn't pack that heft I'm going for), sugar, eggs, a decent amount of vanilla for nostalgia, and almond extract, which adds more life to a vanilla world.

After watching it like a hawk in the oven (overbaked butter cakes are at risk for dryness!), this cake became something that was worth all those sleepless nights wondering if Nick's birthday cake was too dry or if Bernie's needed more vanilla. A reflexive scream of delight on first bite is usually how I know a recipe is where it should be, and this one still does that for me, even having made it zillions of times. It's both small enough and long-lasting enough to make for any kind of tiny family celebration but also, conveniently, versatile enough that if you want to double it into a full-on party cake or turn it into cupcakes, you can do that too.

Cake

1¾ cups (228 grams) all-purpose flour

1½ teaspoons baking powder

¾ teaspoon kosher salt

¾ cup (180 grams) heavy cream, room temperature

6 tablespoons (90 grams) full-fat sour cream, room temperature

2 teaspoons pure vanilla extract

½ teaspoon pure almond extract

½ cup (113 grams) unsalted butter, room temperature

¼ cup (50 grams) unrefined coconut oil, soft but not melted

1 cup (200 grams) sugar

2 large eggs, room temperature

Frosting and decorating

½ cup (113 grams) unsalted butter, room temperature

2 cups (240 grams) powdered sugar

Kosher salt

¼ cup (20 grams) unsweetened cocoa powder, optional

¾ teaspoon pure vanilla extract

¼ teaspoon pure almond extract

2 tablespoons (30 grams) heavy cream (or 1 tablespoon (15 grams) whole milk)

Food coloring, optional

Sprinkles, for decorating

PREHEAT the oven to 350°F. Grease either three 6-inch round cake pans or one 9-inch square metal pan and line the bottoms with parchment paper. Set aside.

IN a medium bowl, sift together the flour and baking powder, then lightly stir in the salt and set aside. In a large measuring cup, whisk together the heavy cream, sour cream, vanilla, and almond extract and set aside.

IN a stand mixer fitted with a paddle, cream together the butter, coconut oil, and sugar on medium high until light and fluffy, 3 to 4 minutes, scraping down the sides of the bowl occasionally with a rubber spatula. Add the eggs, one at a time, beating well after each addition, scraping down the sides of the bowl as needed to combine everything evenly. Reduce the speed to low and add the dry mixture and reserved cream mixture in 2 or 3 alternating additions, mixing until just combined. If necessary, finish up with a couple of stirs by hand with your spatula to ensure that everything is combined. Distribute the batter equally between the pans, spread it out evenly with an offset spatula or back of a spoon, and tap the bottoms on the counter once or twice to eliminate any big air bubbles.

BAKE until the center is springy to the touch and a toothpick inserted into the center comes out clean or with just a few crumbs on it; begin checking for doneness at 22 minutes for 6-inch layers and 32 minutes for a 9-inch square; if it's not done, check frequently until it is. You want to avoid overbaking at all costs. Let cool for 10 minutes in the pans (or, if baking a 9-inch square, you can let it cool fully in the pan), loosen the edges with an offset spatula or butter knife if needed, and turn onto a wire rack to cool completely.

LEVEL off the tops of the layers with a serrated knife so that you can have a cake snack and also some scraps to help you taste test the frosting. (Leveling isn't totally necessary if you're making a 9-inch cake, but you'll want to eat some cake scraps immediately, so . . . go ahead and level.)

TO make the frosting, in a stand mixer fitted with a paddle, combine the butter, sugar, and a good pinch of salt—if you're making chocolate frosting, add the cocoa powder now too, along with another pinch of salt—and mix on low until you're confident that sugar won't fly everywhere, then increase the speed to medium and continue to mix until smooth. (It will seem like there's too much sugar at first, but keep on mixing!) Add the extracts, heavy cream, and food coloring, if using; increase the speed to medium high and continue to mix for a few more seconds, until combined and fluffy. Scrape down the sides of the bowl as needed to ensure that everything combines evenly.

TASTE and make adjustments as desired. By itself, the frosting may taste too sweet, but when spread in a thin layer on the cake, it will be delicious. To accurately taste-test your frosting, spread a thin layer onto a cake scrap.

TO assemble, stack the 6-inch layers up with thin layers of frosting in between each and spread a thin layer of frosting all over the outside of the cake; or, for a 9-inch sheet cake, spread the frosting luxuriously all over the top. Decorate with sprinkles!

STORE leftovers, covered, at room temperature for up to 4 or 5 days.

SOME TIPS

+ This cake is moist enough for you to bake and frost the day before serving. Keep it covered at room temperature until ready to serve. Do *not* refrigerate. This cake *must (!!)* be enjoyed at room temperature! Any colder, and the butter will firm up and it just won't have the softness that it should.

+ Make a double batch of frosting if you plan to add frosting decor in addition to the layer of frosting directed in the recipe. Bernie and I also like decorating with marzipan that has been kneaded with food coloring and cut into cute shapes.

+ Layers can be baked in advance and frozen. To do this, cool them completely, level off the tops, and wrap tightly in plastic wrap, separating the layers with sheets of parchment paper. Freeze for up to a few months. (If you're worried about freezer smells or if you're wanting to keep them longer than 3 months, add a layer of foil on top of the plastic.) You can frost while they're still cold but, if you do, allow ample time, 8 to 10 hours (or overnight), for the cake to come to room temperature before serving.

+ This recipe can also be baked into 18 cupcakes. Begin checking for doneness at 16 minutes and make a double batch of the frosting.

+ This recipe can also be doubled to make three 8-inch layers or six 6-inch layers. Begin checking 8-inch layers at 28 minutes for doneness. I don't recommend baking 2 thicker layers because the increased baking time required can begin to dry them out. Also, the frosting distribution with 3 layers is better.

+ If you only have 1 or 2 cake pans, you can bake in batches, keeping the batter covered at room temperature until it's ready to bake and wiping out the pans and regreasing them in between uses.

DRINKS

My drink of choice is water. Specifically the sweet tap water on the farm, especially in the winter when the cold from the outside makes the water from the tap so perfectly cold but not icy. It's like fancy restaurant water temperature. Water was my pregnancy craving, it's my drink order 99 percent of the time when I go out to eat, it's . . . a dead giveaway to how boring I truly am? I just usually prefer chewing my calories rather than sipping them. I love food (surprise). Drinks, for me, are typically secondary. So for a drink to make it into regular rotation in my life, it not only has to compete with food for a spot in my belly, but it also has to serve a greater purpose: a little buzz, a health kick, a hyper-seasonal thrill. These liquids are overachievers, like those people who start college as sophomores because they took so many AP classes in high school.

FIZZY ZHOUG JUICE

Zhoug is a Yemeni hot sauce that is both super spicy *and* refreshing, thanks to a combination of peppers and loads of fresh herbs. With its frequent additions of cumin and cardamom, it's simply full of sassy personality. A few years ago, I started adding plops of it to my green juice to give me that same sort of wake-up that a Bloody Mary does. As a Bloody Mary lover, I was hooked. (And as a Bloody Mary hater, Nick spit it out, so there's your warning.) Over time, if I didn't have zhoug in the fridge, I just started adding zhoug ingredients, minus the garlic, to my kale and cucumber juice. It's become one of my choice ways to drink my veggies and clear out my sinuses.

I don't like pulling the juicer out for making juice. I wish I'd never bought it! (Do you want a juicer?) Instead, I use my blender to get the juice very smooth, then pour it over ice and top with some fizzy water for extra fun. This way, you're left with an appliance that is much easier to clean, some fiber, and no random pulp to toss.

Oh, and you should definitely spike this if that's the kind of day you're having!

MAKES 2 GLASSES

2 ounces (57 grams/about 1 big handful) chopped kale

1 Persian cucumber or ¼ English cucumber, coarsely chopped

½ cup (20 grams) any mix of flat-leaf parsley, cilantro, and mint

4 slices jalapeño, with seeds

½-inch piece of fresh ginger, peeled

Juice of 1 lemon

1 tablespoon (21 grams) honey

A pinch each of crushed red pepper, ground coriander, and ground cardamom

1 cup (240 grams) cold water

Pinch of kosher salt

Ice

Carbonated water

IN a high-speed blender, such as a Vitamix, combine the kale, cucumber, herbs, jalapeño, ginger, lemon juice, honey, spices, water, and salt and blend on high until very, very smooth. Fill 2 glasses with ice and fill them almost to the top with the green mixture. Top with chilled carbonated water, stir, and enjoy.

FRESH GRAPEFRUIT AMARETTO SOUR

When I turned nineteen, my older sister, Stoopie, gave me her old driver's license in exchange for hanging out with her at the DMV while she got a new one. I used her license to buy amaretto sours at bars in college because they tasted like almondy juice. Though my days of taking down cheap amaretto sours before going to parties in Harlem and ending up at Koronet Pizza on 110th are extremely far behind me, I still enjoy a weekend amaretto sour from time to time. Today they're informed by my very grown-up revelation that pulpy fresh grapefruit juice and fancy maraschino cherries are two of life's great pleasures. On Fridays during citrus season you might find me on the couch, double-fisting my amaretto sour and the leftover can of fizzy water while watching a good big-budget movie, and on noshy nights, there are kettle chips in a nice bowl (not the bag!).

MAKES 1 GLASS

Ice

1½ ounces amaretto

Juice of half a grapefruit (about ⅓ cup), plus a twist of peel for garnish

Extra pulpy!!

½ teaspoon juice from good maraschino cherries (such as Luxardo), plus 1 or 3 (see Note) cherries for garnish

Splash of carbonated water

NOTE: *An even number of any cocktail garnish is bad luck!*

FILL a glass with ice and add the amaretto, grapefruit juice, and maraschino cherry juice and give it a stir to combine. Top with a splash of carbonated water and garnish with cherries and the grapefruit peel.

MATCHA EGG CREAM

Never will I ever turn down an opportunity to drink an egg cream and reminisce about raucous nights at Sammy's Roumanian steak house on the Lower East Side. Nick knows this, so I consider his once-a-farming-season midafternoon suggestion of an egg cream break to be one of his most romantic gestures. He appreciates their quirkiness as much as I lap up the nostalgia.

You may be worried about my access to the required Fox's U-Bet chocolate syrup out here in the Midwest, but let me redirect your worry: I found a substitute that I really like: sweetened condensed milk. *I know!* It's completely sacrilegious, and I am sorry to your Grandpa Murray, but it's an ingredient I always have in my pantry, and it does not require an online order. It gets foamy and frothy and, when mixed with my afternoon pick-me-up of choice, matcha, very pretty.

MAKES 1 GLASS

2 tablespoons (36 grams) sweetened condensed milk (see Note)

½ teaspoon matcha powder

¼ cup (60 grams) whole milk, straight out of the fridge
You want it cold!

Carbonated water, straight out of the fridge

IN a 12-ounce glass, combine the sweetened condensed milk and matcha and mix with a long spoon (or metal or glass straw) until smooth and combined. Pour in the whole milk. And now mix vigorously as you assertively and quickly pour in the carbonated water, stopping when you're an inch from the top of the glass. Continue stirring vigorously until you have a nice layer of foam. Enjoy immediately.

NOTE: *Store leftover sweetened condensed milk in a container in the fridge and add it to coffee or tea, drizzle it on French toast or pancakes, make more egg creams, eat it with a spoon, or any other way. It should last for a week or two.*

CHOCOLATE VARIATION

Sub 1 teaspoon unsweetened cocoa powder for the matcha.

WATERMELON BASIL BUG JUICE

At my old summer camp, every meal was washed down with pitchers of colorful "bug juice," or artificially flavored sugar water that was best identified by color, not flavor. Red and blue were my favorite; purple was good too. (They were probably all exactly the same.) Bug juice fueled us for days of swimming in the lake and evenings flat ironing our hair for Shabbat services. Now that I'm in my adult summer camp days, I make a grown-up bug juice, one that's grown-up by way of using nature's sugar water, from watermelons (not grown-up in the boozy way, but if you want to do that, consider a little vodka). Basil ripped from the garden and a splash of ACV lend just enough flair to make it worth writing home about. The overall mood is pure refreshment.

MAKES 2 OR 3 GLASSES

3 heaping cups (480 grams) coarsely chopped watermelon

4 big fresh basil leaves, plus more for garnish
Mint is also good!

1 tablespoon (15 grams) apple cider vinegar

Ice

Carbonated water, optional

IN a blender, purée the watermelon, basil, and vinegar until smooth. Pour over ice and top with a splash of carbonated water, if desired. Garnish with basil leaves. Cheers!

RHUBARB SHRUB

The first time I had a shrub, I felt like that boy in *The Giver* who sees color for the first time after living all his life in a black-and-white world. My tolerance for sweet cocktails and sodas is low—lower than it should be for someone with such a cake-baking obsession—but adding vinegar to the mix gives these drinks new dimension and puts them in a whole new light. Making a batch of rhubarb shrub syrup is required every spring to give an extra little sparkle to our fizzy water habit. One day La Croix will make a rhubarb flavor, but until then, I'll be adding tiny drizzles of this to my drinks.

MAKES ABOUT 2 CUPS SYRUP

12 ounces (340 grams) rhubarb, coarsely chopped

1 cup (200 grams) sugar

½ cup (120 grams) apple cider vinegar

1 cup (240 grams) water

Carbonated water, for serving

Rosewater, optional, for serving

COMBINE the rhubarb, sugar, vinegar, and water in a saucepan and bring to a boil, stirring to dissolve the sugar. Reduce to a simmer and cook for 10 minutes. Let cool and then strain.

MIX with carbonated water to taste and a teensy drop of rosewater, if desired.

SYRUP stored in an airtight container in the fridge will last for at least a few good weeks.

ACKNOWLEDGMENTS

To the village of humans who poured hard work, energy, love, artistry, taste buds, and all-purpose flour into the making of this book, *thank you*. I am so lucky and grateful to have been able to work with you.

Cassie Jones, Jill Zimmerman, Liate Stehlik, Ben Steinberg, Anwesha Basu, Kayleigh George, Rachel Meyers, Kerry Rubenstein, Renata De Oliveira, and Anna Brower at William Morrow. Jonah Straus, Melina Moser, Hayden Haas, Hillary Reeves, Hannah Opp, Jenna Yeh, Amy Stevenson, Emily Weinberger, Amanda Paa, Tara Melega, Ronde Coletta, and Andy Stabile and my team at ICM.

My trusty squad of testers and advisors: Elaine Ramstad, Nancy Sartori, Jackie Subart, Connie Koenig, Linda Peterson, Mollie Douthit, Lorrie Thoemke, Janice Bahe, Joanne Polifka, Connie DeKrey, Hannah DeKrey, Sandi Sather, Kristiana Sather, Kelsey Sather, Anna Sather, Jason Sather, Roxanne Hagen, Roger Hagen, Renea Wimer, Olivia Wimer, Stephanie Butnick, Tom Kretchmar, Lauren Cohn, Alana Kysar, Natasha Feldman, Lily Diamond, Heather Schneider, Nile Spicer, John Cwiok, Mom, Dad, Teresa, Mia.

The team that brought these photos and illustrations to life: Chantell and Brett Quernemoen, Lisel Jane Ashlock, Hayley Lukaczyk, Ewa Perry, Ian McNulty, Barrett Washburne, Lauren Radel. And the brands that contributed props, wardrobe, and ingredients: Rachel Antonoff, Dakota Timber, Food52, Cuyana, Staub, Lodge, Copper River Salmon, Cambria, Michael Stars, Loup, Webstaurant, Smeg, Ekobo, East Fork, Heath Ceramics, GIR, Williams Sonoma, Pampered Chef, Valrhona, India Tree, Supernatural.

And last but not least, my executive advisory board: Nick, Bernie, and Ira. I love you so much!

INDEX

NOTE: Page references in *italics* indicate photographs.

HarperCollins books may be purchased for educational,
business, or sales promotional use. For information, please
email the Special Markets Department at SPsales@
harpercollins.com.

FIRST EDITION

Designed by Renata De Oliveira
Photographs by Chantell and Brett Quernemoen
Illustrations by Lisel Jane Ashlock

Library of Congress Cataloging-in-Publication Data

Names: Yeh, Molly, author.
Title: Home is where the eggs are : farmhouse food
     for the people you love / Molly Yeh.
Description: First edition. | New York : William Morrow,
     [2022] | Includes index. | Summary:"From the host of
     Food Network's *Girl Meets Farm* and bestselling author
     of the IACP Award–winning *Molly on the Range*, a
     collection of cozy recipes that feel like celebrations" —
     Provided by publisher.
Identifiers: LCCN 2022002983 (print) | LCCN
     2022002984 (ebook) | ISBN 9780063052413
     (hardcover) | ISBN 9780063052420 (ebook)
Subjects: LCSH: Cooking. | LCGFT: Cookbooks.
Classification: LCC TX714 .Y45 2022 (print) | LCC
     TX714 (ebook) | DDC 641.5—dc23/eng/20220416
LC record available at https://lccn.loc.gov/2022002983
LC ebook record available at https://lccn.loc.gov/2022002984

ISBN 978-0-06-305241-3

22 23 24 25 26 LSC 10 9 8 7 6 5 4 3 2 1